WRITING THE FUTURE

Writing the Future

Laȝamon's Prophetic History

KELLEY M. WICKHAM-CROWLEY

UNIVERSITY OF WALES PRESS
CARDIFF
2002

© Kelley M. Wickham-Crowley, 2002

British Library Cataloguing-in-Publication Data.
A catalogue record for this book is available from the British Library.

ISBN 0-7083-1714-6

All rights reserved. No part of this book may be reproduced, stored in a retrieval system, or transmitted, in any form or by any means, electronic, mechanical, photocopying, recording or otherwise, without clearance from the University of Wales Press, 10 Columbus Walk, Brigantine Place, Cardiff, CF10 4UP.
Website: www.wales.ac.uk/press

The right of Kelley M. Wickham-Crowley to be identified as the author of this work has been asserted by her in accordance with the Copyright, Designs and Patents Act 1988.

Typeset at University of Wales Press
Printed in Great Britain by Dinefwr Press, Llandybïe

For Tim

and for my parents

Contents

Acknowledgements		ix
A Note on Quotations		x
Introduction: Critical Views		1
Once and Future Scholarship		3
Current Views: Donoghue and Ambivalence		7
1	**Language as Personal History**	14
	The Prologue of the *Brut*: Laʒamon's Personal History	14
	Language as Cultural Product	21
	Duty to Heritage	28
	Betrayal	36
	Duty, History and Bakhtin	55
2	**The Potential of Writing and Community**	63
	Play, Creation and Intent	65
	Narrator's Intrusions: Voice, Orality and Textuality	70
	Dialogues	77
	The Welsh Connection	82
	Texts, Community and Prophecy	88
	Laʒamon and Bakhtin: Back to the Future	94
3	**History, Prophecy and Possibility**	100
	Magic and Divination: The Supernatural and Natural	100
	Merlin as Laʒamon's Prophet	108
	Prophecy, Possibility and Preaching	126
	Laʒamon and Bakhtin: Textual and Narrative Potential	140
Epilogue		142
Appendix: Overview of Laʒamon's *Brut*		143

Notes	147
Bibliography	163
Index	175

Acknowledgements

I first grew to love Laȝamon's *Brut* in graduate school. When I decided to work on the text, it was a lonely field to play in, but over the years, the community of those interested in the text has grown and thrived, and become one of the great joys of studying and sharing this work. My first acknowledgement, then, goes to the scholars of Laȝamon's *Brut*. From the days in 1987 when two other graduate students joined me in the first session at Kalamazoo on Laȝamon, to the recent fourth International Conference on Laȝamon's *Brut*, held at King's College London as 'Laȝamon 2000', their warmth, enthusiasm and collegial engagement have enriched my efforts.

The original work for this book was my dissertation at Cornell. My thanks for the meticulous feedback of Winthrop Wetherbee and the generosity of Robert T. Farrell in timely and detailed communications to a (by then) long-distance student are still heartfelt. My colleagues at Georgetown University have encouraged and supported me as the work took form, and I am grateful for it and for them. In addition, the anonymous readers for the University of Wales Press made this a better book and have my thanks. I am glad to record here my gratitude also to Rosamund Allen and to Ray Barron and Carole Weinberg, for their translations of the entire text. Not available until after I finished my Ph.D., these versions have allowed many more people to glimpse what Laȝamon accomplished, and I certainly compared my translations here against both. Any remaining errors are on my own head. I am grateful too for the patience and care of the University of Wales Press staff, especially Ceinwen Jones and Duncan Campbell, and the work of Liz Powell on the cover design.

My last and loving thanks are for my husband Tim: he has, quite astonishingly, read everything I have written, often in several drafts, and even when a fair bit is in a language he does not read. 'For a is on treowe monnen׃ treouðe ihalden.'

A Note on Quotations

All quotations from the *Brut* are from the Brook and Leslie edition, and all conventions they use have been copied exactly. Thus line numbers, as per their edition, refer to the Caligula version, and when (rarely) Otho has no corresponding line in Caligula, line numbers are followed by small letters (e.g. 1057a). Other conventions:

- angular brackets < > are used to indicate letters interlined or added in the margin of the manuscript
- round brackets ( ) are used in the Otho version to indicate now illegible readings supplied from Madden's edition of 1847
- square brackets [ ] indicate letters supplied in place of the manuscript reading or as additions
- a vertical line / indicates the end of a line, sometimes occurring between double letters in the text where the word is split between lines.

Parts of chapters 2 and 3 originally appeared in 'Laȝamon's narrative innovations and Bakhtin's theories', in *The Text and Tradition of Laȝamon's Brut*, ed. Françoise Le Saux (Cambridge: D. S. Brewer, 1994). The publishers would like to thank Boydell and Brewer for their permission to reproduce this material.

Introduction: Critical Views

[T]he *Brut* is well worth our attention in its own right. The dull passages are a legacy from its known sources; its vividness, fire, and grandeur, are new.

(C. S. Lewis[1])

Writing the Future demonstrates Laȝamon's use of prophecy as an innovative narrative strategy which unites political and religious ideologies and responds to history. Previous scholarship has presented the *Brut* in rather limited contexts, as mainly of interest to a specialized audience of medieval philologists and literary scholars; yet the text is of interest to the wider audiences for Celtic and especially Welsh literature and history, Middle English literature, and Arthuriana, not to mention those who simply enjoy a fascinating text. This book demonstrates the *Brut*'s importance to those who are concerned with establishing links between literary art, religion and politics in the formation of ideas of nationhood, and it examines some ideological concerns in a crucial period of Britain's formation as Celtic, English and Norman. It also uses Bakhtin's views to suggest new ways of reading Laȝamon's work as reflecting a hybrid community, revealing the dialogic imagination possible in his history and his readers, and the potential for engagement with the text. Thus, exciting questions open up about the roles of oral cultures in creating literary ones, the influence of the Welsh on the evolution of English and British political identities, and the concept of how disparate communities become one in Laȝamon's vision for Britain's future.

The structure of this book is incremental, with each chapter building on the thoughts and conclusions of those previous to it. After the introduction sets out what is known about the manuscripts of the *Brut* and the context of scholarship on Laȝamon's work, it proceeds to respond to the most widely known recent work on the text, and to set up the argument of the book as a whole. The first chapter of *Writing the Future*, 'Language as Personal History', begins by re-examining the crucial prologue to the work, which shows, in its two forms, radical reshaping of that prologue to fit changes in thirteenth-century expectations about authors and texts. The account of Laȝamon's own personal history then gives way to a consideration of language as personal, as a cultural product, especially in the British/Celtic setting of the history and in how language relates to personal history and choices. For Laȝamon, culture can be defined by ethnicity, by religion and by language. He has a keen ear for puns and an interest in how, as others have noted, place names record the changes in populations and conquerors. As an English man, he belongs to a group that has been both conqueror and conquered, uniquely placed to understand the variety of perspectives his history records. By emphasizing heritage and ancestors, he creates a context for language as a measure of honour since, in these early cultures, one's word is one's bond. The crucial aspect which clarifies something of Laȝamon's purpose concerns truth and betrayal: whoever violates truth is open to condemnation, whether British or Saxon. This chapter follows his extensive focus on betrayal in the history of the British and the Anglo-Saxons, ending by discussing his strategy for writing history and modelling behaviour as he does so.

The second chapter, 'The Potential of Writing and Community', looks closely at Laȝamon as a writer to see what innovations and concerns he introduces to the history of narrative and narrative history, considering especially his emphasis on individual potential, both his own and that of his reader, and how it relates to a larger community. By merging aspects of both oral and literate cultures, especially perhaps because he is both preacher and priest, Laȝamon begins to pull his readers into his history in a very real way. The chapter discusses the possible Welsh connection in his work, the role of an oral community in how history is kept and told, the role of the development of preaching and preaching manuals, and how oral prophecy might pull readers into a literate community by linking them to the past through the need for prophecy to be fulfilled. Laȝamon's proximity to Wales and its struggle for survival serves as inspiration for his joining of the natural and the Christian supernatural through prophecy.

The final chapter, 'History, Prophecy and Possibility', demonstrates how Laȝamon's narrative strategy uses Merlin as the focus for prophecy's linking of reader and history. The popularity of the character was assured by Geoffrey of Monmouth's 'blockbuster' before Laȝamon wrote, but Laȝamon could write from his location on the Severn, at the border with Wales and the Welsh March, with an enhanced sense of what Merlin could mean in multiple contexts. He rewrites the character as a Christianized prophet, and with the Welsh story of Arthur as his model, forms his prophetic, homiletic history of past and future. By ending his history six centuries before his own time, those in his time become the future of the history they read. Their duty draws them into the text, or the text out into their lives. Neither Geoffrey of Monmouth, who wrote of the Welsh with disdain, nor Wace, Laȝamon's main source who wrote of Merlin and Arthur and dismissed belief in their return as false, treats the prophecy as true. Laȝamon treats it as not only true, as did the Welsh, but as part of a larger history that will renew the promise of all the peoples of Britain; the idealized vision of Arthur's future political and Christian reality owes much to Laȝamon's sense of history's potential as a literary form.

This study therefore shows how Laȝamon's political and literary vision breaks new ground as a precursor of texts that do what has been called 'cultural work', connecting English narrative in its earliest forms with later shapes and strategies usually identified as 'modern'. The individual becomes the key to a change in history, and Laȝamon's work a call to respond in a dialogue with the text, to make of the present that future which prophecies such as Merlin's promised. It is, in its own way, a call to revolution, spiritual in intent but also practical. Political and religious ideologies unite, and the final result is an open-ended text that works as a literary innovation and dialogue, linking individual choices with overarching historical concerns.

Once and Future Scholarship

Sir Frederic Madden, long appreciated as the discoverer of *Sir Gawain and the Green Knight* among many other medieval pieces, was also the first editor, translator and commentator for Laȝamon's text. As a young scholar helping to restore damaged manuscripts from the Cotton collection, his 'first love affair with the Arthurian legend came from his youthful readings in MS Cotton Caligula A.ix, where he discovered Layamon's *Brut*.[2] This *Brut*, a history of Britain from the time of Brutus, great-grandson of Aeneas, up to the death of the last British king, Cadwalader, exists in two manuscripts; the longer is Cotton Caligula A.ix (hereafter Caligula), the shorter version, Cotton Otho C.xiii (Otho). Caligula was originally dated as the earlier manuscript by fifty years, *c.* 1200, in part because of its longer version and in part because of its more archaic vocabulary. In the 1960s, however, Neil Ker redated the Caligula manuscript and Stanley noted that both manuscripts were therefore roughly contemporary after all, that is, *c.* 1250 or of the second half of the thirteenth century. All assumed differences attributed to the fifty-year gap between the two manuscripts had now to be viewed as dialectal variations of scribes or as products of different traditions but not products of different ages.[3] Most recently, entries in the online Middle English Dictionary have dated the manuscripts as late as 1300, while Elizabeth Bryan's appendix to her 1999 study of the Otho Laʒamon dates Caligula to the second half of the thirteenth century and Otho to 'perhaps the last third of the thirteenth century'.[4] In her second chapter, Bryan notes that the '"original" composition by Laʒamon probably took place fifty to one hundred years earlier, between 1189 and 1236'.[5]

The Early English Text Society edition, edited by Brook and Leslie, to date has only two of the three volumes complete, those of the texts themselves; work on the glossary and critical apparatus is still in progress.[6] Madden's edition, published in 1847, remains the only complete edition of the two texts with commentary and glossary.[7] Selections from the original text were available to students in editions by J. Hall (1924) and G. L. Brook (1963, revised 1983).[8] Only the Arthurian sections in the works of Wace and Laʒamon were published in translation at first: the Everyman series published Eugene Mason's at times inaccurate renderings first in 1912. However, in 1989, a flurry of modern translations of the *Brut* began with an edited prose translation published by Bzdyl[9] and continued with a bilingual edition (Middle English and modern English translation) of the Arthurian section of Caligula edited by W. R. J. Barron and S. C. Weinberg.[10] In 1995, Barron and Weinberg published their full bilingual edition of the Caligula version, allowing access both to the original language and to a fine prose version with excellent notes.[11] In 1992, Rosamund Allen published a fresh translation which then became an Everyman edition, making the text for the first time available to a wide audience while preserving much of the author's liveliness and sensitivity to puns.[12] While Laȝamon's work regularly appeared as excerpts in Middle English survey courses, translations have proven crucial to revived interest in the text.

Madden also was the first to stress Laȝamon's intrinsic interest to English scholars in particular, for he pointed out that the text contained the first versions in English of the King Lear story, the St Ursula legend, the tale of Coriolanus, and the tale of Arthur and his Round Table. For these reasons alone one would expect a rush of scholars to descend on the content of the text, and indeed the Arthurian section at least has received fairly widespread attention. Yet as late as 1978, to take one example, Carolynn Friedlander could quote a comment of 1900 that stated, '[i]t is a remarkable fact that in the mass of comment in the *New Variorum Lear*, Layamon is never once quoted', adding, '[t]hose regrets, voiced by Wilfred Perrett around 1900, have not been outdated'.[13] Only in 1992, and in French, was a discussion 'De Leir à Lear' published.[14] How such a text could be largely ignored both by the nineteenth-century fascination with things medieval and Arthurian and by twentieth-century updaters and revisionists forms an interesting counterpoint to the number of scholars who examined the text's minutiae or who removed the Arthurian section from its context and focused solely on it. Such fragmentary approaches may have occurred because Madden laid out the essentials with authority, as discoverer and gifted first editor. Perhaps he intimidated most from comprehensive interpretations, which helped to break scholarship into two main groups. The first group comprises the linguistic examination of Laȝamon, predictably most active around the early part of the twentieth century and focused on German philological interests. The second involves a mixture of modern nationalism, both English and German, and the fascination of such scholars with limited details in the text rather than with a broader reading of the text in its entirety.

But the most obvious answers to why the *Brut* for so long lacked both a large audience and extensive scholarship concerned with the text as a whole are its length (16,096 long lines or double that if measured in half-lines) and the extended sections of what can only be described as excruciatingly repetitious cycles of brief kingships, as forgettable as the form their description takes; most of these latter passages are unfortunately the earliest parts of the *Brut*, which might dissuade a reader from proceeding to the rest of the text. We might excuse this repetition on the grounds of imitation of sources or supposed accuracy: if a king existed, then he must be named and described, however briefly. To his credit, Laȝamon had a notable champion in C. S. Lewis, as the quotation opening this introduction shows. The text apparently had become increasingly dear to Lewis late in life,[15] and he blamed all the boring bits on Laȝamon's sources. He even makes the noteworthy claim that 'sometimes – rarely, I admit – [the *Brut*] reveals, in a flash, imaginative power beyond the reach of any Middle English poet whatever', including, for Lewis, Chaucer himself.

Such enthusiasm has recently found new voice, with the text finally receiving in-depth attention again. In 1989, Françoise Le Saux published *Laȝamon's Brut: The Poem and its Sources*.[16] Her work meticulously reviews scholarship up to the publication of her book. She argues persuasively for a modern political influence on early German scholarship of Laȝamon, with the evocation of morality and German (via Anglo-Saxon) heritage as not unrelated to the efflorescence of German interest in the text. Germans dominate the scholarship from Wülcker's 1876 publication on Laȝamon's sources[17] to the turn of the century (though certainly the nearly thirty years of silence after the 1847 edition argue for the scholarly domination of Madden's own comments to the exclusion of all others). A survey of work published in the years between 1876 and 1894, for example, includes such topics as proverbs in Laȝamon, verse forms, paragogical 'n', palaeographical study, and Laȝamon's accuracy matched against archaeological knowledge of the late 1800s. Yet all work centred on Germanic dominance in some form, and all scholarship was written by Germans. Not until 1894 does the first article in English appear. Even then it is published in *Anglia* and deals with the relatively minor philological point of open and close 'e'. Le Saux notes in her recent work on sources that bringing Laȝamon within the realm of German rather than merely English tradition 'in the socio-cultural background of pre-world war I Europe, is pregnant with political implication', something she dates to the turn of the century but which the list above shows goes back further still.[18] Her own interest focuses on minority British cultures, itself a political awareness not unrelated to more recent trends in cultural perspectives, one which it will become clear I share.

Certainly the Germans are not alone in wanting to link themselves with a noble heritage. Girouard's suggestive look at chivalry in *The*

Return to Camelot: Chivalry and the English Gentleman shows how pervasive, if altered, its influence was on English gentlemen of the post-medieval centuries, especially those Victorians who became fascinated with the chivalric past.[19] Yet notable here is also how the question of nationalism in Laȝamon remained an active one for readers and scholars centuries later. When British scholars read Laȝamon, they saw him as their own. To take an extreme example, Henry Cecil Wyld, in 1930, saw Laȝamon as 'an English poet', 'in the true line of succession to the old poets of his land',[20] emphasizing Laȝamon's appreciation for the landscape of England and its Anglo-Saxon heroes. When scholars have chosen to consider why this poet wrote in an Anglo-Saxon style about a heroic past, they have had to deal with what Daniel Donoghue has termed the 'apparent inconsistency between its verse style . . . and its content, much of which vilifies the first generations of Anglo-Saxon invaders in Britain and praises their enemies the Britons'.[21] Uncomfortable with this seeming paradox, some scholars have proposed nationalism as a means to reconcile the differences: Laȝamon perceived an essential 'Englishness' as beginning from Anglo-Saxon foundations, and so used Anglo-Saxon forms and vocabulary to emphasize that basis while acknowledging the British roots of the original population. Others have discussed irony as the solution to the contrast of opposing form and context. Both attempts have tried to account for a modern discomfort by proposing solutions which are themselves arguably modern. Because Donoghue is the most recent scholar to create a reading of Laȝamon's work as a whole, because he published after Le Saux's work, and because many of his predecessors in fact chose to focus on the very point he attacks (nationalism), an examination of his views fits well here. He finds Laȝamon in his text exhibiting an overwhelming ambivalence, both towards the past and towards his own time, and he argues that such ambivalence is characteristic of England in the twelfth and thirteenth centuries, views which this book will argue are often untenable for many reasons, not least of which are the Welsh.

Current Views: Donoghue and Ambivalence

Daniel Donoghue's reading can serve as a critical springboard to contextualize this book's argument, as he draws heavily on traditional views of earlier Laȝamon scholars and adds a new view on Laȝamon's attitudes and motivations; publication in the journal of the Medieval Academy of America has assured his article of being perhaps the most disseminated recent work on Laȝamon to medievalists of many disciplines. While other specialists have registered disagreements with Donoghue (perhaps most notably James Noble[22]), I would like to use his perspectives as an opportunity for summarizing his points and positioning this book's argument within past and current views. I do not accept his view of ambivalence as the solution to Laȝamon's seemingly conflicting sympathies, but his argument contains many rewarding insights and usefully contentious points, and, as the best-known recent work, should be treated in detail.

In his 1990 *Speculum* article on the vexed question of what Laȝamon was doing in his text regarding races, history and heritage, Donoghue polarizes critical views in order to steer a course between them, guided by his belief in an essential ambivalence common to both Laȝamon and his culture. He begins by citing a short essay by Borges, presumably because of the authority given by his literary stature and because his pronouncement on Laȝamon is short and pithy. Borges characterizes Laȝamon as childlike in his simplicity and in his ignorance of the Saxon literary models and heritage his choice of English might otherwise suggest, and comments,

> Layamon sang with fervor about the ancient battles of the Britons against the Saxon invaders, as if he were not a Saxon and as if Britons and Saxons had not been, since Hastings, conquered by the Normans . . . Not so dissimilar is the case of the Argentine with no Querendí blood who habitually identifies himself with the Indian defenders of his land rather than with the Spaniards of Cabrera or Juan de Garay.[23]

Borges is best here at perceiving implied reasons for Laȝamon's sympathizing with the native population; I have written elsewhere at more length of Laȝamon's sympathetic ethnography and what it means for his writing and for the Britons/Welsh,[24] and would agree that he often positions himself alongside what seems the less likely but nobler ethnic group. But Borges goes on to invent Laȝamon's historical isolation, the dead-end alliteration of his verse, and his 'rustic jargon':

> He knew nothing of the great verses from which his own were to spring; perhaps he would not have understood them. His curious isolation, his

solitude, make him, now, pathetic. '*No one knows who he is*,' said León Bloy. Of that intimate ignorance no symbol is better than this forgotten man, who abhorred his Saxon heritage with Saxon vigor, and who was the last Saxon poet and never knew it.[25]

The beautiful rhetoric should not blind anyone to its inaccuracy, and Donoghue recognizes the limitations of the piece. But Borges provides Donoghue with a starting-point for his own theory that Laȝamon harboured an ambivalence towards his Anglo-Saxon heritage. To combine the start and finish of Donoghue's article,

> In place of Borges's naively self-hating Anglo-Saxon and everyone else's visionary nationalist . . . I argue that there is no need to reconcile the style and content, because the disparity is consistent with an ambivalence toward the past which Laȝamon demonstrates throughout his chronicle and which can be seen as part of a wider cultural ambivalence in twelfth- and thirteenth-century England . . . Laȝamon does not offer a unifying vision. He comes too late to be an Anglo-Saxon bard and too soon to be a nationalist poet. He remains caught between the old and the new, the Anglo-Saxon and the Anglo-Norman, in an age of competing allegiances, and from his middle position he balances the oppositions within the scheme of a historiographical tradition more complex than most of his modern admirers have allowed. Laȝamon does not abhor his Anglo-Saxon heritage – he cherishes it, but he does so in a way that justifies its decline. This is his final ambivalence.[26]

In placing all of scholarly opinion against a somewhat obscure four-page note by Borges, Donoghue oversimplifies the diversity of opinion. Yet he raises the traditionally important issues in Laȝamon scholarship of nationalism and archaism, calls upon a tradition of writing history whose complexity often escapes literary critics, and credits Laȝamon with 'forging a viable verse style [that] may be one of the least appreciated achievements in early Middle English'.[27] Without question, Laȝamon is underrated as a writer, and Donoghue argues ably for his strengths and sources in writing the first long English poem after the *Ormulum*.

In Donoghue's reading, Laȝamon reverts to Saxon diction and style because he desires stability, though Donoghue carefully points out that the Saxon tradition is not a living tradition at this time, which would seem to undermine his argument: what is stable about a dead tradition? (While it may be seen as static and thus stable, it can equally be seen as more vulnerable and easily lost.) He comments further on the archaic versus the archaistic, the former preserving early forms, the latter imitative of the truly archaic, and sees evidence of both in Laʒamon. He does not comment on why a dead tradition should offer stability rather than nostalgia or anachronism. To bolster his point about Saxon diction and style, he spends a large portion of his article detailing both the use of exhortation as evoking Anglo-Saxon contexts and the semantic weakening and drift in words for 'boast' (*beot* and *gielp*). He also tries to show how Laʒamon changes Wace's chivalric, contemporary warfare to an older form of Germanic foot-soldier confrontation. He admires Laʒamon's prolific invention of poetic compounds, and links him to the Worcester 'tremulous' glossator as a contemporary. The latter provides evidence of having read extensively in Old English, though the 'Tremulous Hand' provides proof that Old English has no living tradition, because he must gloss many of the terms. As Worcester is only ten miles from Laʒamon's church, Donoghue comments that these two men are either independent eccentrics, or part of a movement promoting interest in Anglo-Saxon scholarship and literature. The idea of a 'movement', or better, a small group studying the literature, has merit; perhaps one should consider a teacher/pupil relationship here.

But in discussing the author's own outlook, Donoghue's solution of ambivalence denies any real accomplishment for Laʒamon in visualizing a unifying history, and it skews the perception of the text. Arguing that Laʒamon preserves a tension in two directions, an equilibrium, without promoting one side over the other,[28] Donoghue proposes that the unifying principle of the history is not nationalism, but a providential design that taught Laʒamon 'to accept the Norman Conquest as part of the process of inevitable change, while poetry allowed him to draw solace from the nostalgic ideals of an Anglo-Saxon golden age'.[29] Laʒamon in effect becomes unappreciated because he is a fatalistic romantic, caught in an eternal middle (or muddle), who will not or cannot choose a racial identity, what other critics have called a national identity.

For Donoghue, the idea of nationalism is problematic because of historical considerations, for most historians and commentators argue that it does not develop until the 1230s, after Laʒamon's writing, or that England's own fascination with the Continent promotes internationalism instead (Elizabeth Salter held the latter view).

Donoghue rejects both arguments because he cannot reconcile them with Laȝamon's use of antique diction and aversion to French influence. Instead, he argues that Laȝamon defines his parties by race; he reminds modern readers that Galbraith pointed out in 1941 the fallacy of equating linguistic consciousness with national consciousness (he ignores the contemporary example, geographically next door for Laȝamon, of Welsh nationalism and its identification with language[30]). 'Race' here Donoghue defines primarily as the *Anglen*, English, and the *Brutten*, British/Welsh, in a broad cultural context: 'by "race" (Laȝamon's *leod*) I do not mean a narrow definition simply based on birth but one that adds to it a cluster of associations that include language, social structures, and a common myth of origin.'[31] He rejects the overly romantic reader who sees Laȝamon 'as a kind of resistance fighter against the linguistic invasions of the French language, which becomes the equivalent of seeing him as the defender of a national literature', singling out especially '[p]erhaps the most sustained example of this fallacy' of identifying linguistic and national consciousness as R. W. Chambers's *On the Continuity of English Prose from Alfred to More and His School*.[32]

Donoghue sees Laȝamon as heightening racial antipathies, and for a purpose. Citing the tradition of Gildas, in which history is presented and judged according to God's law, he sees Laȝamon as operating in a 'typological manner through an exegetical method'.[33] For him, twelfth-century history saw Gildas and Wulfstan's warnings vindicated with the conquest by the Normans. Despite only one mention by Laȝamon, Donoghue contends that the typological approach allows the author to write of the Normans without having to mention them again. Laȝamon constructs his poem for solace, allowing the clash between style and content to free him from spelling out the analogy to the Norman conquest which the Anglo-Saxon conquest provides. Typology allows history to repeat itself, and Laȝamon can reconcile himself and his people to conquest because it is part of a cyclic pattern of change.

The idea of ambivalence may well have an attraction because it too is a modern viewpoint: moral relativism in the modern age and our inability to distinguish between good and evil are much discussed in the media, for example. Such an ambivalence on our part, if it exists, might predispose us to accept Donoghue's ideas, though a lack of resolution to problems also characterizes medieval genres such as debate poetry. Yet scholars have consistently commented on

Laȝamon's individualized tone; he has presented his narrator as having clear opinions, so that readers of whatever literary persuasion must begin with his depiction of what is acceptable and what is not. Donoghue's presentation of ambivalence, lack of nationalism, and providential design imply a fatalism in the text which does not seem valid, even if ambivalence is understood as the unwillingness to choose rather than the inability to choose. True, individual warriors are often fatalistic or *fey*, in an echo of Anglo-Saxon *wyrd*, and such occurrences fit well with a return to other aspects of an Anglo-Saxon context. But Laȝamon's emphasis on the individual and his honour, on the value of keeping one's word, counters a providential design that undercuts any individual act. Indeed, the fundamental causes of problems, according to men such as Gildas and Wulfstan, are man's sinful behaviour, his choices and his failure to honour his Lord, thus betraying him. While human frailty may occur cyclically, it is due to choice, not predetermined action. Death or temptation may be set before anyone, but how one faces them is not. For Laȝamon, individual honour, whether held as *trowþe* or betrayed by *swikedom*, and whether of lord (such as Arthur) or Lord, is a means to communicate why such patterns occur and what solutions are available.

Donoghue finishes by reiterating that Laȝamon uses diction cleansed of foreign elements out of a desire for stability, and that his love of books is similarly motivated, because he sees them as a stable source of wisdom. He sees Laȝamon's phrase that Arthur will come to help the *Anglen* as 'a kind of paninsular gesture of unity against outsiders', adding that it is, if true, 'the only such glimpse in Laȝamon and postpones the day of national unity to the dim and indefinite future'.[34] In my view, Donoghue omits the clear indications of an 'us/them' mentality which Laȝamon constructs concerning heathens and Christians *instead of* nationalism or race identity. He also gives too brief a consideration to prophecy. The prophecies of the Sibyl (recorded in Augustine and others and incorporated into popular perceptions in songs) and those of Merlin have more intrinsic worth to Laȝamon than Donoghue allows. Further, while Laȝamon resurrects a glorious past in his form and content, his concerns prove very contemporary once the details of language and perspective emerge. The emphases on Merlin and on Arthur thus become clearer in their link to Welsh historical prophecy, and Arthur becomes Laȝamon's quintessential example of a Christian lord who represents the almost archetypal story of truth and betrayal. Yet

Laʒamon continues the story to the last Celtic ruler, and wraps a prophecy that speaks to his own time into the future of those British whose history he records. Nationalism is only one method of 'unifying': Christianity and a common future are two others, and the Welsh emphasis on political prophecy in the twelfth and thirteenth centuries provides a close and relevant encouragement to use of their history by Laʒamon. Donoghue overlooks crucial evidence of prophecy linked to the Welsh, preferring to emphasize *Anglen* as evoking a 'paninsular unity' impossibly in the future, and unattainable. While the aim may well be paninsular unity, it is imminent, not delayed.

In contrast to Donoghue's views, this book argues that Laʒamon, his vision of the future and his warnings and prescriptions combine to create a much more proactive solution which does not deny race or ethnicity but subjugates them to the larger questions of ethics and, ultimately, religion. It proposes to read history the way Laʒamon would while recognizing the projection and problems inherent in that aim, following indeed the tradition Donoghue recommends, of salvation and providential history. But here Christianity and a man's individual responsibility in that context are most important, because arguably those considerations are closer to what Laʒamon as a priest near the March of Wales would have perceived. He certainly revives the Anglo-Saxon past and its literary forms; just as clearly, he praises the Britons.[35] But Laʒamon's unity is Christian and ethical, that is, distinguishing between right and wrong more than any detailed doctrinal theology, and what Donoghue terms ambivalence oversimplifies praise and blame as racial, as many other scholars have done in perhaps the most consistent misreading of the text.

As I said at the beginning of this introduction, in thinking through Bakhtin's views on how language and the novel work in society, I came to new ways of reading Laʒamon's work as reflecting a hybrid community in active dialogue. Throughout this book, I read aspects of Laʒamon's work from within the confines of the text and history. Then, in parallel, after discussion of the medieval text, Bakhtin's views are used to stimulate rethinking what Laʒamon offers us, reading the *Brut* as a dialogic text which participates in and shapes a community with many voices: British, English, Danish, Christian, non-Christian, past, present and future.[36]

1
Language as Personal History

> One notices, if one will trust one's eyes,
> The shadow cast by language upon truth.
> (W. H. Auden, 'Kairos and Logos')

The Prologue of the *Brut*:
Laȝamon's Personal History

Nearly everyone begins by pointing out that Laȝamon's prologue lists his personal details, his three main written sources, the possibility of oral sources and his methodology, before ending with a pious prayer and invocation. Typically, scholars mention that two manuscripts exist, Cotton Caligula A.ix, the longer and so presumed more accurate text, and Cotton Otho C.xiii, which removes many sections, updates obscure or archaic vocabulary and is heavily damaged. Then they proceed, fairly or unfairly, to use Caligula (as this study does) unless discussing specifically the differences in the texts, scribes or orthography. Critics have repeated certain not necessarily correct observations: he knew of Anglo-Saxon poetry even if he did not know exactly how to reproduce the forms; his work is mainly a translation of Wace but it incorporates, especially in the Arthurian section, extended descriptions taken to be Laȝamon's own since we have no other confirmed sources; he doubtless used the extensive library at Worcester to study, though we have only a general idea of what he read. Few scholars have questioned that Laȝamon wrote his own prologue. Yet certain inconsistencies emerge which seriously call this assumption into question, at least in the Otho version, which has at the least been revised. While we cannot establish for certain that Laȝamon wrote his own prologue in the Caligula A.ix version, we can compare the two versions for their notable divergences. The process provides clues to how others perceived his text, for example, in Otho as one based on spiritual authority, something not as emphasized in the Caligula version. In Bzdyl's translation of the *Brut*, he comments on differences in the prologues briefly in a footnote to the introduction:

> A more speculative possibility is that the prologue was written by someone other than Layamon after the poet's death. Significantly, only in the prologue is the poet referred to in the third person; in the poem proper, the author uses 'I' when speaking of himself.[1]

While speculative, the possibility should have received more attention than it has because scholars have based many assumptions on it, not least the date range of the text and the actual sources used. Before the prologue, Caligula has 'Incipit hystoria Brutonum' (The history of the Britons begins), while Otho starts, 'Incipit Prologus libri Brutonum' (The Prologue of the book of the Britons begins). As noted in the Brook and Leslie edition,[2] Wanley's transcription of the badly damaged Otho MS[3] has 'Incip. lib.' after the Prologue's 'Amen', before line 36. From the first, then, the Otho text distinguishes prologue and book more carefully, while Caligula clearly states that the work is a history. A fuller look at the prologue uncovers substantial disagreement; here, Caligula will be reproduced, with differences in Otho cited in discussion. Caligula begins:

> An preost wes on leoden⁄ Laʒamon wes ihoten.
> he wes Leouenaðes sone⁄ liðe him beo Drihten.
> He wonede at Ernleʒe⁄ at æðelen are chirechen.
> vppen Seuarne staþe⁄ sel þar him þuhte.
> on-fest Radestone⁄ þer he bock radde.
> Hit com him on mode⁄ ⁊ on his mern þonke.
> þet he wolde of Engle⁄ þa æþelæn tellen.
> wat heo ihoten weoren⁄ ⁊ wonene heo comen.
> þa Englene lond⁄ ærest ahten.
> æfter þan flode⁄ þe from Drihtene com.
> þe al her a-quelde⁄ quic þat he funde.
> buten Noe.⁊ Sem⁄ Iaphet ⁊ Cham.
> ⁊ heore four wiues⁄ þe mid heom weren on archen.
> Laʒamon gon liðen⁄ wide ʒond þas leode.
> ⁊ bi-won þa æðela boc⁄ þa he to bisne nom.
> He nom þa Englisca boc⁄ þa makede Seint Beda.

An-oþer he nom on Latin/ þe makede Seinte Albin.
⁊ þe feire Austin/ þe fulluht broute hider in.
Boc he nom þe þridde/ leide þer amidden.
þa makede a Frenchis clerc/
Wace wes ihoten/ þe wel couþe writen.
⁊ he hoe ʒef þare æðelen/ Ælienor
þe wes Henries quene/ þes heʒes kinges.
Laʒamon leide þeos boc/ ⁊ þa leaf wende.
he heom leofliche bi-heold. liþe him beo Drihten.
Feþeren he nom mid fingren/ ⁊ fiede on boc-felle.
⁊ þa soþere word/ sette to-gadere.
⁊ þa þre boc/ þrumde to are.
Nu bidde[ð] Laʒamon alcne æðele mon/
for þene almiten Godd.
þat þeos boc rede/ ⁊ leornia þeos runan.
þat he þeos soðfeste word/ segge to-sumne.
for his fader saule/ þa hine for[ð] brouhte.
⁊ for his moder saule/ þa hine to monne iber.
⁊ for his awene saule/ þat hire selre beo. Amen. (Caligula 1–35)

(A priest there was among the people; Laʒamon he was called.
He was Leovenath's son; merciful may God be to him.
He lived at Areley at a noble church
upon the bank of the Severn; well it seemed to him,
fast by Radestone; there he read books/a Missal.[4]
There came into his mind a fine thought,
that he would tell of the noble in England,
what they were called; and whence they came,
who first took English land
after the flood that came from the Lord
which here slew all alive that it found
except Noah and Shem, Japhet and Ham
and their four wives that with them were on the Ark.
Laʒamon went travelling widely throughout the people
and acquired the noble books that he took as authoritative.
He took the English book which St Bede made.
Another he took in Latin, which St Albin made
and the fair Austin who brought baptism here.
He took the third book, laid it there amidst them,
which a French clerk made;
Wace he was called, who knew well how to write,
and he gave it to the noble Eleanor
who was Henry's queen, the high king.
Laʒamon laid down this book and turned the leaves.

He lovingly beheld them, merciful be the Lord to him.
Feather quill he took with fingers and composed on book vellum
and the truer words set together,
and those three books pulled into one.
Now Laȝamon asks of every noble man
for Almighty God['s sake?]
that he read this book and learn this advice,
so that he say these accurate words together
for his father's soul who brought him forth,
and for his mother's soul who reared him to manhood,
and for his own soul that it may be better. Amen.)

Caligula proceeds to tell us there was a priest 'on leoden' called Laȝamon; in Otho, he is 'in londe'. While the distinction is minor, the stress on a people (*leod*) is important in Laȝamon's work, as is the link between the people and the land (*lond*). The confusion or substitution is interesting. The next line produces even more of a contrast: in Caligula, he is Leouenað's son, in Otho, his father is Leucais. The difference here emerges as more than scribal error, and not a mistake Laȝamon himself was likely to make. Leouenað is Anglo-Saxon, while Leucais links to religious contexts, specifically Luke the evangelist (or, less likely, perhaps to a Luces in the text, either the king under whom Christianity is introduced to the Britons, or the Roman emperor overcome by Arthur in the *Brut*). The name Leouenað occurs in the Domesday records (1086) for Worcestershire three times, once referring to Leofnoth the priest, and twice elsewhere to a Leofnoth who may or may not be two separate people by that name:

(1) In WICH . . . reddeƀ T.R.E. ƥ annu. LX soliđ 7 C. mittas salis. 7 XXXI. burgsis redđ. XV. soliđ 7 VIII. den . . . Leuenot pƀr.I. salina redđ. X. soliđ.

(In Droitwich . . . before 1066 they paid 60*s*. a year and 100 measures of salt . . . Leofnoth the priest (holds) 1 salt-house which pays 10*s*.)

(2) Isđ Rađ ten MORE. Leuenot tenuit 7 potuit ire q voluit.

(ROCKMOOR. Leofnoth held it; he could go where he would.)

(3) Isđ. W. ten BELLEM. Leuenot tenuit. tan regis.E. Ibi.III. hidæ.

(BELL (Hall). Leofnoth, a thane of King Edward, held it. Three hides.[5])

Line 3 in the prologues goes on to place Laȝamon at 'Ernleȝe/ Ernleie', which in Caligula has an 'æðelen are chirechen' (noble church) and in Otho places Laȝamon 'wid þan gode cniþte' (with the good knight). (Hereafter, phrases before a slash are from the Caligula manuscript, after the slash, from Otho.) Are we to understand that the church was a manor church? Was the knight his father or his patron, or even both? Both texts agree that he thought it pleasant there upon the Severn, reading his books near or at Radestone/ Radistone, which may have had a small monastic community. He gets the idea to 'þa æðelæn tellen / þe ristnesse telle' of England, what men were called and whence they came – in short, a story of origins for a land, from the Flood on; note that the starting-point is a biblical analogy of men's origins. Both texts agree that Laȝamon travelled widely. Though we do not know what 'widely' could mean to whoever wrote at the time, in Caligula again he goes widely among the 'leode' while in Otho he goes 'so wide so was þat londe'. The phrase could refer to collecting material from oral sources, and some scholars have speculated that this is so. At the least, he saw the countryside of his area. Caligula then says, in a line not matched in Otho, that he obtained (*bi-won*) the books he needed for his work (*þa he to bisne nom*). If this is true, he undoubtedly had some personal resources with which to purchase the books, or personal connections to a book owner or library, or else he was able to make his own copies. Both texts then go on to name the three texts which have perplexed scholars of Laȝamon from the beginning. Caligula names the English book of Bede, Otho the same. The second book is a Latin text by 'Seinte Albin' and 'þe feire Austin' in Caligula, in Otho a Latin text by 'Seint Albin' alone. The third in Caligula is one by Wace, 'A Frenchis clerc' who gave his text to Ælienor, the queen of Henry II. Otho, however, says the third book is one by 'Austin. þat follo[s]t bro[s]te hider in', that is, who converted the Anglo-Saxons. All references to Wace, Henry and Eleanor are omitted.

The rest of the section is fairly close in both manuscripts. Laȝamon turns the pages of the book(s), reads lovingly (*leofliche/loueliche*), takes quill in hand and writes the 'truer' (Caligula) or simply 'true' (Otho) word. Then Laȝamon (in the third person) bids each good man for love of God to read and to pray. The differences in the two versions are interesting: Caligula tells a reader to 'leornia þeos runan', *runan* usually meaning advice or counsel in the *Brut* itself, that he say these true (*soðfeste*) words together (implying unity, or a set oral presentation versus solitary reading?), and that the requested prayers be for his father, his mother and his own soul. Otho is shorter: he bids men to read this book, that they say these true words together, and pray for those who 'hine to manne strende' (raised him) as well as for himself.

Clearly the largest differences between the texts concern Laȝamon's father and Laȝamon's sources – yet these details are among the most specific and important. That Laȝamon would write this section in the third person but use such a form nowhere else seems noteworthy though not impossible. While the author's prologue in the Middle Ages is a commonplace, as is the modesty topos (imitating St Paul), we still do not expect the variation on key information that we find here. As an Anglo-Saxon name, Leovenað is fairly unusual, and so perhaps more unlikely as a mistake or invention. The Domesday evidence suggests that the name at least existed in the right region in the early Norman period. All this debate, then, makes Leucais seem an addition, though the motivation for the change is as yet unclear.

The creation of a prologue with biographical information fits well with what we know of twelfth-century demands for teaching and studying texts. Minnis notes that the 'most popular series of headings employed in twelfth-century commentaries on *auctores*' included 'the title of the work, the name of the author, [and] the intention of the author'. In the early thirteenth century, new headings emerged, due to the influence of Aristotle, based on his four major causes: efficient (the *auctor*), material, formal (style and structure) and final (his objective); 'Two of the most important concerns which this new interest produced are considered in detail, . . . [the writer's] individual literary activity and his individual moral activity.' Minnis's example is Lathbury's life of Jeremiah, described as prophet, writer, priest, virgin and martyr. These generic attributes echo in references to Laȝamon's priesthood, scholarly activity, named sources and piousness:

> To be 'authentic', a saying or a piece of writing had to be the genuine production of a named *auctor*. Works of unknown or uncertain authorship were regarded as 'apocryphal' and believed to possess an *auctoritas* far inferior to that of works which circulated under the names of *auctores*.[6]

While Minnis is mainly discussing scriptural exegesis, and his *auctores* are spiritual authorities, the concerns both of identifying a writer so that his character could be known and of his claim to his own work and its reliability would be general ones.

As for sources, no one questions that Wace is the dominant source for the text, yet Otho omits it entirely. Either the reviser is very ignorant, or he has a reason to omit the mention of the French or Normans. The book of Albin and Austin, whether two sources or one, has never been satisfactorily identified; given the conflicts enumerated, we can see that it may well be the invention of a later reviser, who need not know Laȝamon's actual sources as such, but may be constructing a prologue to fulfil a reader's expectations. Certainly, for instance, Geoffrey of Monmouth's work of history has a similar problem with identifying the unknown British source he claims was available only to him; such antique and rare sources lend authority and appeal. The omission of Wace from Otho, however, seems a crucial one, especially given the arguments over Laȝamon's nationalism or intention. Only ignorance of Wace's text could allow for a non-political motivation in omitting Wace and his patrons, and, even then, merely not knowing the source would not be reason enough to omit it. Importantly, the omission of Wace separates the book by Albin and Austin into two, one by each: it omits the only *secular* source, and so creates the impression that all Laȝamon's sources were *auctores*. This change argues strongly for the prologue in Otho being at least as significantly altered by a commentator or editor of Laȝamon, not by the author himself.

That suggestive point implies that at least one contemporary thought such secular information should be cut. It reflects a sensitivity to Laȝamon's text by a contemporary that belies Donoghue's perception of Laȝamon and his time as essentially ambivalent. It implies, in fact, someone clearly wanting the text to have religious authority behind it. We know that the Church was extending its influence in the area and in Wales (a discussion follows in chapter 3), and that sovereignty and partisanship played a part. Someone clearly perceived the moral implications and possibilities of Laȝamon's work, his *intention*. Therefore Donoghue's stress on, for instance, those who had land in Normandy and in England, and their need to choose, while offered as a case of ambivalence,[7] instead can easily imply more charged and divisive loyalties. Such tensions erupt almost constantly in Laȝamon's *Brut*, often due to invaders, but just as frequently due to internal strife. Instead of ambivalence, therefore, Laȝamon demonstrates an awareness of the varied customs, desires and needs that his own multicultural society was experiencing, and the threat of civil disruption it could entail. Perhaps that constitutes the main reason for his consistent concern for *treope*, and for those who betray their word, their lord or their people. Instead of minimizing the differences among the many peoples in Britain, he presents the dangers and the possibilities realistically, and shows how he prefers Christianity as a unifying factor. It ensures both honour, because of a personal moral code, and a future in which mankind has choice and visionary potential.

Language as Cultural Product

To begin looking at Laȝamon's history itself, one must consider Laȝamon and language, and especially his understanding of the relationship of language and culture, of language as a cultural product. Perhaps language is Laȝamon's starting place for discussing history because it constitutes the most obvious and immediately apparent difference between peoples, even between regions. As an English-speaking priest living in the border region near the Severn, he could hardly be unaware of Welsh struggles with the English. In fact, he ends his work by conferring Wales on Cadwalader's descendants, as if to emphasize the right of Welsh survival as the last remnant of an older British heritage. But since Laȝamon's concern for language is a topic often invoked in discussions of nationalism and his sources, examining his references and sensitivity to language itself and its relationship to culture and to religion will clarify his treatment of his own hybrid culture.

The opposition of natives versus foreigners has often caused scholars to comment on Laȝamon's nationalism or insularity. Yet he seems not so much concerned with homogeneous nationalism as with recording the differences within a nation's regions. He seems interested in voicing the claims of both the British/Celts and the Saxons; yet we need not accept ambivalence to explain this duality. For Laȝamon, his land's heritage (not to mention that of his region near the Severn) is mixed: he can lay claim to both cultures, and write of British history in English. Interestingly, this claim links to a medieval Christian perception discussed by O. B. Hardison and picked up by Maureen Quilligan. Quilligan cites Hardison's work on the mass and Christian drama where, before communion, the faithful are 'the Chosen People longing for the fulfillment of prophecy . . . Following the Communion, the congregation assumes still another role. Allegorically it becomes the disciples and apostles receiving the blessing of Christ.' Quilligan notes,

> Fluidly fluctuating between a consciousness of themselves as historical Hebrews and as present Gentiles, the congregation is, at any time, literally within the role the metaphorical or 'allegorical' (in old parlance) interpretation would assign to them.[8]

While at first glance ambivalent, this fluctuation, or (better) fluidity, should be read not as an inability or unwillingness to choose (clearly these people would see themselves as Christian), but as a sign of historical perspective, the past alive in the present, a dual heritage: while at any given time the congregation may be predominantly Hebrew or Gentile in its performance of a role, Christianity allows them to see themselves as multiple and also one.

The bond of Christianity is larger than that of a nation, and many of the incidents used as problematic evidence for nationalism gain clarity when the religious element emerges. This religious aspect and Laȝamon's moralistic tone would also be relevant to the question of *auctoritas*: 'To have "intrinsic worth", a literary work had to conform, in one way or another, with Christian truth; an *auctor* had to say the right things.'[9] For example, when Vortiger falls in love with Rouwenne, he is a British Christian who is manœuvred into the situation by her father, Hengest, a Saxon heathen. In the scene of their initial meeting, Rouwenne offers Vortiger a drink (in a manner that prefigures her later poisoning of his son) according to a Saxon custom. Keredic interprets her act for Vortiger:

> Hit beoð tiðende/ inne Sæxe-londe.
> Whær-swa æi duȝeðe gladieð of drenche/
> þat freond sæiðe to freonde/ mid fæire loten hende/
> Leofue freond wæs hail/ þe oðer sæið Drinc hail.
> þe ilke þat halt þene nap/ he hine drinkeð up.
> o[ð]er uul me þider fareð/ ꝯ bithecheð his iueren.
> þenne þat uul beoð icumen/ þenne cusseoð heo þreoien.
> þis beoð sele laȝen/ inne Saxe-londe.
> ꝯ inne Alemaine/ heo beoð ihalden aðele. (ll. 7149–57)

(It is the custom in Saxon lands
Whenever any retinue is gladdened with drinking
That friend says to friend with a fair, noble gesture,
'Dear friend, wæs hail [to your health]'; the other says, 'Drinc hail.'
The same one who holds the drinking bowl, he drinks it up.
Another full one is brought there and given to his companion.
When that full one is come, then they kiss three times.
This is good manners in Saxon lands
and in Germany this is held as noble.)

Vortiger predictably likes this custom and adopts it, which Laʒamon credits as the introduction of the custom to all Britain. Vortiger answers Rouwenne 'an Bruttisc⁄ ne cuðe he nan Ænglisc' (l. 7159) (in British – he did not know any English), and so 'þurh þa ilke leoden⁄ þa laʒen comen to þissen londe' (l. 7163) (through that same people the custom came to this land). Again, the link of people, custom, land and language emerges. But Laʒamon adds his own comment: 'þat wes swi[ð]e ladlic þing⁄ þat þe Cristine king. / luuede þat haðene maide⁄ leoden to hærme' (ll. 7172–3) (that was a hateful thing, that the Christian king loved that heathen maid to the harm of the people). The possible pun of *leoden* as 'led' and as 'people' is not unlikely, and the cause-and-effect construction ending in harm should not go unremarked.

But to return to Laʒamon and language more specifically. Some scholars have made much of Laʒamon's own name and the Scandinavian element 'law', even to tracing his references to custom (*laʒen*) and declaring them as a primary fascination of his. This attempt stretches the evidence, to put it mildly. Signifying elements of a name do not predetermine the interests of anyone, and discussions of customs and law are an aspect, not a dominant theme, of Laʒamon's interest in variation in cultures – though, if it were, he is much closer to being an anthropologist than a lawyer. *Medieval* readers may well have focused on *laʒen* because of his name (see the previous comments from Minnis), but that would have led them to his interest in cultural variation, not to an insistence on any law or custom of a particular people as dominant. Acknowledging differences and maintaining them need not imply an ambivalent inability to choose, but a keen eye for individuality. In any case, he several times refers to his own language as English while stressing British history and culture, and clearly pictures his audience as English, most obviously in writing in that language. Lines 1455–6 mention Kaer Leir, and he adds that it is the city 'þa we an ure leod-quide/ Leirchestre clepiað' (that we in our people's speech call Leicester). A similar comment about legions, 'þa we clipieð ferden' glosses *fer-rædene* (l. 3002) which were in that same day called legions, 'þe weoren on þan ilke dæʒen/ legiuns ihaten' (l. 3003). Interestingly, one of the effects of rehearsing many names for one place is to show that the place survives as a constant; for Laʒamon, the land survives, no matter what men do. There remains a constant base for any cycle of change.

In the larger cultural context, languages mirror cultural changes, the cyclical constant paradoxically made of change. Thus, the *Brut* opens with a Trojan settlement by Brutus of the island that then takes his name, Brutaine. In fact, Laʒamon says the settlers spoke *Troinisce*, and that afterwards they called this language *Brutunisc* (l. 987). Fascination with the romance of Troy and its tragedy existed throughout Europe, and, much as earlier Anglo-Saxons had linked their genealogies with the gods', so writers of the twelfth century and after traced their countries' origins to famous Trojan ancestors. But before a thousand lines of the poem have flowed, Laʒamon has already cut to the end of his work to mention that Gurmond drove out the Britons, that he was Saxon from a part of Germany called *Angles* (later we find he is African but allied with Saxons), that from the Angles came the English, and that they called the land *Engle-lond*. He adds, 'þa Englisce ouer-comen þe Brutuns/ ⁊ brouhten heom þer neoðere. / þat neofer seoððen heo ne arisen/ ne her ræden funden' (ll. 997-9) (The English overcame the Britons, and brought them down so far that never since have they arisen nor found their counsel/had their say). He mentions that the name Britain still sticks fast in places, however (l. 981), presumably where Celts survive. In fact, the Welsh consistently used 'Britain' and 'Briton' through the twelfth century, not abandoning usage until late in that century in favour of Cymry (the name for people and land were the same). Almost immediately after, Laʒamon gives the first of many place-name derivations which scholars have long noted and studied separately (for example, the extensive work by Blenner-Hassett[10]), the strongest initial indication that for him the land speaks of its heritage through the names men give it. He speaks of New Troy, called Trinovant by the Trojans and especially loved by the king Lud. As a result, the people come to call it after him, Kærlud, afterwards called Lundin. When the English came they called it Lundene, but when the French conquered and brought their customs (*leodðeawe*), they called it Lundres (ll. 1013–31). Not content with a mere rehearsal of names linked to peoples, Laȝamon adds,

> þus is þas burh i-uaren/ seððen heo ærest wes a-reræd.
> þus is þis eit-lond/ i-gon from honde to hond.
> þet alle þa burhȝes/ þe Brutus iwrohte.
> ⁊ heora noma god/ þa on Brutus dæi stode.
> beoð swiðe afelled/ þurh warf of þon folke. (ll. 1032–6)

> (Thus has this city fared since it first was raised.
> Thus has this island gone from hand to hand,
> so that all the cities that Brutus wrought
> and their good names which in Brutus' day stood
> are entirely destroyed through changes in the peoples.)

He later repeats the same heritage for the place with some additional commentary. Instead of the French, though, he refers to the Normans in a passage frequently quoted by those who would argue Laȝamon's political intentions are to denounce the overlords. It is the only time he mentions Normans directly.

> Seoððen comen Normans/ mid heore nið-craften.
> and nemeden heo Lundres/ þeos leodes heo amærden/
> Swa is al þis lond iuaren. for uncuðe leoden/
> þeo þis londe hæbbeð bi-wunnen. and ef[t] beoð idriuen hennene.
> And eft hit biȝetten oðeræ/ þe uncuðe weoren.
> ⁊ falden þene ælden nomen/ æfter heore wille.
> of gode þe burȝen/ ⁊ wenden heore nomen.
> swa þat nis her burh nan/ in þissere Bruttene.
> þat habbe hire nome æld/ þe me arst hire on-stalde. (ll. 3547–55)

> (Afterwards came the Normans with their evil ways
> and they named it Lundres; this people they ruined.
> So has all this land fared because of uncouth/foreign people,
> who have won this land and afterwards are driven hence.
> And after, others got it who were foreigners,
> and abandoned the old names of the good cities,
> according to their will, and changed their names,
> so that there is here no city in this Britain
> that has its old name which people first established.)

While *nið-craften* is clearly a derogatory reference, the context of the quotation, especially when placed alongside the earlier, similar reference, shows Laȝamon as more closely concerned with the loss of older names. Loss of names silences heritage. It produces a misleading homogeneity and ignorance of the past. Laȝamon, however, writes not merely descriptive history but prescriptive history as well. He rehearses the names to preserve them as truth: recall his request to learn these true words and say them together (not edited?), but also to remind people that change is a constant. (Here, I agree with Donoghue's point on cyclical change, though within a different setting.) He seems fascinated with variety in peoples, languages and customs, perhaps showing this even in his own varied forms of verse. Laȝamon clearly also values the ability to remember history and the ability to speak well, often in another's language, and here his fascination for variety emerges in multilingualism. If the prologue contains any truth, Laȝamon himself knew at least English and even Anglo-Saxon, Anglo-Norman French and Latin, a far cry from the simple country priest some would make him.[11] Indeed Elizabeth Salter comments precisely on these languages in an essay on early thirteenth-century culture and literature that

> facility in the three languages – Latin, French and English – was admired in men of culture and education: as early as 1181–2, Walter Map commented of Gilbert Foliot, Bishop of London, that he was 'vir trium peritissimus linguarum, Latine, Gallice, Anglice, et lucidissime disertus in singulis . . .', and the same may have been true of Grosseteste. Roger Bacon in his *Compendium Studii Philosophiae* (1271–2) takes it for granted as desirable that the English should speak three languages: English, French and Latin 'sicut maternam in qua natus est'; it may be significant that he places English first – 'ut nos loquimur Anglicum, Gallicum et Latinum'.[12]

Thus, when Julius Caesar looks for two messengers, he specifies that he wishes men 'þe wel cunnen a speche' (l. 3639), which can mean simply that they should be eloquent, but may mean able to converse in British, as they are being sent to Cassibellaunus as initial contacts.[13] When discussing the abilities of Magan, the wise man whom Vortiger calls to confirm if Merlin's mother's story can be true, Laȝamon describes him as knowing the craft that dwells in the sky (astrology), being able to advise and see afar, and being able to tell 'of ælche leodspelle' (l. 7863). I am tempted to translate such a phrase as knowing each people's tale of history or origins, as it is Merlin's origins he is called to confirm. (Laȝamon uses a similar construct, 'a leoda ne a spella' (l. 903) to say that no one had ever heard the names of twenty giants who followed Geomagog, either among the people, as in oral history, or in tales.) Again, he speaks of *leod-scopes* who sing about Arthur, perhaps implying by the term a person who sings specifically about a people; in that context, however, he adds the interesting comment that such singers sing neither all truth nor all lies, but that never had a king so great as Arthur existed, 'for þat soðe stod a þan writen/ hu hit is iwurðen' (l. 11468) (that truth stood in the writing, how it happened). Again, the reliance on books to preserve the truth reinforces the claim for truth in the prologue.

For Laȝamon, history allows accomplishments to many groups, not simply the one Laȝamon himself might favour. He clarifies the history of Anglo-Saxon law, for instance, when he declares (following Geoffrey) that Mercian law was not codified by Alfred the Great but originally written by a wise British queen called Marciane, hence *Mærcene laȝe* in *Bruttisc*. He says instead that Alfred translated it:

Seo[ð]ðen þer-æfter. monie hundred wintre/
com Alfred þe king. Englelondes deorling/
and wrat þa laȝen on Englis. ase heo wes ær on Bruttisc/
and whærfde hire nome on his dæȝe. and cleopede heo Mærcene laȝe/
Ah þet I þe sugge. þurh all þing/ ne makede heo noh[t] ærst Ælured king.
ah heo makede þa quene/ þe me Mærcie cleopede.
and Ælured heo seide on Englisc/ þis is seoð ful iwis. (ll. 3147–53)

(Then many hundred winters after that
came Alfred the king, England's darling,
and wrote the law in English, as it was first in British,
and changed its name in his day and called it Mercian Law.
But this I tell you through everything, King Alfred did not make it first,
but the queen made it, whom people called Mærcie,
and Alfred said it in English: this is absolutely true.)

But what of knowing the languages of others? Clearly the example above is a benefit to the Anglo-Saxons and, in the case of Vortimer and Rouwenne, Vortimer's knowledge of Saxon might, in Laȝamon's implication, have saved him: 'þe king heo uæire under-uæng/ to his fæie-siðe. / Fortimer spæc Bruttisc/ ⁊ Rouuenne Saxisc. / þan king þuhte gomen inoh/ for hire spæche he loh' (ll. 7472–4) (The king responded fair to her, to his undoing/fey doom. Vortimer spoke British and Rouwenne Saxon. The king thought it entertainment enough; he laughed at her speech). She poisons him, with a play on words of which Laȝamon was surely aware: she offers a bowl (*bolle*) of wine with poison, but soon after, the lines read 'þat *atter* heo halde in þat win. / seoðen heo þa *cuppe*/ bitahte þan kinge' (ll. 7481b–2). *Atorcoppe* is Old English for spider, something suitable to Rouwenne's long-plotted revenge and available as a *double entendre* only to those in Laȝamon's audience who knew English (or Old English?), unlike Vortimer. Similarly, in a parallel situation, the British are injured by a foreigner who knows their tongue. When King Wiðer fights the Romans of Claudius, the Roman Hamun disguises himself as a Briton and begins to strike down his own people in order to get close to the king. Notably, he can accomplish this infiltration not just because he kills his own but because 'his speche wes al Brutisc/ Brut swulc he weoren' (l. 4639) (his speech was entirely British, as if he were a Briton). Language is the key to power and survival. Knowing several, not merely one's own, increases such power. There is no ambivalence about the limitations of a single nationality or language here.

Laȝamon uses language and the history of peoples as a key to domination and loss. The British early on lose their domination after the deaths of Belin and Brennes, who conquered Rome, until the time of Arthur. When Arthur and Howel go to the aid of Lincoln, which Childric, emperor of Germany besieges, Arthur sends in a messenger to tell the city he arrives at midnight. They are to come forth and trap Childric between them, and 'we heom sculleð tellen/ Bruttisse spelles' (l. 10281) (we'll tell them British tales). History, the past, lives in the present, in language and in the invocation of British history to would-be conquerors; importantly, against the Continent the British can triumph once again, as they had not done since the time of Belin and Brennes. In fact, the claims of Belin and Brennes, ancestors of the Britons, reinforce the link between heritage, language and duty which will contain Laȝamon's moral messages.

Duty to Heritage

The link to the past is directly through ancestors, who play a large part in Laȝamon when descendants claim honour and rights to inheritance or land. Perhaps such a view of ancient heritage plays a part in Laȝamon's feeling of loss when any place name is superseded and lost to another. For the Picts, for example, who get wives from Ireland, language and race are one, for 'þurh þa ilke wifmen⁄ þa þer wuneden longe. / þat folc gan to spelien⁄ Irlondes speche' (l. 5021) (through those same wives who lived there long, that folk began to talk the speech of Ireland). Among many examples, Arthur invokes his ancestors Belin and Brennes when deciding to cross to the Continent and fight Rome. But even more, he cites emperors that came from Britain, such as Constantine, whose mother was British ('he wes Helene sune⁄ al of Brutten icume', l. 12509), and Maximien, who was king of Britain before he became emperor (ll. 12512–16), ending, 'And þeos weoren mine ælderen mine aððele uore-genglen' (l. 12517) (And these were my elders, my noble forefathers). Similarly, when Walwain and two others confront Emperor Luces as messengers, both sides invoke ancestors as determining their rights to rule. Luces reminds Walwain of Julius Caesar, while Walwain cites Brennes and the fact that the Romans lost Britain many years before (ll. 13184–92).

Soon after, Quencelin, a knight of Luces's *cunne* (kin), insults all the British as boastful but without honour, and Walwain kills him, setting off a chase of the three British messengers back fifteen miles to Arthur's camp. Walwain turns back several times, because he 'icneo þene reme⁄ of þane Romanisce men' (l. 13235) (understood the shout of the Roman men) and can understand the insults they hurl after the British. He had been fostered in Rome and knighted there, 'For Walwain cuðe Romanisc⁄ Walwain cuðe Bruttisc. / he wes iued inne Rome⁄ wel feole wintre' (ll. 13099–100) (for Walwain knew Roman, Walwain knew British; he was raised in Rome full many winters). In one of his encounters, he kills the Roman knight Marcel and tells him to tell his *spelles* in hell to Quencelin and others, an echo of Arthur's comment to Colgrim after killing him. In that passage, Arthur mockingly compared Colgrim's defence of a hill to trying to climb to heaven, but gaining hell with his dead kin instead: 'þu clumbe a þissen hulle⁄ wunder ane hæȝe; / swulc þu woldest to hæuene⁄ nu þu scalt to hælle. / þer þu miht kenne⁄ muche of þine cunne' (ll. 10698–700) (you climbed this hill, wondrously high, as if you wanted to get to heaven. Now you shall go to hell, where you should recognize many of your kin). Walwain, in another echo of the same battle sequence, specifically Arthur's admonition to Lincoln's people, cries that 'þus we eou scullen techen⁄ ure Bruttisce speche' (l. 13248) (thus we shall teach you our British speech). Instead of bowing to Rome and speaking its language, he equates superiority and domination with the triumph of his own tongue, and thus of his people. Indeed, shortly after, a warrior called Beof of Oxene-uord, seeing Arthur's men lose ground, rallies them by advising that they show they are of the same kin or breed, 'of are cuðða' (l. 13350), and must show their *cniht-scipe*. Soon after, when the British have once again triumphed and taken a key Roman prisoner, Petreius, Arthur says, 'Wulcume Petreius. / Nu ic þe wulle teche. Bruttisce spæche' (ll. 13392–3) (Welcome, Petreius: now I will teach you British speech).

The friction between Britons and Saxons especially has its clearest example in Hengest and his actions. What he does has a direct relationship to language (as sworn word) and to ancestors (as victims of betrayal of that word). After Hengest has been exiled in Vortimer's time and then recalled once Vortiger rules again, Hengest plots vengeance, and Laȝamon emphasizes betrayal once again. In the space of ten lines (7570–80), he mentions *swike* (treachery) in some form five times: Hengest plots treachery, 'þohte swike'; he was angry, as is every man who considers himself 'bi-swikeð' (betrayed); he thought to betray ('swiken þohte') the king who had his daughter, for there is no man who may not be overcome by 'swike-dome', and so Hengest becomes 'þe swike'. By line 75590 he has become 'þe leod-swike' (the people's traitor), and twice more within fifteen lines he is the knight 'swikelest' (most treacherous). The concept of treachery relates to language, heritage and oral culture, where a man's word is his bond, and is one of Laȝamon's two most pervasive themes; the other is Christians versus heathens. (A fuller discussion of treachery follows in the next section of this chapter.)

When Hengest has won and divided up the country among his followers, the British do not forget his actions. According to Laȝamon, the British name the sections of the country to include the word *sæx*, an Anglo-Saxon form of knife, to remember Hengest's treason:

> Brut<tes> scupten þan londe nome/ for Sæxisce monnen scome.
> 7 for þan swike-dome/ þat heo idon hæfden.
> for þan þe heo mid cnifen/ biræueden heom at liue.
> þa cleopeden heo þat lond al/ Æst-sæx West-sæx.
> 7 at þridde/ Middel-sæx. (ll. 7676–80)

> (The British gave the land names for the shame of Saxon men,
> for the betrayal they had committed.
> Because they deprived them of life with knives,
> thus they called all that land Essex [i.e. East-*sæx*] and Wessex
> and the third part Middlesex.)

Laȝamon clearly understands that the place names contain the name 'Saxon' in them, as he has already used these terms in the passage immediately before this one to describe which of Hengest's men received which sections (ll. 7661–70). But he links the heathen Saxons with their weapons, and makes their name a sign of their betrayal: notably, Hengest's act becomes one that constitutes shame for all his men, and they are implicated along with him. Again, people, language and their actions in history are linked and preserved in names.

More than names, British memory retains the betrayal of their ancestors by the Saxons. Even so, Christianity softens the reaction until treachery re-emerges, this time in violation not simply of a secular bond but of an oath sworn with religious considerations. Arthur initially pardons Childric, the German emperor, when Childric loses a battle and is caught 'like a fox chased by hounds'. He does so for markedly Christian sentiments. He sends Childric and his followers home, for they 'Tellen tidende⁄ of Arðure kinge. / hu ich heom habbe ifreoied⁄ for mines fader saule / ⁊ for mine freo-dome⁄ ifrouered þa wrækchen' (ll. 10425–7) (will tell tidings of Arthur the king, how I have set them free for my father's soul and because of my generosity spared the wretched). But, as Laȝamon sadly informs us, Arthur is 'aðelen bidæled' (lacking good judgement), and no one dares tell him he has made a mistake. When Childric pretends to leave but returns to kill churls, knights, wives, maidens, book-learned men and shepherds, Arthur arms with his famous arms and armour, all individually named in a mix of British and English, and summons his men. Carrying Caliburn his sword, Ron his spear, wearing Uther's helm Goswhit and his own shield Pridwen engraved in red gold with the likeness of Mary, Arthur invokes Christianity, ancestry and vengeance. The linguistically mixed names of his arms emphasize the unification of these variations under Christian motivation as Arthur proclaims:

> Lou war her biforen us⁄ heðene hundes⁄
> þe sloȝen ure alderen⁄ mid luðere heore craften.
> and heo us beoð on londe⁄ læðest alre þinge.
> Nu fusen we hom to⁄ ⁊ stærcliche heom leggen on.
> ⁊ wræken wunder-liche⁄ ure cun ⁊ ure riche.
> ⁊ wreken þene muchele scome⁄ þat heo us i-scend habbeoð
> þat heo ouer vðen⁄ comen to Derte-muðen.
> ⁊ alle heo beoð for-sworene⁄ ⁊ alle heo beoð for-lorene.
> heo beoð for-demed alle mid Driht/tenes fulste. (ll. 10564–72)

(Look where here before us are heathen hounds
who slew our ancestors with their treacherous power
and who are to us in the land the most loathly of all things!
Now let us charge them, and fiercely set on them,
and wreak vengeance gloriously for our kin and our kingdom
and avenge the great shame with which they have dishonoured us
when they came to Dartmouth over the waves.
And they are all forsworn and they are all lost:
they are utterly doomed with the Lord's aid.)

Vengeance is for kin, country and the shame dealt the British, but with heathens as its specific object. Many years later, when Cadwalan is king of all England and having difficulty with Oswy, St Oswald's brother, Penda requests men to kill Oswy, as Penda had previously killed Oswald through treachery (*swike-dome*). Cadwalan is unsure, and asks Penda to retire while he and his men deliberate. Cadwalan wishes to send a messenger to see why Oswy has not come to court along with all his other lords (Penda has in fact lied, saying Oswy refuses). But a king of south Wales, Margadud, angrily rejects that option. He pointedly says they should let the English fight the English: Penda is English and a former enemy, though reconciled now with Cadwalan and linked to him through marriage to Penda's sister (l. 15516). But the English disinherited the British, leaving them only the western edge (Wales), and most importantly, they betrayed the Christian British king through a heathen woman. 'Let dogs fight with dogs', says Margadud:

> þa comen Englisce men/ mid heore ufele craften.
> heo weore wiʒel-fulle/ and þis lond al biwunne.
> and biswiken heore lauerd sonen/ and alle his leoden.
> ⁊ ʒiuenen heore kinge/ ane heðene quene.
> þa comen of Sex-londe/ þa leoden us beoð laðe.
> þurh þere quene/ ure cun aqualden here.
> and swa habbeoð Englisce men/ ure icunden at-heolden.
> þet we nauere seoððen/ bi-sechen hit no mihten.
> Penda king is Englisc/ and Oswy al-swa ful iwis.
> Let þu þa hundes/ hannen to-gaderes.
> eiðer freten oðer/ swa hund deð his broðer.
> and leten heore whelpes/ whæruen heom bi-sides.
> elc oðer quelle/ þat þer nan quic no leue. (ll. 15803-15)

(Then came English men with their evil ways.
They were cunning and won all this land,
and soon betrayed their lord and all his people
and gave their king a heathen queen
who came from Saxony; that people is loathly to us.
Through their queen they killed our kin here.
And so English men have held on to our birthright
such that ever since, we cannot hold it.
King Penda is English and Oswy also, certainly.
Let dogs fight together,
let each tear at the other as a hound does his brother
and let their whelps turn on them besides,
let each kill the other, so that none leave there alive.)

The echoes in both speeches, Arthur's and Margadud's, are apparent, and strongly negative concerning the English. They betray, they are heathen, they killed ancestors, they are animals and aliens. (The initial phrase strongly resembles the one cited above for the Normans.) But note that in both cases the speeches are those of historical figures, not Laȝamon's own comments. His comments are reserved for bad judgement and situations such as his regret over a Christian marrying a heathen. He clearly includes the idea of such a mismatch in all discussions about the incident, and links such betrayals of Christian unity to betrayal of people and ultimately land. In a few instances, Laȝamon uses constructs that seem almost to make characters the land personified. After Arthur kills Colgrim, he laughs and speaks with boisterous words, 'mid gomenfulle worden' (l. 10693), in the same passage about Colgrim's trying to get to heaven and meeting his Saxon kin in hell, including Hengest. Arthur in mockery or scorn says, 'nu ich al þis kine-lond/ sette an eower ahȝere hond. / dales dunes/ al mi drihtliche uolc' (ll. 10696–7) (Now all this realm I place in your possession, dales and downs and all my worthy folk). Later, Cador, just before slaying Colgrim's ally Childric, says fiercely, 'Abid abid Childric/ ich wulle þe ȝefen Teinewic' (l. 10790) (Hold on, hold on, Childric – I'll give you Teinewic [the hill which Childric defends in his last resort]).

Of course, Arthur follows the example of many earlier Christian kings, though he is the best. His father, Uther, fights in his crippled old age a lifelong enemy, Octa. In the past, Octa had been both enemy, as a heathen, and ally, converted to Christianity. He has, however, reverted to heathenism and thinks to take the kingdom since Uther is ill and Arthur is in Brittany. But Uther calls on God, especially conscious of being in Verulam where St Alban was martyred, and invokes ancestors, God and his saints together, imparting a sacred link to all three:

> Iþenche[ð] on eoure aldren/ hu gode heo weoren to fehten/
> Iþenche[ð] þene wurðscipe/ þat ich eou habbe wel biwiten.
> ne læten ȝe næuere þas hæðene/ bruken eoure hames.
> þæs ilke awedde hundes/ walden eouwere londes.
> And ich wullen bidden Drihten/ þat scop þæs dæies lihten.
> ⁊ alle þaie halȝen/ þa an hæfene hæhȝe sitteð.
> þat [ich] on þissen felde/ mote beon ifroured. (ll. 9746–52)

> (Think of your ancestors, how good they were at fighting.
> Think of the honour that I have well bestowed on you.
> Do not ever let these heathens take our homes,
> these same rabid hounds rule your lands.
> And I will pray to the Lord who created the light of day
> and all the saints who sit in heaven on high
> that I may be aided on this field.)

By now, the vocabulary echoes are clear: heathens are hounds who are not to have the land, and memories of ancestral warriors are to inspire the defence. In fact, Uther wins and, recalling how Octa derisively taunted that Uther thought to thrust down the Saxons with his crutch (ll. 9720–1), Uther wryly comments that a wondrous thing, a miracle even, has happened: 'nu haueð þeos dede king/ þas quiken aqualden' (l. 9781) (now has this dead king slaughtered the living). Given his previous reference to ancestors (*aldren*), the subtext of *their* triumph too is suggested, an ancient wrong corrected, the past alive in the present. The Christian overtone of a dead king's triumph over the living should not escape unremarked, however.

The ancient Christianity of Britain, predating Augustine's mission, is a source of pride to the Britons even before Uther, and perhaps also to Laȝamon, given his location and his priesthood. When Augustine baptizes the English, and then calls for the seven British bishops and the monks of northern England and Bangor to attend him, they write him an indignant response. Not only does he baptize their enemies (and so remove one of the main inspirations for opposition), but he claims an authority he does not have. Their pride is injured, and they remind him of their heritage:

Language as Personal History

Ne beo we na-wit under him/ þe is ihaten Austin.
ah we beo on londe/ heȝe men and stronge.
and habbeoð ure irihte/ of ure arche-biscope.
þe wuneð inne Karliun/ godd clarc and wel idon/
þa haueð his cantel-cape on. of Gregorie þan pape/
and mid wurð-scipe mucle/ haldeð his wike.
For no scal hit nauere iwurðen/ a þissere worlde-richen.
þat we auere buȝen/ Austine þan uncuðen.
for he is ure fulle ifa/ ⁊ his iferen al-swa.
For Austin is iboȝen hidere/ in-to þissen londe.
and haueð i-fulleȝed þene king/ Cantuaren aðeling.
Aðelbert ihaten/ heh inne Anglene.
and he hafueð ifunden here/ hundes heðene.
þa comen of Sexlonde/ mid Gurmu[n]de þan kinge.
þeo he alle fullehte ð/ and to Gode fuseoð.
þeo haldeoð ure kinelond/ mid unrihte on heore hond.
Cristine we beoð alle/ and of Cristine cunne.
and ure elderne swa weoren/ agan is þreo hundred ȝeren.
and heo beoð neowene icumen/ and Cristindom habbeoð under-numen.
and Austin heom fullehteð/ and to Gode fuseoð.
For þan we hine hatiȝen uulleð/ <heren h>[ine nulleð]
nauere to ure liue. no scullen we him wurðen liðe. (ll. 14843–64)

(We are not in any way under him who is called Austin [Augustine],
but we are high men and strong in this land,
and have our rights from our archbishop
who lives in Caerleon, a good and well educated cleric
who has his cope from Gregory the pope,
and who with great honour holds his office.
For it shall not ever happen in this world's kingdom
that we ever bow to Austin the foreigner,
for he is fully our foe, and his followers also.
For Austin is come here into this land,
and has baptized the king, the royal one of Kent
called Athelbert, important among the English,
and he has found here heathen hounds
who come from Saxony with Gurmund the king.
All these he baptizes and urges to God.
They hold our family lands unjustly in their hands.
Christians we are all, and of Christian kin,
just as our ancestors were, starting three hundred years ago.
And they are newly come, and have accepted Christianity,
and Austin baptizes and urges them to God.
Therefore we mean to revile him and will not listen to him;
never in our lives will we ever be happily obedient.)

Elsewhere, *uncuð* is the mark of the foreigner, as is the term *unleoden* for invaders (l. 3459). It also has the meaning of someone alienated from the group, as when the knights of Arthur riot and Rumareth's son declares he will put an end to the fight between 'uncuðe kempen' (l. 11377). These same men are those who swore allegiance to Arthur and, while technically they are from many countries, it is their action which occasions the term, not their origins or nationalities. Rumareth's son himself is from Winet-londe, usually understood as meaning the Wends, equivalent to the *winedas* of 'Widsith'. So too Arthur speaks of alienation when recounting his dream about Modred's and Wenhauer's treachery. In the dream, he sits atop a hall with Walwain, and Modred and Wenhauer tear the hall apart beneath him; he refers to the content of his dream as 'spelles uncuðe' (l. 14062), a strange vision where those he loves turn against him. Thus, Augustine is not merely a foreigner to the Britons, attempting to usurp the place of their archbishop who was also appointed by Pope Gregory: he has alienated himself from British Christians by baptizing their enemies and giving them equal or greater status, ignorant of British feeling and memories of rights and betrayal. Laʒamon may be attempting fairness at this point; apparently of Anglo-Saxon extraction himself, he nevertheless frequently admits the claims of other groups, notably those of the native Britons, in his day the Welsh. His insistence on 'soþe' approaches the aims of modern historians to produce objective or at least balanced truth about the past. That is not to say, however, that his presentation is free of editorial or scholarly comments, any more than historians today can claim total objectivity, or wish to.

Betrayal

That we can discern Laʒamon's own perspectives remains in keeping with his emphases on personal honour, fallibility and responsibility. Nowhere is that clearer than in his consistent and constant repetition of treachery and betrayal. *Swiken* becomes the cause of political unrest, underlines oral culture's emphasis on word as honour, and marks those who betray or reject Christianity. Political and religious betrayals link the sacred and profane in a way that parallels Laʒamon's larger depiction of prophecy as a link of the infinite and finite. But the betrayal of a people begins with the individual.

The verb *swiken* occurs throughout the text as perhaps the most frequent verb associated with changes in power and rulership. Laʒamon uses specific terms such as *leod-swike* and *lauerd-swike* to describe particular betrayals of a people and a lord. Therefore, Anacletus, captured by Brutus and sent under threat of death to lead his king into ambush, is called *leodene swike* (l. 378), though he does what Brutus requires in order to save his own lord's life. The betrayal is emphasized by a proverb about how his own army and leader could believe him: there is nowhere any man so wise that he may not be betrayed – 'Nis nawer nan so wis mon⁄ þat me ne mai bi-swiken' (l. 379). When Uther's father Constantine dies, he is stabbed by a Pict in his household who was 'al-swa his broðer': the Pict entices him into an orchard having first knelt before the king and 'þus leh þa *leod-swike*. biuoren his lauerd' (l. 6459) (thus lied the people's traitor before his lord). Hengest, before betraying Vortiger at Amesbury, secretly tells his own men to bring knives after swearing to come weaponless: 'Þus heo hit speken⁄ æft heo hit to-breken. / for Hængest þe *leod-swike*⁄ þus he his gon learen' (ll. 7589–90) (Thus they said it and after they broke it, for Hengest the people's traitor, in this way he taught his followers). Soon after, when Vortiger tries to build his castle against Hengest on Mount Reir, the walls fall and a false sage named Ioram calls for the blood of a boy without a father. Merlin challenges him to tell the truth, calling him 'Ioram *leod-swike*' (l. 7926), presumably because his lies place the kingdom and its people, not simply Merlin, at risk.

A similar specific term, *lauerd-swike*, is used solely by Arthur. In setting up his laws, he returns land to any who had lost it unless he was a traitor to his lord or a perjurer forsworn; then the man himself is lost: 'bute he weore swa fule biwite⁄ þat he weore *lauerd-swike*. / oðer touward his lauer[d] man-swore⁄ þene þe king demde for-lore' (ll. 11047–8). Later, when Roman messengers bring Luces's unwelcome requirements, the British are about to kill them for their presumption when Arthur leaps up 'like a lion'. He chides them for punishing a messenger's loyalty to his lord despite danger, and says death would only be justified if he betrayed his lord (as the Pict did Constantine): 'þet he weore *lauerd-swike*' (l. 12408). Ironically, Arthur himself is betrayed by Modred and Wenhauer; betrayal of *lauerd* and of *leod* unite in his case.

More telling than such individual terms, however, is the consistent emphasis on those who *swiken* and on *swikedom*. Without exception, every major story contains betrayal or concern about betrayal. It is worthwhile here to consider something Brian Stock writes on a related topic about the interaction of orality and literacy. In discussing forgery, he comments on its rise due to the new emphasis on written documents as proof of claim:

> In oral culture a forger was not a person who altered legal texts; he was a traitor. He betrayed the relationship not between words and things but between men.
> Only through the wedding of property claims to a written record of title did the opposite point of view come to prevail.[14]

Laȝamon accurately locates betrayal and treachery in a pre-literate, oral culture where reputation depends on a man's word and his ability to keep troth. Perhaps this location of truth as between men, not things and words, partially accounts for his use of dialogue when his sources have no such exchange, the need to put words in a man's mouth and make him take responsibility. Perhaps too this accountability is why Arthur, upon hearing Frolle's acceptance of single combat, says with such satisfaction, 'hit bicumeð kinge⁞ þat his word stonde' (l. 11841) (it becomes a king that his word should stand). (The prophecy about Arthur, notably, is that the wild boar 'scal al þa *swiken⁞* swenien mid eiȝe' (l. 8034) – all the traitors he shall destroy with terror.) Frolle actually wishes Arthur had backed down, but will not now renege because his standing as a king is at stake. That Laȝamon wishes to emphasize truth in this account may be partially in reaction to the treachery of men.

Swikedom, betrayal or treachery, often takes place within a family, as when Membriz was counted among the greatest traitors, 'swike mid þan meste', promising peace with his brother; but soon he undid the peace ('ah sone he makede unfrið') and *bi-swac* his brother Malin (ll. 1274, 1279, 1304).[15] As a corrective, his good son Ebrauc 'heold swiðe god grið⁞ ne breac na man his frið' (l. 1312), a syntactic inversion of what Membriz did: Ebrauc kept a strong peace, and no man broke it. But the first real concentration of family betrayal in deed and in words comes with the story of Leir and his daughters, the first English version of this tale. (Leir is of course Shakespeare's Lear, but preceding him are the Welsh Llŷr and Irish Lir, sea gods.) Ironically, by testing his daughters verbally, Leir becomes the victim of orality: he trusts that his daughters will not lie, and he also accepts too shallow or literal a meaning. We know Gornoille is lying because Laȝamon describes her as quite wary, 'swiðe wær' (l. 1482). Regau responds 'mid rætfulle worden' (with discreet or prudent words) in Caligula, but in Otho, 'mid worde⁄ and noht mid heorte' (l. 1502) (with mere words and not with her heart). Cordoille, on the other hand, hears the lying ('iherde þa lasinge') and decides – 'heo wolde suge seoð⁄ were him lef were him lað' (ll. 1513, 1515) (she would tell the truth, no matter if it pleased or angered him). She is also the only one to swear by her god, Appollin. Because she does not embroider the truth, Leir disowns her, but is soon disinherited by his other two daughters. Regau's husband Hemeri is a warning of what will come: he betrayed his old father, 'his alde fader *bi-swake*' and so presumably has had practice to guide his wife in doing the same. Almost immediately after, Leir bemoans his state in which he has only five knights allowed to his service: 'Wela weolla. wella. hu þu *bi-swikest* monine mon. / Þenne he þe treoweðe alre best on⁄ þenne *bi-swikes* tu heom' (ll. 1704–5) (Alas, alas, how you betray many a man: when he trusts you best of all, then you betray him). He travels to France, to his disinherited Cordoille, sending a knight to her while he waits in a field. The knight says to her, 'beoð ba þine sustren⁄ touward him *forsworene*' (l. 1758) (both your sisters have forsworn themselves to him). Eventually, Cordoille restores Leir to power, and he in turn gives the rule of his kingdom to her; she only loses it because the Scots, including her nephews Morgan and Cunedaigius, invade. Taken prisoner, in wrath she kills herself, but nephew Morgan himself later suffers betrayal. His knights, hating his people and his land ('þeo ne luuede noht þas leoden. ah laið heo hem weoren', l. 1896), talk him into invading the land of Cunedaigius: 'þus speken þeos *swiken*⁄ and spileden mid worde⁄ / swa long heo hine lærde. þat he heom ileuede' (ll. 1905–6) (Thus spoke those traitors, and spilled forth words for so long to their lord that he believed them). Again, the spoken word misleads. Cunedaigius slays Morgan in Wales, and it was 'þet lond. þurh Morgan. Margan ihæten' (l. 1930), that is, Glamorgan, an area of south-east Wales, was named for this man.[16]

The next concentration of betrayal occurs in the Belin and Brennes episodes. The two are sons of Donwal, loving brothers, with the elder, Belin, ruling more land and with Brennes his sworn man. Through bad advice, Brennes marries without permission, and Belin tellingly says upon hearing the news, 'Wa wurðe a þon broðer⁄ þe *bi-swikeð* þene oþer' (l. 2222) (woe betide the brother who betrays the other). Seven years of fighting follow, until the brothers face each other on the field for a life-and-death battle. At this point, their mother, Queen Tonuenne, dresses in rags and goes barefoot to Brennes to confront him. She reminds Brennes that he has allied himself with *unleoden*, and has broken his word: 'Aðes him [Belin] swore׳ *swiken* þat þu noldest' (l. 2514) (You swore oaths to him that you would not betray him). She reminds him that, once Belin is slain, Brennes will never have another brother; in the end, she reconciles the two and they become the greatest power in Britain before Arthur. In many ways, the language used about them and the events concerning them are directly analogous to the Arthurian sections.

They come to Rome, as Arthur will, and conquer. The Romans in turn swear to accept them as lords: '⁊ æðes we sulle[ð] þe swerien׳ þat we þe nulle[ð] *swiken*' (l. 2694). (The promise *not* to betray is later repeated several times whenever a king becomes Arthur's man without a battle.) Here, the Romans soon contemplate treachery, and promise hostages. The king sits silently while the traitors speak: 'Þe king wes stille׳ ⁊ þa *swiken* speken ille. / he weonden þat hit weoren soð׳ þat heo iseid haueden' (ll. 2705–6) (The king was silent and the traitors spoke evil. He thought that it was true, what they had said). Then *þa swiken* return to Rome. Belin and Brennes, however, are aware of the treason ('weoren warre. / of þon *swike-dome*', ll. 2752–3), and defeat the traitors. The ability to concede mercy in return for oaths, but to discern treachery, will be crucial also to Arthur later on.[17]

> Vortiger þat isæh. þe Wurse him wes ful neh׳
> ofte he hine bi-ðohte. wæht he don mahte׳
> hu he mihte mid *læsinge*. i-quemen þan kinge׳
> Nu þu miht iheren. hu þes *swiken* him gon uaren. (ll. 6630–3)

> (Vortiger saw this, the Worse/Devil was quite close to him;
> often he thought to himself what he might do,
> how he might gratify the king with lies.
> Now might you hear how this traitor went forward.)

Vortiger surrounds himself and the king with Picts; given his father's death, Constance should have suspected but did not. Therefore, Vortiger can spoil his Pictish friends and prime them to do his treachery for him. He tells Constance that the Picts will fight for him, 'ah wale þat nuste þa king. of his þohte naðing، / ne of his *swike-dome*. þe he dude þer-æfter sone' (ll. 6697–8) (but alas that the king did not know anything of his thoughts, nor of his treachery that he did soon thereafter). From this point, the concentration of *swike* forms in the section increases markedly.

Vortiger first lies to the Picts, telling them he has spent his fortune on them and cannot steal from the king; he must leave to serve another, and so dismisses them: 'Nusten noht þas cnihtes. wæt þe *swike* þohte. / Vortiger wes fæc، for her he his lauerd *bi-swac*، / þe cnihtes heolden hit for *soh*. þat þe *swike* sæide' (ll. 6740–2) (The knights did not know what the traitor thought. Vortiger was sly, for here he betrayed his lord and the knights held what the traitor said as true). The Picts resolve to find the king, get drunk and murder him, ridding themselves of the monkish king Constance so as to please Vortiger; their leader Gille Callæt drinks and talks with the king, but '*swiken* he þohte' (l. 6770). Once the murder is done, Vortiger tells the people that Constance mistakenly loved the Picts too much, and that he himself was ruined by having to support them. As a result, the Britons slaughter the Picts when they come to Vortiger expecting a reward. Laȝamon leaves no doubt who is truly to blame, as he refers to Vortiger as 'þe *swike* wes ful derne' (a quite devious traitor) three times in just over twenty lines (ll. 6789, 6799, 6805) and again just before he calls on the Britons to kill the Picts (l. 6839). Merlin too makes his guilt clear later. Speaking to Vortiger, he says, 'Þu lettest slæn Costanz. þe wes king a þis lond، / þu lettest þine Peohtes، hine ladliche *biswiken*' (ll. 8011–12) (You had slain Constance who was king in this land; you had your Picts betray him cruelly).

Davies's comments on Vortiger here are extremely relevant. In his history of Wales, Davies comments that

> The Welsh were inordinately proud of their past; . . . But their pride was balanced by profound [*sic*] sense of loss and shame – the loss of the sovereignty of Britain and shame at the oppressions (W. *gormesoedd*) which the Island of the Mighty had suffered at the hands of alien races. Such a sense of deprivation and failure often led to despair, to a deep conviction of the Britons' sinfulness and a sense of shameful contrition in the face of ineluctable divine retribution. Equally it could and did beget a bitter resentment against those who had, willingly or otherwise, aided and abetted the Saxons to deprive the Britons of the sovereignty of Britain. In this gallery of villains none was more reviled than Gwrtheyrn, or Vortigern, one of the Three Dishonoured Men of the Islands of Britain of

Welsh lore. But the Welsh coupled their own sense of failure and betrayal with a bitter enmity towards the Saxons, the heirs of Hengist and Horsa, or the children of Rhonwen as they were called.[18]

Several familiar elements in Laȝamon emerge here, enough to give pause before dismissing Welsh influence on his work. The section on Vortiger and Vortimer takes up more space than any other section concerning an individual except Arthur, and Le Saux's chart shows 444 lines added to this section in Laȝamon. It seems quite striking that the greatest villain and the greatest hero of British tales have such emphasis, and that the two are linked by the character Merlin, also expanded in Laȝamon. Similarly, the emphases on treachery, on sin and retribution, and on the betrayal of Rhonwen (Rouwenne) and the Saxons all find substantial attention in Laȝamon's work. He shares many of the same concerns as the Welsh of his time.

The next incident of betrayal is, in fact, the cited episode with Rouwenne. Vortiger, afraid of the vengeance of Constance's brothers Ambrosius and Uther because he was killed 'þurh *swicfulle* laȝen' (l. 7041), allies with the Saxons. Laȝamon's catchphrase for Vortiger here, constantly repeated, is 'of ælchen ufel he wæs wær' (of every evil he was aware/knowledgeable). Vortiger is also aware of the Picts and their threat; despite voiced misgivings about the paganism of Hengest and his men, he accepts their aid. He tells them, 'ȝe ne ileoueð noht an Criste. / ah ȝe ileoueð a þene Wurse⁄ þe Godd seolf awariede. / . . . Ah neoðeles ich wulle eou at-hælde. an mine anwalde. / for norð beoð þa Peohtes' (ll. 6958b–9, 6961–2a) (You do not believe in Christ but you love the Devil whom God himself damned . . . But nonetheless I will keep you in my retinue, for north are the Picts). Christianity continues to be a factor in negotiations between the two. When Hengest sees that Vortiger is in a precarious position, he asks for a castle, and that he may send for his family, including his daughter Rouwenne. Vortiger grants the latter request, but will grant no castle or city, 'for ȝe haldeð þa hæðene laȝe⁄ þat stod on eoure ælderen dæȝe. / ⁊ we haldeð Cristes laȝe⁄ ⁊ wulleð auere an ure dæȝe' (ll. 7071–2) (for you hold to heathen customs that stood in your elders' days, and we hold to Christ's custom, and always will in our lives). As a result, Rouwenne arrives and later marries Vortiger, cementing his alliance. Notably, at their marriage, despite Vortiger's comments on religion, 'he imakede heo to quene. / al after þan laȝen⁄ þe stoden an hæðe[ne] dæȝen. / nes þer nan Cristindom⁄ þer þe king þat maide

[n]o[m]. / ne preost ne na biscop⁄ ne nauere ihandled Godes boc. / ah an heðene wune he heo wedde' (ll. 7178b–82a) (he made her his queen all according to the customs that stood in heathen days. There was no Christianity when the king took that maid, no priest nor bishop ever handled God's book, but in heathen fashion he wedded her).

The difficulties become obvious soon enough, and the Britons go to their king to tell him what his sin has brought them to:

Þu ært þurh us bald king⁄ inne þissen Brutene.
⁊ þu hafuest þe biwunnen⁄ ⁊ hærm muchele sunnen.
ibroht heðene folc⁄ ȝet hit þe ihærmeð.
⁊ þu letest Godes laȝen⁄ uor uncu[ð]e leoden.
⁊ nult ne ihæren ure Drihten⁄ for þissen hæ[ð]ene cnihten.
⁊ we þe wulleð bidden⁄ for alle Godes sibben.
þat þu heom bilæuen⁄ ⁊ of þine londe driuen . . .
⁊ ȝif heo alle beoð hæðene⁄ ⁊ þu ane Cristine.
nulleð heo nauere longe⁄ habben þe to kinge.
buten þu a þine daȝen⁄ a-fo hæðene laȝen.
⁊ bilæue þe hæhȝe Godd⁄ ⁊ luuie heore Mahimet. (ll. 7264–70, 7276–9)

(You are through us a bold king in this Britain,
and you have brought on yourself harm and great evil,
brought heathen folk. You may yet be punished –
and you abandon God's law for foreign people
and will not listen to our Lord on account of these heathen knights.
And we wish to ask you that all for the peace of God
you forsake and drive them from your land . . .
And if they are all heathen and you a Christian,
they will not for long have you for a king
unless you all your days follow heathen laws
and abandon the high God and love their idols.)

The British call an assembly in London, and 'al þat folc þider com⁄ þat luueden þene Crist/ten-dom' (l. 7305) (all the folk who love Christianity attend). They choose Vortimer as king, and exile Vortiger and his Saxon allies. As mentioned above, the division is between Christians and heathens: 'Þa wes Vortimer⁄ Cristine king þer. / Uortiger his fader⁄ fulede þan hæðenen' (ll. 7309–10) (then was Vortimer Christian king there, and Vortiger his father followed the heathen).

This situation causes Rouwenne to plot to betray Vortimer, the good son of Vortiger, after the exile gives her cause for vengeance.

He, despite kinship, recognizes his father's error but blames the heathens. In conversing with St Germain, he comments on how he will reinstate Church land, condemn heathen custom and support the claims of widows (through their *lauerdes quide*, with 'quide' the Anglo-Saxon term for a will taken from what must have originally been an oral text, a 'quote'). He adds,

> ꝥ þus we scullen an ure daȝen⸱ aniðeri Hengestes laȝen.
> ꝥ hine ꝥ his hæðene-scipe⸱ þæ he hider brohte.
> ꝥ minne fader *biswak*⸱ þurh *swike* his cra[f]tes.
> þurh his dohter Rouwenne⸱ mine uader he uor-radde.
> ꝥ mi uader swa uuele agon⸱ scunede þene Cristindom.
> ꝥ þa hæðene laȝen⸱ luuede to swiðe. (ll. 7415–20)

(Thus we shall in our days cast down Hengest's laws
and him and his heathenness that he brought here;
and he betrayed my father through his traitorous ways.
Through his daughter Rouwenne he led my father astray
and my father most evilly did refuse to practise Christianity
and loved heathen laws too much.)

But Vortimer's Christianity does not save him, as Rouwenne's vengeance can use it against him: 'Rouwenne heo bi-þohte⸱ whæt heo don mahte. / hu heo mahte hire fader wreken⸱ hire freoudene deað' (ll. 7434–5) (Rouwenne considered what she might do, how she might avenge her father and her friends' deaths). Laȝamon comments, with an echo of his comment about Constance earlier (ll. 6697–8), 'Wale þat þe gode king⸱ of hire þonke næs wær. / þat he nuste þene *swikedom*⸱ þe þohte þa luðere wimman' (ll. 7445–6) (Alas that the good king was not aware of her thought, that he did not know the treachery that the wicked woman intended). She asks to convert to Christianity, 'þe *swic-fulle* wimman' (l. 7468), and he welcomes her. Laȝamon invokes our attention, saying, 'Hercne nu muchel *swikedom*⸱ of þere luðere wimmon. / hu heo gon *swiken* þer⸱ þene king Uortimer' (ll. 7470–1) (Listen now to the great treachery of this wicked woman, how she began there to betray the king, Vortimer). In the next ten lines, she is treacherous twice by Laȝamon's vocabulary, when he describes how this woman carries on while the king is ignorant of her betrayal: 'Hærcne hu heo toc on⸱ þ[i]s *swicfulle* wimman' (l. 7475), 'for Uortimer þe gode king⸱ of þan *swikedom* nuste na-þing' (l. 7485). Twelve lines later, she can deceive Vortiger as well, though he himself was so used to deceiving. She instructs her followers to lie to the traitorous Vortigern, saying that his son intended to besiege him; Vortigern believes it all (they should 'luȝen Uortigerne⁊ þat his sune hine wolde biliggen. / ⁊ Vortigerne þe *swikele* king⁊ ilæfde þare læsing', ll. 7496–7).

That Rouwenne comes of treacherous kin emerges clearly when we return to accounts of Hengest. As mentioned earlier, Hengest is referred to by some form of *swike* five times in just over ten lines as he contemplates vengeance (ll. 7470–80). He is also a *leod-swike*, and twice referred to as *swikelest* (ll. 7590, 7594, 7609). Even the components of some verbs seem to indict him: Laȝamon has him urge on his men by crying '*Aswikeð* mine cnihtes' (l. 7647), where the verb asks them to stop, but the echoes are of treachery. The British preserve the Saxons' treachery in their use of *sæx* names 'for þan *swike-dome*⁊ þat heo idon hæfdon' (l. 7677) (for the treachery they have committed).

Hengest continues to be a focus of treachery and its vocabulary, and Laȝamon's overwhelming emphasis makes clear that nationalism or ethnic pride does not feature here for this English writer. When Vortiger has burned to death, Hengest rallies his troops to attack Aurelius, but he is still the most treacherous of knights, 'cnihten alre *swikelest*' (l. 8131). Aldolf, in the ensuing battle, prays for an encounter with Hengest because of his treachery at Amesbury: Hengest '*biswac* mine leofe freondes⁊ mid longe his sæxes. / bisiden Amberesburi' (ll. 8176–7a) (betrayed my dear friends with his long knives at Amesbury). When Aldolf captures Hengest, he immediately reminds him of 'Ambresburie. / þer þu þa sæxes droȝen⁊ and Bruttes of-sloȝen. / mid muchele *swike-dome*⁊ þu mi cun sloȝe' (ll. 8248–50) (Amesbury, where you drew knives and slew Britons with great treachery – you slew my kin). When Hengest's fate is debated, as mentioned earlier, Aldolf's brother the bishop Aldadus reminds Aurelius that Hengest is the most hated man to their people, a heathen hound doomed to sink into hell 'for his *swike-dom*' (l. 8297). Indeed, to avoid a fate similar to his, Octa and his men beg for baptism, and swear not to betray them: 'aðes heo sworen⁊ *swiken* þat heo nalden' (l. 8430). The same Bishop Aldadus counsels mercy, to his later regret. Even once Hengest is dead, the memory of their betrayal continues to pain the Britons. Aurelius, wishing to commemorate Amesbury's dead, sends for Merlin, who agrees to bring Stonehenge from Ireland to the field 'bi Amberes-buri⁊ þe is brad ⁊

swiðe muri. / þer wes mid cniuen׃ þi cun idon of liuen. / þer wes moni bald Brut׃ *biswiken* to þan deðe' (ll. 8563–5) (near Amesbury, [the plain] is broad and quite pleasant. There with knives were your kin robbed of life, there was many a bold Briton betrayed to the death). Davies's Welsh emphasis on Vortiger and his betrayal with the Saxons has a long life in Laȝamon's work and in Britons' memories.

The next concentration of treachery concerns the poisoning of Aurelius. Vortiger's son Passent, living as an outlaw in Wales, accepts the offer of Appas to murder his enemy Aurelius. Appas poses as a physician, but, perhaps more important to Laȝamon, 'he wes an hæðene gume׃ ut of Sax-londe i-cume' (l. 8813) (a heathen man from Saxony), who comes to Aurelius 'swulc hit weore an hali mon׃ þe hæðene deouel' (l. 8817) (as if he were a holy man, the heathen devil). Much of what he does echoes vocabulary previously used of Rouwenne and of Hengest; this is not surprising as he is also Saxon, but suggestive since he too poses as Christian and uses poison. Again, Christianity is used against believers, for Appas cures men for love of the Lord ('for luue of mine Drihtene', l. 8841). Laȝamon sadly writes, 'ah whar is æuere æi mon׃ a þisse middel-ærde. / þe þis wolde wenen׃ þat he *swiken* weore' (ll. 8843–4) (but where is there ever any man in this middle earth who would believe this, that he was a traitor). Appas, again 'þe haðene mon' (l. 8848), plies the king and his retainers with bits of spice: '⁊ þan kinge he gon dæle׃ muchel canele. / ⁊ gingiuere ⁊ licoriz׃ he hom lefliche ȝef. / alle heo nomen þat lac׃ ⁊ he heom alle *bi-swac*. / Þeos *swike* feol a cneowe׃ at-foren þan leod-kinge' (ll. 8855–8) (and to the king he dealt out much cinnamon, and ginger and licorice. He lovingly gave them. They all took that gift, and he betrayed them all. This traitor fell to his knees before the people's king). He offers the king *atter* to drink, then 'Forð wende þe *swike*' (l. 8869a) and in quiet secrecy stole out of the town ('mid stilleliche rune׃ bistal of þan tune', l. 8871). Thus, treachery again governs a change of kings: Constantine was murdered by a Pict, as was his son Constance at Vortiger's behest and by his Picts; Vortimer, son of Vortiger, was poisoned by his stepmother Rouwenne; and Aurelius is poisoned by Appas the heathen Saxon.

Uther, perhaps predictably at this point, is also poisoned by Saxons, who choose six men for the task. Their leader is Colgrim, 'Hængestes mæie׃ monnen him ⁊ leofuest' (l. 9788) (Hengest's kinsman and dearest of men to him). They pose, 'þas *swiken*' (l. 9818), as beggars, noble men robbed of their status by the Saxons but piously praying for Uther's recovery. Uther agrees to take them in, ironically echoing Appas by saying he would do so for the love of God, 'for mines Drihtenes lufe' (l. 9844). The *swikele* come to him, and ponder how to kill him. They empty six ampullae of poison into his well, 'þa weoren ful bliðe; þæ *swiken* on heore liue' (l. 9867) (the traitors were quite happy with their lives). Later, two knights bear two gold bowls of poison to the king: each scene of betrayal echoes the others, reinforcing them all.

Arthur's time, however, offers a respite, with peace reinforced by the emphasis on *not* betraying. Arthur's conquests are the greatest since Belin and Brennes ruled, and his reputation becomes so established that war becomes unnecessary: kings surrender without a fight. Thus, the Scots come out of their hiding places, after the women have pleaded with Arthur, and 'aðes heo sworen/ *swiken* þat nalden' (l. 10951) (they swear oaths that they will not betray). Not without relevance, just before this ceremony, the women have reminded Arthur that both he and the Scots are Christian, and that the Saxons, who forced the Scots to obey, were 'heathen hounds'. They make the telling point that if Arthur destroys the Scots, he will be just like the heathens: 'Heo us duden swiðe wa/ þu us dest al swa. / þa heðene us hatieð/ þe Cristine us sari makieð' (ll. 10933–4) (They did us great harm, and you did it to us also. The heathens hate us and the Christians make us suffer). Given the history Arthur knows, the comparison could scarcely be more damaging.

Other people surrender to Arthur without having to plead, or even justify past warfare. Ælcus of Iceland almost grudgingly swears on the relic in his sword 'likien swa me liken/ nulle ich þe nauere *swiken*' (l. 11233) (like it or not, I will never betray you). Gonwais of Orkney, a heathen, promises sixty ships of fish as yearly tribute 'and aðes he swor gode. *swiken* þa[t] he nolde' (l. 11254) (he swore good oaths not to betray). Doldanim of Gutlonde seems especially anxious to please, as he brings his two sons by a Russian princess and agrees to send seven thousand pounds: 'Þat ic wulle swerien. þat nulle ich næuere *swiken*. / ah here ich wulle þe mon bicomen/ þi mon-scipe is þa mare. / *swiken* nulle ich nauere/ swa longe swa beoð auere' (ll. 11282–4) (That I will swear, that I will never betray but here I will become your man; your honour will be the greater for it. I will never betray, for as long as forever). Finally, Æscil of Denmark sends enormous amounts of tribute and hostages, and greetings to say later he would swear he would not betray Arthur: 'seoððen he wolde swerien/ *swiken* þat he nalden' (l. 11640). All of these kingdoms are notably Scandinavian in settlement (though the settlement of Iceland so early is anachronistic); Laȝamon's own name suggests he may have such ancestry himself, which could explain such detail as names which do not occur in his sources. (It is yet another instance where oral sources may have been helpful.)[19]

The stress on those who will not betray Arthur increases the effect of Modred's treachery with Wenhauer, as does the fact that Modred is the brother of Walwain, Arthur's dearest and best knight. So many years of peace and honour fall apart because 'treouðe nefde he nane/ to nauer nane monne' (l. 12712) (good faith he had none at all, never for any man), not even to his uncle Arthur or his aunt: 'Arðures suster sune/ to þere quene wes his iwune. / þat wæs ufele idon/ his æme he dude *swike-do[m]*' (ll. 12715–6) (Arthur's sister's son made love to the queen; that was evilly done. He committed treachery against his uncle). In an echo of earlier lines where soul opposes *sæl* (mercy), Laȝamon comments that ever after these two lovers were hated so 'þat nauer na man nalde/ sel bede beoden for heore saule. / for þan *swike-dome/* þat he dude Ar[ð]ure his æme' (ll. 12733–4) (never would any man offer a prayer for their souls, on account of the treachery he committed against Arthur his uncle). Modred's lack of *treouðe* (troth, truth, loyalty, good faith) is only foreshadowed in the lines above; Laȝamon creates a singular echo when the giant of St Michael's Mount, having raped and killed, asks Arthur for mercy. Arthur has asked him who his kin are and where he is from, and the giant answers that he will tell: 'Al þis ich wulle don/ and þine treoðe under-fon. / wið þat þu me let liuien/ and mine leomen hælen' (ll. 13026–7) (all this I will do and accept your troth, provided you let me live and heal my limbs). Incensed, Arthur has Beduer behead him. The implication is not simply that the giant thinks he has room to negotiate, but that acceptance of Arthur's *treoðe* is conditional rather than unquestionable. Only someone whose own *treoðe* fluctuates would say such a thing to Arthur.

Modred's treachery emerges only through the account of a messenger, not by his own admission. While dreams before waking are understood as prophetic in the Middle Ages and so will be discussed as such in the final chapter, here we can say that Arthur's dream of betrayal draws the truth from the messenger who has come from Modred. After telling his dream, Arthur hears the messenger deny its truth but then add, 'ȝif hit weore ilu[m]pe . . . and he hafde al þus idoʒ mid his *swike-dome*. / þe ʒet þu mihtest þe awreken' (ll. 14026a, 14030–31a) (if it were to come to pass . . . and he had thus done all with his treachery, then yet you might avenge yourself). Arthur, anguished, cries, 'Longe bið æuereʒ þat no wene ich nauere. / þat æuere Moddred mi mæiʒ / wolde me *biswiken*. for alle mine richen. / no Wenhauer mi quene . . .' (ll. 14036–39a) (For as long as forever I will not believe that, that Modred my kinsman ever would betray me, for all my wealth, nor Wenhauer my queen . . .). The messenger then gives up his effort to protect Arthur and admits the truth. Arthur tells his men, and swears not only to kill Modred and the queen but their supporters; 'alle ich wulle for-donʒ þa biluueden þen *swike-dom*' (l. 14066) (I will destroy all who believed in that treachery). The ensuing encounter between Arthur and his betrayers goes against Modred; he cannot then even keep faith with those who support him:

> Modred þa þohteʒ what he don mihte.
> ⁊ he dude þereʒ alse he dude elles-whare.
> *swike-dom* mid þan mæsteʒ for auere he dude unwr<a>ste.
> he *biswac* his iuerenʒ biuoren Winchestren.
> and lette him to cleopienʒ his leofeste cnihtes. anan.
> and his leoueste freond alleʒ of allen his folke.
> and bi-stal from þan fihteʒ þe feond hine aʒe. (ll. 14180–86)

> (Modred then thought what he might do
> and he committed there as he did elsewhere
> treachery of the worst kind, for always he was deceitful.
> He betrayed his companions before Winchester
> and had summoned to him immediately his dearest knights
> and all his dearest friends from all his folk
> and stole away secretly from the fight – may the Fiend take him.)

Arthur and his kingdom fail, and treachery once again becomes a regular occurrence. The next time it appears, the circumstances echo Arthur and Modred as well as previous betrayals, because Conan helps kill *mid attere* his uncle in order to rule after him; he kills Constantine as well as Constantine's sons, although he is Constantine's sister's son. Sure enough, the echoes heard take form when Carric rules. Laʒamon also introduces a strange comment on his name, saying that although the king was a noble Briton, he was mocked by being called Kinric, 'and ʒet on feole bockenʒ his nome me swa writeð' (l. 14406) (and still in many books men so write his name). Bzdyl adds in his translation this is 'a Saxon name'.[20] Le Saux runs through various scholarly opinions by A. C. L. Brown and Visser before concluding that Visser was convincing in matching the name to a Welsh triad, mentioning 'Kerric y Gwyddyl' and an entry in the *Annales Cambriae* (for 616), 'Ceretic obiit.' She is less convinced, as Visser was, that it derives from *cynnhrig*, Welsh for 'primitive' or 'aboriginal'. Unexplained in either case is why a non-Welsh-speaker would introduce a Welsh pun as a Saxon name; in my own view, it is a point in favour of possible Welsh oral sources. In any event, poor Carric falls prey to Gurmond, originally from Africa but allied to heathens from all over and especially to the Saxons. Hearing of Gurmond's might, Hengest's surviving kin consider 'hu heo mihten *biswik[e]n⁊* Karic of his richen' (l. 14466). They join with Gurmond, and Carric and his men end up besieged in Cirencester. Carric proves an able commander, and Laȝamon comments that the city was won only because Gurmond engaged in trickery, '*biswiken* wið-innen' (l. 14577). A heathen offers to take the city – 'a-waried wurðen he forþan', says Laȝamon (l. 14586) (for that may he be damned), and Gurmond promises an earldom. The stress here is on 'heathen', as both the knight and Gurmond are consistently referred to by this term. The city is taken by a scheme involving sparrows, fire carried in nutshells by the birds, and the subsequent destruction of the city by burning when the birds return to their nests in the eaves of the city. Carric escapes to Wales, and no one sees or hears of him again.

The last concentration of this extensive focus on betrayal occurs in the final section on Cadwalan and Penda. A short initial reference to betrayal occurs in the section concerning Cadwalan and Edwin to introduce the later, fuller treatment. Born on the same day, they were raised together and lived lovingly until Cadwalan accepted bad counsel that invoked unnecessary pride. That easy acceptance of betrayal becomes something Cadwalan tolerates in those around him. After much fighting, Cadwalan flees for shelter to Ireland, and Edwin rules: 'Wa wes Cadwalan⁊ þat he wes on liuen. / for he bigon þene *swike-dom⁊* uppen his sweord-broðe[r]en' (ll. 15234–5) (Woeful was Cadwalan that he was alive, for he committed treachery against his sword brother).

Having later captured Penda, Cadwalan receives his knight sent to negotiate on his behalf. Laȝamon comments on truth here in reference to the good man sent, 'for a is on treowe monnen⁊ treouðe ihalden' (l.

15496) (always in true men is troth held). Recognizing such a truth, apparently, Cadwalan will accept Penda as his man: 'treouwe mon auere beon⁄ neouwar min herm iseon. / likede swa him likedeð næue[re] me *bi-swike*' (ll. 15508–9) (a true man ever be, and never seek my harm, and never willingly or unwillingly betray me). The phrasing echoes that of Ælcus above. Penda does manage to be true to his lord, though he often betrays others to hold to that loyalty. For example, in a meeting that resonates with the one at Amesbury, Penda slays St Oswald by bringing weapons to what was supposed to be a truce meeting. He had thought about how he might betray Oswald, 'hine bi-þohte⁄ *swiken* hu he mahte' (l. 15656), and Laȝamon calls Penda the most treacherous of all kings, '*swikelest* alre kinge' (l. 15673) who betrayed St Oswald, 'þe Seint Oswald *biswac*' (l. 15694), to make his disapproval clear. When Penda tells what he has done, Cadwalan approves, but Laȝamon adds, 'Hit likede wel þan kinge⁄ buten for ane þinge. / hit of-þuhte him ful sone⁄ for þan *swikedome*' (ll. 15697–8) (the king was well pleased, except for one thing: he repented it quite soon because of the treachery). Laȝamon has changed this scene to make Cadwalan eager to dispose of all opposition. Le Saux notes,

> Laȝamon gives [Oswald] a heroic death, like that of Vortimer, Uther or Arthur: through treason . . . By comparison, both Wace and Geoffrey state that Oswald won the battle of Heavenfield, but was finally killed by the joint forces of Penda and Cadwalan.[21]

Le Saux sees the scene as emphasizing Cadwalan as a 'megalomaniac'. Though she recognizes the treason, she does not see how pervasive a theme it is, and that the point is not a heroic death (Vortimer's and Uther's deaths by poison seem particularly *non*-heroic in an English context) but the contrast between faith (hence the stress on *Seint* Oswald at the end) and not keeping faith (*swiken*).

The final mention of betrayal returns once again to the by now archetypal scene of treachery, Vortiger and Hengest, for Margadud reminds Cadwalan of how the Saxons *biswiken* their ancestors (l. 15805) with a heathen queen: let the English fight the English so that we do not have to. This isolation echoes once again at the end of Laȝamon's text, for Yuni and Iuor return to Wales and leave the Saxons to rule England; but they do so only so long as it takes for prophecies to be fulfilled and for God's will to be accomplished. Rome, prophecy and Wales are linked.

Why such an extensive and pervasive concern with *treousian* and *swikedome*? The reason needs to be stronger than a mere assertion that men are fickle and treacherous, and only God is trustworthy. Such a moral could easily have been stated outright, though undoubtedly the contrast between mortal faith and divine concern was real. The portrayal of such a pervasive and consistent thread in history can teach in several other ways, however. Analogy or allegory, for example, can extend the meaning of an incident beyond its limited depiction of a set event. Such is in fact the justification for some scholars to argue that Laȝamon deeply resents his Norman overlords and that the entire work vilifies them by praising his ancestors – but then we encounter the problem that he praises the British more than the Anglo-Saxons. So more recent scholars have hedged and agreed cautiously that while he rejects the Normans, he does so without any depth of resentment. Le Saux comments on his ambiguity:

> Where the Welsh are accepted but culturally ill-defined, the Normans are explicitly rejected, whilst Laȝamon displays a firm grasp of their language, and betrays some knowledge of their literature. The Normans are *de facto* integrated within the narrative fabric of the *Brut* as the Welsh are not – though the poem is obviously not directed towards the Normans.
>
> The poem is focused on the English people, written in the English language, eschewing excessively learned detail, making use of proverbs and local references (such as Milburga). Laȝamon gives them a more prestigious pedigree than 'standard' histories, and provides them with an answer to the problem of legitimacy posed by the Normans, in distinguishing them from those mere conquerors by the force of weapons, but also with regard to the Welsh, whose prior claims are subtly denied. Laȝamon's *Brut* reads as an attempt to create a new foundation myth, that could give his countrymen both moral justification and the incentive to survive.[22]

She has sidestepped the issue of Laȝamon's emphasis on the British often at the expense of the Saxons because she has not recognized his greater concern for their religious beliefs, not their nationalism or race. Instead of a national foundation myth designed for a particular ethnic group, he is creating a history that anticipates a culture where Christianity is the unifying force. The Welsh have more ancient claims to that religion in Britain, but the multitude of saints for the Saxons allows both cultures their own ways within the larger context.

Like Le Saux, Daniel Donoghue can write trying to have it both ways also. He too implicitly accepts using Laȝamon for analogy, but in a limited way:

> In addition to the prevailing ambivalence between Laȝamon's Anglo-Saxon style and anti-Anglo-Saxon content, one can draw other parallels between Laȝamon's contemporary situation and the historical past. One of the main lessons of the chronicle is that rulers, no matter how virtuous and powerful like Arthur, finally suffer defeat and die. Change is constant, and in the typological scheme history repeats itself as the guiding providential design unravels. At the same time, Laȝamon's writing style hearkens back to a golden age with classical, timeless ideals: a past preserved, however, imperfectly, in the language of poetry. The lessons of history, then, taught Laȝamon to accept the Norman Conquest as part of the process of inevitable change, while poetry allowed him to draw solace from the nostalgic ideals of an Anglo-Saxon golden age.[23]

That men die is scarcely the point, especially as Arthur is specifically described as *not* dying no less than three times. Twice Merlin says he will not die: 'Longe beoð æuere׀ dæd ne bið he næuere' (l. 9406) (so long as forever lasts, he will never be dead), and 'of þas kinges end׀ nulle hit na Brut ileue. / buten hit beon þe leste dæð׀ at þan muchele dome. / þenne ure Drihte׀ demeð alle uolke. / Ælles ne cunne we demen׀ of Arðures deðen' (ll. 11504–7) (of this king's end, no Briton will believe it, unless it be the final death at the great judgement when our Lord judges all folk. Otherwise we do not know how to judge of Arthur's death). 'Bruttes ileueð ȝete׀ þat he bon on liue' (l. 14290) (Britons believe still that he is alive) Laȝamon affirms after Arthur's final battle; Arthur himself had previously foretold his journey to Avalon to heal, whence he would return (ll. 11508–17). But more than this point, Donoghue freezes Laȝamon's significance into a classical, timeless past, what Bakhtin called the valorized past, and so 'cheats' him of a real achievement, his inclusion of prophecy, and its influence on the form and meaning of the book. While he does mention relevant aspects, such as the 'historiographic typology begun by Gildas and continued through Bede and Geoffrey of Monmouth' and 'divine providence',[24] he does not seem to develop an understanding of *how* relevant such concepts can be.

In addition to analogy, typology and allegory, which link past and present, and which Laȝamon does and might be expected to use as a priest,[25] this history invokes the future based on personal response and responsibility, something perhaps more suited to a sermon (such a possibility is discussed in chapter 3). Laȝamon need not have looked far into his past to find a fitting model for such condemnation of *swikedom*; among many choices, Wulfstan's *Sermo Lupi ad Anglos* has an extensive section that emphasizes many of the concerns just discussed:

> Understandað eac georne þæt deofol þas þeode nu fela geara dwelode to swyþe, ⁊ þæt lytle getreowþa wæran mid mannum, þeah hy wel spæcan . . . Forþam her syn on lande ungetrywþa micle for Gode ⁊ for worolde, ⁊ eac her syn on earde on mistlice wisan hlafordswican manege. And ealra mæst hlafordswice se bið on worolde þæt man his hlafordes saule beswice, ⁊ ful micel hlafordswice eac bið on worolde þæt man his hlaford of life forræde oððon of lande lifiendne drife, ⁊ ægþer is geworden on þysan earde . . . And git hit is mare ⁊ eac mænigfealdre þæt dereð þysse þeode. Mænige synd forsworene swyþe forlogene, ⁊ wed synd tobrocene oft ⁊ gelome.
>
> (Understand properly also that for many years now the Devil has led this nation too far astray, and that there has been little loyalty among men although they spoke fair . . . For there are here in the land great disloyalties towards God and towards the state, and there are also many here in the country who are betrayers of their lords in various ways. And the greatest betrayal in the world of one's lord is that a man betray his lord's soul; and it is also a very great betrayal of one's lord in the world, that a man should plot against his lord's life or, living, drive him from the land; and both have happened in this country . . . And yet what is injuring this nation is greater and also more multifarious. Many are forsworn and greatly perjured, and pledges are broken over and again.)[26]

The emphasis on the breaking of oaths and betrayal of a lord, even of his soul, finds solid echoes in the *Brut*. Later, towards the end of his sermon, Wulfstan comments on an illustrious predecessor, also preaching against sins of a people, and, as Laȝamon will after him, he recommends how to understand the past:

> An þeodwita wæs on Brytta tidum Gildas hatte . . . Þurh fulne eac folces gælsan ⁊ þurh oferfylla ⁊ mænigfealde synna heora eard hy forworhtan ⁊ self hy forwurdan. Ac utan don swa us þearf is, warnian us be swilcan, ⁊ soþ is þæt ic secge, syrsan dæda we witan mid Englum þonne we mid Bryttan ahwar gehyrdan . . . And utan word ⁊ weorc rihtlice fadian ⁊ ure ingeþanc clænsian georne ⁊ að ⁊ wed wærlice healdan ⁊ sume getrywða habban us betweonan butan uncræftan.

There was a historian in the time of the Britons called Gildas . . . [T]hrough the foul extravagance of the people and through gluttony and manifold sins, they destroyed their country and they themselves perished. But let us do as is necessary for us – warn ourselves by such things. And it is true what I say; we know of worse deeds among the English than we have anywhere heard of among the Britons . . . And let us order words and works aright, and earnestly cleanse our conscience, and carefully keep oath and pledge, and have some loyalty between us without deceit.[27]

Duty, History and Bakhtin

Gervase of Canterbury, in his preface to a history written in Latin in 1163, gives an idea of what historians were to do and how, and gives what sounds suspiciously like a genre distinction in the process, at least to twentieth-century ears:

> Historici autem et cronici secundum aliquid una est intentio et materia, sed diversus tractandi modus est et forma varia. Utriusque una est intentio, quia uterque veritati intendit. Forma tractandi varia, quia historicus diffuse et eleganter incedit, cronicus vero simpliciter graditur et breviter. 'Proicit' historicus 'ampullas et sesquipedalia verba'; cronicus vero 'silvestrem musam tenui meditatur avena'. Sedet historicus 'inter magniloquos et grandia verba serentes,' . . . Proprium est historici veritati intendere, audientes vel legentes dulci sermone et eleganti demulcere, actus, mores vitamque ipsius quam describit veraciter edocere, nichilque aliud comprehendere nisi quod historiæ de ratione videtur competere. Cronicus autem annos Incarnationis Domini annorumque menses computat et kalendas, actus etiam regum et principum quæ in ipsis eveniunt breviter edocet, eventus etiam, portenta vel miracula commemorat. Sunt autem plurimi qui, cronicas vel annales scribentes, limites suos excedunt, nam philacteria sua dilatare et fimbrias magnificare delectant. Dum enim cronicam compilare cupiunt, historici more incedunt, et quod breviter sermoneque humili de modo scribendi dicere debuerant, verbis ampullosis aggravare conantur.

(The historian and the chronicler have one and the same intention and use the same materials, but their modes of treatment are different and so is the style of their writing. Both have the same object in view because both eagerly pursue the truth. The style of treatment is different because the historian marches along with a copious and eloquent diction, while the chronicler steps simply and briefly. This historian 'pours forth swelling phrases and words half a yard long'; the chronicler 'practises a woodland muse on a humble oaten pipe'. The historian sits 'among men who are impressive talkers and string together grand words . . . It belongs to the historian to strive after truth, to charm his hearers or readers by his sweet and elegant language, to inform them of the true facts about the actions, character and life of the hero whom he is describing, and to include nothing else but what seems in reason to be appropriate to history. The chronicler reckons up the years . . . and the months and kalends . . . briefly sets forth the actions of kings and princes and what takes place in those same years and months, and mentions also events, portents, miracles. But there are very many who, while writing chronicles or annals, go beyond their proper limits, for they delight to make broad their phylacteries and enlarge the borders of their garments. Setting out to compile a chronicle, they march along in the manner of a historian, and try to weight with swelling words what they ought to have said shortly and in unpretentious language after the manner of ordinary writing.)[28]

Several points emerge as important here: a historian is *expected* to write elaborately and elegantly, to produce an effect both for the ear and for the eye; he is to produce the truth; and he is to describe both actions *and* the character of any heroes present, with those heroes apparently central to the recounting of history. Gervase states also that both the mode and the style differ in history and chronicles, though not the basic facts. He does not specify where the additional material of the historian (such as 'true facts about the actions, character, and life of the hero') comes from, unless we are to suppose that historians have special skills in perception of chronicle material. He goes on to add that the differences between historians and chroniclers sometimes blur, and attributes that to a fault, namely the self-importance or pride of chroniclers. Important for now, however, Gervase's emphasis on truth accords with Laȝamon's *soþere* and *soþfeste word* described in the prologue. Laȝamon too desires to inform readers of more than bare facts: he elaborates on the character of his historical figures for moral purposes, a tendency that predates Laȝamon as far back as the 890s, as demonstrated in the *Anglo-Saxon Chronicle*.[29]

I used Auden's lines at the beginning of this chapter because the phrase 'the shadow cast by language upon truth' seemed so apposite. Laȝamon wishes to show us truth, but his truth is mediated by the conscious manipulation of language, itself necessarily limited by what the writer understands, what readers understand. Bakhtin understood this inexact match of perception when he created the term 'heteroglossia'; he wrote of the conflict between language as a fixed system of transcription and the influence of context. When people communicate, they do so attempting to minimize aspects not shared by both. By definition, however, all transcription must be inadequate, with written language even more so than conversation, since the nuances of tone, gesture and pronunciation are missing. Writers can attempt to compensate by style, what Holquist, writing on Bakhtin, refers to as 'the sum of the operations performed by the poet in order to accomplish the violence necessary to mark the text off as literature'.[30] While Laʒamon wrote as a historian, we have seen that his concerns are often with language and its place, and given his poetic form and the rhetorical expectations Gervase mentions, we can discuss his work in ways usually reserved for literature instead of history.

Denis Donoghue, in his *Ferocious Alphabets*, discusses the supplanting of language A (his example is Irish) by language B (for example, English), and a theory that a native speaker of A learns uses of B that are grammatically compatible with A. In his example, that process yields Irish English: 'In time, his masters find it charming if he exhibits some of the old forms of defeated A, translated more or less directly into B.'[31] While Laʒamon is clearly not writing in French, he *has* used a French source as his main text, and his version is markedly archaicized. According to Donoghue's ideas, his choice of text, the time since the Conquest, and the abatement of perceived threat allows Laʒamon to get away with his history in English. Notable, though, is the acknowledgement of change such adaptation admits. Thus I cannot accept Laʒamon as having rejected French out of nationalism. He need not have accepted Wace's text on Arthur as a source at all, having perfectly suited texts by Geoffrey of Monmouth if he desired them. He chose Wace's text, and so accepted its value if not its form. Like place names, the story of Britain itself can have many languages.

As stated above, Laʒamon is notable for his even-handed treatment of claims rivalling the Anglo-Saxons', probably in part because he sees religious orientation as more important. Yet his interest in varied cultures and languages, and his representations of them in place names as an integral part of his history, call to mind Bakhtin's thoughts on epic and the novel. While I do not accept Bakhtin's definitions without argument, they provide useful starting points. For Bakhtin, the epic has three main features:

(1) a national epic past – in Goethe's and Schiller's terminology the 'absolute past' – serves as the subject for the epic; (2) national tradition (not personal experience and the free thought that grows out of it) serves as the source for the epic; (3) an absolute epic distance separates the epic world from contemporary reality, that is, from the time in which the singer (the author and his audience) lives.[32]

The novel has a similar list:

(1) its stylistic three-dimensionality, which is linked with the multi-languaged consciousness realized in the novel; (2) the radical change it effects in the temporal coordinates of the literary image; (3) the new zone opened by the novel for structuring literary images, namely, the zone of maximal contact with the present (with contemporary reality) in all its openendedness.[33]

Bakhtin sees all three aspects of the novel as interrelated and occasioned by a specific 'rupture' in European civilization: 'A multitude of different languages, cultures and times became available to Europe, and this became a decisive factor in its life and thought.'[34] That same crucial factor emerges both in the past about which Laȝamon writes and in his own post-Conquest time, a transitional period when genres, languages and regions are in flux. Bakhtin speaks of the 'new cultural and creative consciousness' in a polyglot world where the time 'of national languages, co-existing but closed and deaf to each other, comes to an end'. He adds,

The naive and stubborn co-existence of 'languages' within a given national language also comes to an end – that is, there is no more peaceful co-existence between territorial dialects, social and professional dialects and jargons, literary language, generic languages within literary language, epochs in language and so forth.
All this set into motion a process of active, mutual cause-and-effect and interillumination.[35]

We have seen that Laȝamon can look at his past from a distance, and that such a view corresponds to the epic; but he also can look at languages from a distance, enumerating the history of place names and the historical tensions ('no more peaceful co-existence') they represent, while also using such puns as *atorcoppe* and an Anglo-

Norman source for 'interillumination' and cause-and-effect constructions of history. In epic, Bakhtin says, beginnings and founders become extreme '*valorized* temporal categories', with memory the 'source and power for the creative impulse . . . There is as yet no consciousness of the possible relativity of any past.'[36] This last comment seems inapplicable to Laȝamon, which brings us to the relevance of the novel in discussing his work.

Why discuss the novel, epic and Laȝamon together, given that the novel generally is discussed as a modern genre, with the exception of Greek novels (romances)? Bakhtin's theories of the novel gain their power from his rejection of periodization and ability to describe the novel as an old, though the youngest, still-evolving genre, unlike, say, tragedy. Holquist summarizes the situation:

> Syncretic chronicles of such genres as the ode, the lyric or tragedy may be written extending back to classical times, because each such history will have as its subject a set of formal characteristics so fixed – from the earliest days of European culture – that nuanced modulations (in their surface features, at least) can be recognized with relative ease. It is probably for this reason that such discursively homogeneous genres accord so well with received ideas about the periodization of general history into such chapters as 'classical antiquity,' the 'Age of Louis XIV' and so forth.
>
> So militantly protean a form as the novel raises serious problems for those who seek to confine it to the linear shape of most histories. The difficulty is compounded if we recognize further that such histories usually begin by presupposing the very organizing categories that it is the nature of novels to resist.[37]

He goes on to compare histories and novels. Histories 'insist on a homology' between the form imposed to create a narrative explanation and the sequence of what is told. A novel 'dramatizes the gaps that always exist between what is told, and the telling of it, constantly experimenting with social, discursive and narrative asymmetries (the formal teratology that led Henry James to call them "fluid puddings")'.[38] Given the critical opinions of Laȝamon's metrics, his varied pace and mode and, not least, his introduction of substantial passages of dialogue, his work more closely resembles the description of novel above than of history. Indeed, Denis Donoghue comments that dialogue itself is a concert of rival voices, taking possession of the entire space in creating a semblance of company (that is, in dramatizing the gaps of linear history); he too adds a quotation from

Henry James, from his preface to *The Awkward Age*, a novel noted for the domination of dialogue, to explain the power diologue confers: 'To make the presented occasion tell all its story itself'.[39] When people and land and language are one, an imposed dialogue becomes the voices of the land's history itself.

Holquist offers a brief definition of the novel for Bakhtin: 'whatever force is at work within a given literary system to reveal the limits, the artificial constraints of that system'.[40] Given scholars' confusion over what forms Laʒamon uses for narrative and metrics, and his location in a transitional period, it is possible that he is experimenting with the 'constraints' of a system. Salter comments on Laʒamon's creativity:

> Wace surprisingly, on one occasion, invents without prompting from Geoffrey . . . [but it] cannot wholly account for what we find in Laʒamon's *Brut*. Familiarity with other kinds of works must have persuaded Laʒamon towards large-scale transformations and relocations of subject matter. For it is not only the range of his illustrative topics but also the ingenuity with which he develops them which distinguished his simile-making from that of his most obvious sources. The effect of these descriptive 'excursions' . . . is both decorative and enlarging in an imaginative sense.[41]

Certainly an attempt to imitate Anglo-Saxon poetry or even Latin heroic poetry in Middle English requires adaptation and sometimes new forms. In addition, though, his formulation of the epic past has new aspects to it: dialogue has already been mentioned, but he also includes plentiful proverbs and aphorisms, linguistic observations and, perhaps most important, an open ending linked to prophecy. He prefigures such an ending with Arthur's own passing; though he adopts the fact from Wace, he elaborates by adding a voyage to Avalon with Arthur's cure from an Elvish woman's herbal remedies. He then adds a passage about how Arthur does not die, and Britons expect him to return to them; he himself comments that Merlin has foretold that *an* Arthur will come, to the *English*. (Madden, the original editor, was so confused by this that he considered the change a scribal error.[42]) Such an ending to Arthur's section allows the future and the past to link across the present. The specificity of *the* Arthur becomes broader, *an*, and the past of British rule encompasses their English successors and all who come to live in a land by that name.

By Laȝamon's time, the Normans are as much part of the English country as any previous people. Laȝamon links people and place to language and heritage, in order to present duty as at once historical and Christian. But duty can be betrayed; choice allows prophecies to fail. What of the novel's open-endedness?

In terms of epic and novel, Bakhtin describes the epic world as having no room for 'any openendedness, indecision, indeterminacy' because it is a timeless, distanced past, self-contained'. It is isolated

> from that eternal present of children and descendents in which the epic singer and his listeners are located, which figures in as an event in their lives and becomes the epic performance. On the other hand, tradition isolates the world of the epic from personal experience, from any new insights, from any personal initiative in understanding and interpreting, from new points of view and evaluations. The epic world is an utterly finished thing . . .[43]

Clearly Laȝamon's world of the *Brut* is not 'finished'. Not only does his admiration for varied cultures and heroes survive, something perhaps open to being termed mere epic valorization, but his entire history loses its point without its prophecies and open possibilities of the future, without ancestors who have descendants free to remember duty and heritage, and to choose. He actively participates in his presentation of the past by commenting on it and by placing words in the mouths of his heroes. These actions sound suspiciously like what Bakhtin would describe as the role of the novelist:

> The novelist is drawn toward everything that is not yet completed. He may turn up on the field of representation in any authorial pose, he may depict real moments in his own life or make allusions to them, he may interfere in the conversations of his heroes, he may openly polemicize with his literary enemies and so forth. This is not merely a matter of the author's image appearing within his own field of representation – important here is the fact that the underlying, original formal author (the author of the authorial image) appears in a new relationship with the represented world. Both find themselves now subject to the same temporally valorized measurements, for the 'depicting' authorial language now lies on the same plane as the 'depicted' language of the hero, and may enter into dialogic relations and hybrid combinations with it (indeed, it cannot help but enter into such relations).[44]

What Laȝamon accomplishes as a writer by placing himself on the same plane as the language of the hero is the subject of the next chapter.

2
The Potential of Writing and Community

History is subjective because it is tied to language, determined by strategies, and inherently narrative. Like all the human sciences, history depends on language not only to express the results of its findings, but also to formulate the objects it studies, the questions it asks, and the whole relationship between those who construe the past and the past that they construe. Human imagination and understanding are mediated through, if not created by, language. This is particularly true of that domain of experience that we designate as the past: the only way to recuperate it and 'make sense' of it is to pull it into language . . . The tripartite division – that of past, present, and future – with which we make our experiences into sense and keep them distinct from one another is essentially verbal, and hence linguistic: language governs our thought and creates the past . . . Despite our fondness for cause-and-effect thinking, both causes and effects depend on what we look for, our ability to see, and the patterns in which our understanding works.[1]

Misunderstood, these assertions by Peter Allen could lead us to conclude with a fatalism or ambivalence much like that of which Laȝamon is frequently accused by readers. But finding meaning in a text inevitably links us to that text: 'relevancy' may be subjective but nevertheless remains a real goal of many readers and commentators. (It was, for example, the main objective of biblical exegesis, since the meaning of the Bible and writings of the Fathers was literally of vital importance to how men were to live.) Laȝamon turned to the past, one he deliberately limited in duration to the death of Cadwalader, and has as a result been termed nostalgic or archaic and old-fashioned. Yet the tension between that past and what he might have meant by turning to it continues to draw scholars to his work. In discussing modern readers and texts, Allen comments that

[t]he text is approximate, partial, and changeable, and can therefore never offer a firm basis for establishing anything like a 'true' meaning. Meaning

comes only when a particular individual interacts with the text, and is therefore necessarily subjective.[2]

As argued, Laȝamon interacted with the texts he used, and with the past he reconstructed, placing himself and us on the same plane as his events, as Bakhtin discussed. What is unremarked here is that such interaction inevitably argues for *meaning being not simply necessarily subjective but necessarily contemporary.*

To locate Laȝamon in his own text, or to attempt to do so, we can begin by trying to uncover his voice and perspectives in clues small and large. While these details may seem more appropriate initially to my earlier discussion of language, here the difference is between language as a cultural product and language as manipulated by an author for his own ends. Here we move into areas which preserve clues to what Laȝamon may have thought about a particular event or sequence of events. Many of the details of word choice, such as puns original to Middle English instead of to Anglo-Norman French, new compounds, transition and variations in structure, can show his hand as well. Even Laȝamon's preference for written over oral sources tells us something of his thoughts and of his place in his own time, moving beyond the identification of a people with its language and heritage to this man's identification with the language that he uses. Ruth Morse comments on history and how medieval authorial intent could manipulate the past:

> Historical example formed part of the thesaurus of rhetorical exercises in the largest sense. The past was the central subject, the one most worth writing about if one was to take a secular theme – or even if one was to use a secular theme to demonstrate God's hand in history. While there was an assumption that one of the things that distinguished historical from fictional examples was that they referred to events that had really happened, there was also recognition that, since the 'historical' and 'fictional' styles overlapped when the events they narrated were verisimilar, no foolproof method of distinguishing the one from the other could be established . . . Particularly when events came to be thought of as a method of interpreting God's purpose in guiding human history toward its eschatological conclusion, what the events signified went well beyond what they were. Admixtures of invention, elaboration, and embellishment were a method of stylization *in order to* make the past comprehensible . . . [L]ike the orator, the historian had reasons to move and persuade his audience, and the idea of the disinterested preservation of the past is part of the claim to a trustworthy *ethos.* Creating or avoiding a particular

narrative voice is one of the historian's many choices; the use of annotation or commentary allowed multiple tones.³

I would suggest that those many choices and multiple tones help readers see what Bakhtin called the dialogic imagination at work in Laȝamon's *Brut*.

Play, Creation and Intent

Laȝamon's choices for rhyme and wordplay often reveal an almost ironic view of an event on which he is otherwise silent, and help delineate his voice as writer. Earlier, I mentioned his connection between Saxons and *saex* and *Welscen* and *wæl*. But for more striking connections involving commentary in puns or wordplay, Laȝamon will often use personal names. Thus, Laȝamon describes Maelgod as 'ful god' but only insofar as he is *swike*: 'swike he wes ful god' (l. 2198), creating the irony and expressing an opinion about the mismatch of name and reality which links the English language to Laȝamon's own personal views. A similar contrast occurs when Julius Caesar has Androgeus send his son Cenan as hostage '⁊ þritti ȝi[s]les oðere⁊ he sende him to Oðeres' (l. 4248) (with Othere the tower Caesar built on the Continent, a foreign [other] land). Even Caesar's name does not escape: several times it is paired with the internal rhyme *saer*. When Caesar and Androgeus ambush Cassibellaunus, 'þes kinges heorte wes ful *sær*⁊ he wende þat hit weore Ce*sar*' (l. 4312) (the king's heart was full sore; he thought that it was Caesar). Here the anguish and Caesar are one. In a later episode, King Wiðer and his men rebel against the emperor Claudius. Claudius' noble, Hamun, sees the success of Wiðer and his men just before deciding to impersonate a Briton: 'Hamund biheold Wiðer⁊ ⁊ his wiðer-happes' (l. 4623) (Hamun beheld Wither and his hostile feats). The king and his men are not simply linked together, they are linked to their action of resistance, of being against (*wiðer*) the emperor. At times, Laȝamon's wordplay is more blunt: he describes how Arthur surrounds his enemies the Scots so completely that 'þa weoren Scottes⁊ ilhalden for sottes' (l. 10881) (then were the Scots taken for sots/fools). Only somewhat less obvious is his comment about Isemberd's apostasy: 'ne mihte he na wurse don. / for Crist seolue he for-soc⁊ and to þan Wursen he tohc' (ll. 14565–6), where he could not do worse than to go to the Worse (the Devil). At times, Laȝamon manipulates rhyme even to comment on cause and effect.

Thus Cassibellaunus could lament, 'Wale wale un-ræd⸵ mani cniht þu makest dæd' (l. 3995): the direct result of bad counsel is death.

Laȝamon also links rhymes and slant rhymes to underscore a particular meaning for more abstract terms. When Merlin dictates his needs for being able to remain open to powers of prophecy, he states that boasting and merry company cause his spirit to be angry and still: '⁊ binimeð me min wit⸵ ⁊ mine wise word for-dut. / þenne weore ich *dumbe⸵* of æuer-ælche *dome*' (ll. 8554–5). The slant rhyme and alliteration emphasize the connection. Laȝamon also frequently pairs the verb 'to obey' with 'lord' as another example of a more abstract connection. So Brennes 'seide þat he [Duke Seguine] wolden *hæren⸵* and halden hine for *herra*' (l. 2440), and he receives the duke's daughter for his wife as reward; when the French throw off Caesar's rule after the British have beaten him, they proclaim 'Nulle we him nauere *hæren*. ne hælde for ure *hærre*' (l. 3825), and Caesar must buy their goodwill; when Ælcus the king of Iceland 'dude al so wis mon' (l. 11215) and acknowledged Arthur as his lord without a fight: 'Ich þe wullen *heren⸵* swa mon scal don his *hærren*' (l. 11223). He too reaps a generous reward. Similar wordplay emerges when Julius speaks of conquering Britain, giving as his reason 'al hit is min *aȝen*. þat ic iseo mid min *æȝen*' (l. 3647). A virtually identical line describes Vespasian when he comes to France before invading Britain: 'þa ȝet hit wes al his *aȝen*. þat he isæh mid his *aȝene*' (l. 4849). While owning all that one sees may itself be a formula, the construction echoes Laȝamon's technique elsewhere. A related form suggests that at the least he appreciated the use of such a link between sight, greed and war. Writing of Aurelius' and Uther's siege of Vortiger at Mount Cloard, he describes their tactic of cutting down trees to fill the castle's ditch. But they do so because 'þa heo *iseȝen⸵* þat heo *siȝen* næfden' (l. 8084), again with a connection of sight and battle over claims to rule, this time seeing no victory.

Further delight in homonyms and puns crops up in gruesome circumstances involving souls and mercy. When the Christian British beat the heathens under King Melga, they do so in part because 'þa æhte wif-men⸵ wæpmonnes claðes duden heom on. / ⁊ heo forð wenden⸵ tow/ward þere uerde' (ll. 6405–6) (the valiant women put on them warrior's clothes and they went forth to the army). Afterwards, the men watch the 'play' (*þat gomen*) of the women as they tear enemy stragglers to bits, '⁊ beden for þere *seole⸵* þat hire neuere *sæl* nere' (l. 6425) (and prayed for his soul that he would never come near bliss). A parallel lack of sympathy occurs in a more suggestive context, when

Aurelius takes counsel on destroying Hengest. Bishop Aldadus tells the story of Saul, king of Jerusalem, and his enemy, Agag of the Amalekites, who was allied with the Devil ('þe Wurse him wes ful nieh', l. 8302). (A previous selection established the link of heathens and the Devil if we needed it.) In Aldadus's tale, Saul's men take Agag, and the prophet Samuel beheads him in the marketplace and cuts him to pieces to scatter in the streets. Bishop Aldadus recommends a similar course of action, for similar motivations. He sees the two occasions as exactly parallel: 'þus tok Samuel on⸱ and swa þu aȝest Hengest don' (l. 8337). Needless to say, Aldadus's advice is followed, and his own brother Aldolf kills Hengest. Aurelius, though, has the body buried 'after heðene laȝen' (again Laȝamon's insistence on accurately acknowledging different customs), though Aurelius 'bad for þere *sæule⸱* þat <hire> neuere *sæl* neore' (l. 8346). He manages to echo Saul's name and the previous line in the Melga episode, and the reference to the Devil being *nieh* prevents the nearness or approach of mercy, *sæl neore*.

Laȝamon's use of compounds has been noted frequently by scholars, though much argued over in terms of number and source, and so they too constitute evidence of his concern for word choice. Françoise Le Saux, in her work on sources, raises the relevant points of whether compound nouns were a natural part of Laȝamon's style or came from a deliberate attempt to recreate an effect of Old English poetry.[4] Reviewing Oakden's work,[5] she states that 261 compounds were not used by any other Middle English writer, and most do not occur in Old English poetry. About one-third of his compounds, however, while not used by Middle English poets, do appear in other Early Middle English works, such as the *Ancrene Riwle*, distinguished by its practical or utilitarian intent. She also reviews the thesis of Gibbs,[6] who questions Oakden's criteria and concentrates on the semantic fields of the compounds. He concludes that Laȝamon's compounds cluster into two major groups: those concerned with war and warfare, and those concerned with the concept of 'leod'. He also notes the absence of sizeable clusters of compounds in passages not from Wace. Le Saux ends by writing, 'What comes clearly through the works of both Oakden and Gibbs is that Laȝamon's use of compound nouns is fully conscious.' His compounds form 'part of a *living* vocabulary for the poet, who used them according to the context and according to their meaning'. She adds, 'A further proof that Laȝamon's compounds must have been widely intelligible is that . . . the Otho scribe retains 203 of them in his modernized version.'[7]

In addition to word choice, Laȝamon's reworking of Wace's material indicates something of his interests and approach. Le Saux conveniently collects evidence for expansion and reduction of Wace's material in Laȝamon in a chart which is reproduced in abbreviated form here. She also corrects the common mistake of referring to Laȝamon's work as twice the length of Wace's by pointing out that when printed as long lines, Laȝamon's *Brut* is 16,095 lines long, while Wace's *Roman de Brut* has 14,866 lines. Given only some 1,250 lines' difference in length and Laȝamon's acknowledged expansion of several sections including the Arthurian one, she concludes that he must have 'considerably *compressed* certain episodes of Wace'.[8]

Subject matter	Length difference in Laȝamon
Aeneas, Ascanius, Brutus before arrival in Britain	197(–)
Brutus in Britain, Locrin, Camber, Albanactus	27(–)
Guendoleine to Bladud	19(–)
Leir and Cordoille	25(+)
Margan, to Rival and successors	2(–)
Ferreus, Porreus, Judon	3(+)
Stater to Dunwale	7(+)
Belin and Brennes	26(–)
Gurguint to Lud	30(–)
Cassibelaune (Caesar's invasions)	127(–)
Tenauntius, Kinbelin	55(+)
Wider, Arviragus, Marius, Coil	123(+)
Luces to Coel	29(+)
Constantin, Octaves, Maximian, Constantine	153(+)
Vortigern and Vortimer	444(+)
Aurelius	172(+)
Uther	263(+)
Arthur	
(a) to the conquest of France, incl.	1021(+)
(b) to his death	902(–)
Constantin to Malgo	21(+)
Carric and Gurmund	11(–)
Augustine's mission, to the Bangor massacre	15(–)
Minor kings	15(–)
Cadwallan	207(+)
Cadwalader	28(+)
Yvor and Yuni, conclusion	6(–)

As Le Saux notes, the chart shows a clear trend towards compression at the beginning of Laȝamon's English version, not just in the beginning but even in the famous sections such as the one concerning Belin and Brennes, or Caesar's invasions.[9] Her comment that 'the period of the birth of Christ onwards (Kinbelin) starts a strong movement towards expansion' correlates with my earlier point concerning Laȝamon's focus on Christianity. Surprisingly, however, while the Arthurian section is greatly expanded in its first section, the second section, after the conquest of France, is greatly reduced, the whole being only 2.7 per cent longer than Wace's version,[10] but differing greatly in treatment and detail.

Laȝamon's creativity or lack thereof has featured in most discussions of his work. Salter felt that, while Laȝamon did indeed display allegiance to his past, Stanley had overstated the case for deliberate archaizing while others had overstated his uneven style and form. (Pearsall, as she notes, called Laȝamon 'a massive erratic in the history of English'.) She writes:

> the *Brut* is an extremely varied composition: if, as Stanley argues, Laȝamon was at times self-consciously 're-animating fossils of an extinct art form' and advertising the English past 'by putting up *ye olde* signs' he was also at times assimilating that past, with its pre-Conquest literary traditions, into the present. In fact, we might reasonably hold that while parts of the *Brut* bear witness to an 'antiquarian activity' by Laȝamon, other parts witness to his equally strong concern with the adaptation of older literary forms for newer purposes.[11]

Those 'newer purposes' remind us of Morse's earlier comments on interpreting the past to make it comprehensible and significant. In an early section of her study on *Truth and Convention in the Middle Ages*, Morse uses the examples of Geoffrey, Wace and Laȝamon to demonstrate how many 'voices' an incident could have. The scene is Cador's comments before a potential battle, on whether peace makes men 'soft'. In Geoffrey, Cador laughs and, after noting British indulgences of the previous five years, says God has led the Romans to them so that 'in pristinum statum nostram probitatem reducerent' (they will restore our honesty/uprightness to its former standing). Morse then turns to Wace, who 'first expanded Cador's defence of war by adding more general sentiments on the relative demerits of peace . . . [then] added a few words on the benefits of peace, which he put into the mouth of Gawain, who was not even present in the first version'.[12] She notes that details such as anaphora, here the beginning of several lines with the same word or phrase, plus Cador's change of tense to stress what he dislikes, show Wace's manipulation of the incident. Her last example is from Laȝamon: 'he dramatized it as a fully fledged debate, and incidentally suppressed any hint of humour. His version gives Gawain an angry riposte which defends peace.' She adds, after quoting the passage, that 'what appeared in French to be a neutral statement of an argument, now appears to be characterized by the way he replies in the early English (and archaizing) heroic mould . . . the arguments create the character rather than vice versa.'[13] Later, Morse amplifies her perception that arguments may not be for characterization at all, but for their own sake, with the speaker a secondary consideration. What emerges from her comparisons, for our purposes, is a clear indication of authorial intent.

Narrator's Intrusions: Voice, Orality and Textuality

While we can discern an emphasis or perspective in his word choice and his manipulation of expansion or revision, however, the most obvious voice of Laȝamon (or the one most likely to be identified as his) emerges in the narrator who provides us with clear transitions between episodes, placing himself in the story ('I') or making us all part of a group that follows the sequence ('we'). Laȝamon seems to reserve the first-person singular pronoun especially for his comments on place names or personal names.

> For heore beire nome⁄ ich þe wulle telle.
> þe an hehte Gabius⁄ þe oðer Prosenna. (ll. 2635–6)

> (For both their names I will tell you:
> the one was called Gabius, the other Prosenna.)

> Kæir Usch. heo næmde⁄
> and seoððen heo wes ihæten. Kair Lion⁄ ich wullen seggen þe for wan.
> (ll. 2995b–6)

> (Caer Usk he named it
> and afterwards it was called Caer Leon; I will tell you why.)

> Seo[ð]ðen her com oðer mon-cun/ þe heo cleopeden Kaerliun.
> Nu ich þe habben iseid/ hu hit is igan. of Kaerliun bi Glom-margan/
> Fo we ȝet to Beline to þan blisfulle kinge. (ll. 3013–15)

> (Later another race of men came here who called it Caerleon.
> Now I have told you how it comes to be Caerleon of Glamorgan.
> Let us turn again to Belin, to the blessed king.)

[concerning the place called Galli or Wale-broc]
> Nu ich habbe þe i-raht/ hu he hauede þene nome icaht.
> for nu an auere-mare/ is þe nome þere. (ll. 5408–9)

> (Now I have explained to you how it acquired the name;
> for now and evermore it is the name there.)

Laȝamon's interest in place names is testified to in Blenner-Hassett's studies. Such interest and the accompanying use of the first-person pronoun suggest that 'I' reflects a real personal comment or expression. In other words, it is not a convention, but Laȝamon's own voice. Accepting that suggestion, we can look at other evidence for his intrusion into the history.

Three times, Laȝamon writes of himself telling about an event in a *spelle* or tale. When Cassibellaunus celebrates victory with a ceremony worshipping Apollo, Laȝamon describes it and then turns to the feast that follows. 'þer-of ich wulle þe tellen/ selcuðe spelles' (l. 4039) he says (thereof I will tell you excellent stories), and proceeds in a manner that will echo in later descriptions of Arthur's feasts at religious holidays:

> Weoren in þeos kinges cuchene/ twa hundred cokes.
> ꝗ ne mæi na man tellen/ for alle þa bermannen.
> Islaȝene weoren to þon mele/ twælf þusend ruðeren sele.
> ꝗ þritti hundred hærtes/ ꝗ al swa feole hinden.
> of þan fohȝel-cunne/ ne mai hit na mon kennen.
> ꝗ al þat wæl ꝗ al þat gold/ þe wes ȝeond al þeos kinges lond.
> hit wes al isomned/ [at] þere sereuunge.
> Nes hit nauer mid soð itald/ seoððen þeos weoruld wes a-stald.
> þat weore on ane stude/ swulc ȝifueðe istured.
> ne of alche þinge swulc riche-dom/ iȝiuen ꝗ under-fon. (ll. 4040–49)

> (Two hundred cooks were in the king's kitchen
> and no man may tell of all the servers.

Slain for the meal were twelve thousand fine cattle,
and thirty hundred harts and as many hinds.
Of how many bird types no man may know to tell,
and all the wealth and all the gold that was throughout the king's land,
it was all gathered at the serving forth.
It was not ever truly told since this world was created
that in one place were such gifts supplied as provisions
nor such richness in all things given and accepted.)

In parallel passages about Arthur, for example, Laȝamon states that, no matter how skilled, no one could describe half the joy at Arthur's return to London: 'Ne mihte na mon suggen/ nære he na swa hende. mon. / of halue þan blissen/ þa weoren mid þan Brutten' (ll. 12091–2) (No man might say, were he ever so skilled a man, half of the joys that were amongst the Britons). Nor could anyone name all those present at a Whitsunday feast in Karliun: 'To tellen þat folc of Kairliun/ ne mihte hit na mon idon' (l. 12165). No one could tell the amount of wine and ale at the same feast ('ne mai hit na mon suggen on his tale/ of þan win and of þan ale', l. 12196), nor could anyone, learned or lewd, tell half of the richness of Arthur's Karliun that day:

Nes he næuere i-boren/ of nan cnihte icoren.
i-læred no læwed/ a nauere nare. leode.
þe cuðe him i-telle/ an æies cunnes spelle.
of halue þan riche-dome/ þe wes inne Kairliune.
of seoluere and of golde/ and gode iweden.
of hehȝe iborene monnen/ þa inne hirede wuneden.
of horsen and of hafueken/ of hunden to deoren.
and of riche iweden/ þa a þan hirede weoren.
⁊ of alle þan folke/ þe wuneden þer on folde.
wes þisses londes folk/ leodene hendest itald. (ll. 12288–97)

(That man was never born of any chosen knight
learnèd or lewd of any country whatsoever
who knew for himself how to tell in any race's story
half of the richness that was in Caerleon
of silver and of gold and excellent garments,
of high born men who lived in the royal court,
of horses and of hawks, of hounds for hunting,
and of rich clothing that was in the court,
and of all the folks who lived there in the world
the folk of this land were accounted the most beautiful.)

Laȝamon appears here to intrude storytelling techniques, clearly marked as such, by mentioning men who tell about such things as feasts, and by using increased alliteration and rhyme to tie such sections together, as if evoking stories normally heard aloud rather than read alone. The inexpressibility of detail is a common formula in romance, for example.[14] The question of oral and written sources was a contemporary concern for Laȝamon, as Brian Stock observes:

> [T]hroughout the eleventh and twelfth centuries an important transformation began to take place. The written did not simply supersede the oral, although that happened in large measure: a new type of interdependence also arose between the two. In other words, oral discourse effectively began to function within a universe of communications governed by texts. On many occasions actual texts were not present, but people often thought or behaved as if they were . . . And the writing down of events, the editing so to speak of experience, gave rise to unprecedented parallels between literature and life: for, as texts informed experience, so men and women began to live texts.[15]

When Laȝamon refers to what he *says*, he in fact refers to what he wrote, though he may also be thinking of his text read aloud. When he refers to how men cannot tell something, however, the context of excess belongs to literature, not history. In Laȝamon's time, romance described such scenes, but he does not mention books, only 'men'. That need not preclude texts, of course, but Stock's observation that people often behaved as if a text existed even when it did not points to a perception of what constitutes truth and authority, a perception evolving during Laȝamon's lifetime (and perhaps not unrelated to the problematic prologue and its three sources). Morse comments,

> From the point of view of the development of history as a discipline – and historians were self conscious – overt dramatization suggests a failure of intent here. That is, strict adherence to the truth of what happened was sacrificed to 'pathos'. This shift in emphasis toward moving and persuading the audience turned history closer to other kinds of writing: tragedy and epic were the highest genres to which historians aspired, but fiction, 'poetry', of the kind now categorized as 'romance' also played a part in giving shape to a plot and in speculating about character . . . The defence of invention – where defence might be thought to be needed – comes through two claims which present themselves as moral. Since examples gain force when they are true, history may be said to be superior to poetry. Since true examples are more forceful than precepts alone . . . history may be said to be superior to

moral philosophy. While neither of these claims was to go unchallenged, the poets and philosophers having rather a lot to say for themselves, they remained commonplaces of the arguments . . . [T]ruth is *morally* superior to fiction . . . The implication of this kind of instrumental use of the past is that the report may be manipulated on moral grounds, and this remained acceptable practice. It makes the past something analogous to a text which can be represented, interpreted, and translated.[16]

Thus, though Laȝamon writes a history or book and states 'Her mon mai arede، of Arðure þan king' (l. 11337) (here men may *read* of Arthur the king) and his twelve years of peace, seven lines later he can write, 'Ich mai sugge، hu hit iwarð، wunder þæh hit þunche. / Hit wes in ane ȝeol-dæie، þat Arður in Lundene lai' (ll. 11345–6) (I may *say* how it happened, wondrous though it seems. It was on a Yule day that Arthur lay in London). On other occasions he describes his effort more specifically by using the term *boc-spelle*, a written tale, to describe what he is doing. He describes Aurelius on Whitsunday at Amesbury, sanctifying Stonehenge and creating two bishops (ll. 8726–37) 'al-se ich þe wulle telle، a þisse boc-spelle' (l. 8728) (as I will tell you in this book tale). Elsewhere, Uther lies ill but wishes to join Lot in battle at Verulam, and Laȝamon says he will now tell us in this written tale what Uther did: 'Nu ich þe wulle tellen، a þissen boc-spællen. / hu Uðer þe king uu[nd]ede hine seolven' (ll. 9691–2).

The distinction between oral and written text may have been especially involved for churchmen and priests since, in addition to being *ilarede* or *boc-ilarede* (learnèd/book-learnèd), they preached, an act Laȝamon uses the term *lar-spelle* to describe (ll. 5068 and 5069). Note too that the echoes heard from something like Wulfstan's text are from a *written* version of a text for *oral* delivery, a sermon preached and recorded. (For a fuller treatment of Laȝamon and preaching, see the following chapter.) Brian Stock notes:

> such rough-and-ready texts perhaps created the first lay listening audiences. From them it was a short step to vernacular translations of Latin lives (or vice versa) and the reconstitution of the reading public through hagiography, *chanson de geste*, romance and lyric.[17]

For Laȝamon in particular, Salter comments that

> [I]t is doubtful whether he would have made any very rigid demarcation of the provinces of homily and chronicle . . . Although Laȝamon does not

intend to subject his historical narratives to the judgment of the homilist [here I disagree with Salter] . . . he must have been conscious of a strong medieval tradition of historical writing which crossed the boundaries of chronicle and homily [she cites Bede, one of his 'sources' from the prologues] . . . he must also have been conscious of other literary traditions such as that of the Saint's Life, in which history, sermon and heroic drama are inextricably mingled. There seems no serious obstacle to the idea that he met the demands of his historical subject matter with a form already proved for its durability and flexibility in a homiletic field; those demands were often, in any case, the same as the demands made by homily.[18]

His own training may have induced Laȝamon to make such a link. Discussing the training of medieval students, Morse writes

> The very scarcity of written texts of any kind meant that students memorized what they read, or what they heard read out to them. This meant, as well, that they proceeded only very slowly, since a few lines a day are all that can be absorbed on this method, whether one is memorizing the Psalter or Virgil. In the twelfth century, John of Salisbury, an early and exceptional classicizing scholar . . . describes his own teacher, the famous Bernard of Chartres . . . John says that at the end of each day students would compose and deliver sermons to each other (this was Christian training for twelfth-century clerics); this was probably a means of putting into practice the literary techniques they had been studying during the day. Turning literary study to Christian use by improving the students' ability to preach was both justification of literary study and demonstration of the use to which it was meant to be put. The preacher replaces the Orator.[19]

Without question, however, churchmen in Laȝamon are identified with books and textuality; his reference above to the learnèd and lewd or uneducated ('i-lǣred', 'lǣwed') who cannot 'i-telle; an æies cunnes spelle' (ll. 12289–90) (tell any kind of story that expresses the grandeur of the occasion) contrasts those who read and write with those who do not. He apparently recognizes that both have abilities and that those two groups do not tell stories or recount events in similar ways, nor do they necessarily preserve the same information. Laȝamon emerges as less judgemental here than we might be, with our references to preliterate or illiterate groups. For him, *lǣwed* men still have something to offer, though he elsewhere expresses his wish to rely more on texts, and so to write things down in order that truth be preserved, an accurate reflection of changing attitudes in his day.

For Laȝamon and his time, book-learning was the prerogative of the Church and a mark of Christianity. Given my earlier argument that he is much concerned with the difference between Christians and heathens, with the latter as a threat, texts enter that realm of concern and bolster his preference for the written text. In his many depictions of clashes between Christians and heathens, he repeatedly describes Christians not in terms of the proper noun but in terms of texts. Helena, Constantine's mother and discoverer of the True Cross, he describes as 'wel itæht⁄ on bocken heo cuðe godne cræft' (l. 5448) (well taught; she had good knowledge of books). When Hengest triumphs, 'alle þe cuðe a boken⁄ þa feorme for-soken. / for þa hæðene men⁄ weoren hæhst an hireden. / ꝩ þæt Cristine hired⁄ for hæne wes ihalden' (ll. 7202-4) (all who were literate (or knew the Bible) forsook the feast, for the heathen men were highest among the retinue and the Christian retainers were held as least). When Vortimer is chosen king because his father Vortiger allies himself with the heathen Saxons, the nobles take counsel before choosing, among them 'biscopes' and 'þa boc-ilæred men' (l. 7298), with the result that 'þa wes Vortimer⁄ Cristine king þer. / ꝩ Uortiger his fader⁄ fulede þan hæðenen' (ll. 7309-10) (then was Vortimer a Christian king there and Vortiger his father followed heathen ways). When Aurelius summons his followers to council (*hustinge*), they include again bishops and 'þa boc-ilærede men' (l. 8435); Aurelius has just followed the advice of Bishop Aldadus and required Octa and his Saxons to convert to Christianity. Churchmen have similar authority when along with earls and warriors ('eorles ꝩ beornes') the 'boc-ilarede men' (l. 9894) send for Arthur when heathens poison Uther. (The echo of heathen Rouwenne's act is unmistakable, especially as Laȝamon chooses to put the poison both times in *amppullen*, and have the kings drink from bowls of gold *mid attre*.)

Elsewhere, Archbishop Piram is described as 'witful on bocken' (l. 11027) much as Helena was, and being literate is linked with persecution of such Christians. When Childric ravages the countryside, he commits atrocities, echoing those of Wulfstan's sermon:

> þa cheorles heo uloȝen⁄ þa tileden þa eorðen.
> heo hengen þa cnihtes⁄ þa biwusten þa londes.
> alle þa gode wiues⁄ heo stikeden mid cnifes.
> alle þa maidene⁄ heo mid morðe aqualden.
> and þaie ilærede men⁄ heo læiden on gleden.
> Alle þa heorede-cnauen⁄ mid clibben heo a-qualden. (ll. 10457-62)

(They drove away the churls who tilled the earth,
they hanged the knights who governed the land,
all the good wives they stabbed with knives,
all the maidens they laid low in murder,
and the learnèd men they laid on fiery coals.
All the boy servants they clubbed to death.)

In another section, Ælfric the evil king, also seen as a threat to Christians, is visited by many representatives such as monks, hermits and white canons (*munekes, eremite, masse-preostes, clærkes, canones white, biscopes*) with *Godes mærkes* on them, unspecified. He asks them to assemble in a field where he will send his decision after taking counsel about allowing them to remain. Instead, without advice, he sends 1,400 men with battle-axes. These men '[mid] unrihtes sloʒen; al þat heo neh comen. / Heo ualden to grunde; fiftene hundred. / and fife and sixti anan. selere monnen. / *boc-ilerede men;* balu wes on uolken' (ll. 14919–22) (slew with injustice all that they came near. They felled to ground fifteen hundred and sixty-five very excellent men, book-learnèd men; disaster came on the people). What the various types of churchmen have in common is clear when Laʒamon refers to them as a group; 'God's mark' is not unrelated to being *boc-ilerede*.

Dialogues

Laʒamon makes a point of acknowledging both oral and written forms, and in fact creates a unique compromise by inventing dialogue, a form that mimics speech, in his historical, written text. He also writes as if speaking to a reader, clearly shown in his transitions. Some transitions merely emphasize the presentation of truth, as with how something got its name. So, for example, he describes the West-mering stone and finishes, 'Nu þu hafuest soð *iherd;* for wham hit swa hatte' (l. 4975) (Now you have heard the truth, for what reason it is so named). His phrase creates a link between his text and truth (as in the prologue), but also implies a responsibility on the hearer's/reader's part to accept and perhaps replace a previous idea with his account. He does the same earlier in an example already cited, when describing the origin of the name Caerleon: 'Nu ich þe habben iseid; hu hit is igan. of Kaerliun bi Glom-margan' (l. 3014). He will also use the common ground of having related an event as a shared experience, as when he describes (emphasis added) how the Romans who accept Belin's rule can return to Rome in peace 'a[nd] bi-cumen þes kinges mon⁄ alse *we* hit ær cuðden' (l. 2971) (and become this king's men as we proclaimed before), under 'Belin *ure* hæʒe king' (l. 2974) (our high king). The most interesting aspect of the last reference is what follows it; in Laʒamon's text, dialogue appears without marking in the text, but in this example the world of the reader and Laʒamon suddenly becomes the world of the history. What could be interpreted as a quoting of the king's proclamation by someone high up on the walls (l. 2965) blurs into an identification with the scene. The full lines read: 'And Belin ure hæʒe king⁄ hit bi-tæcheð Brenne. / þe scæl bi-læuen here⁄ and beon *eower* kæisere' (ll. 2974–5) (And Belin our high king entrusts [Rome] to Brenne, who will remain here and be your Caesar). What started as something we learned before in the text shifts to a place where both we and the Romans themselves ('you') identify Belin as our high king. Such conflation creates exactly the situation Bakhtin described where the author exists on the same plane as does his hero, and can enter into 'dialogic relations'.[20] Laʒamon, however, insists not merely on dialogue in his text or between himself and his text (as when he injects commentary on an event), but dialogue that involves us as well on that same level. Perhaps this clue tells us why he does not abandon the oral element: it suggests intimacy and allows him an immediacy that distanced narration or mere moralizing could not accomplish.

Thus he pulls us along or shifts the scene by acknowledging that *we*, together, must follow events. '⁊ seoððen wæs þæ king dæd⁄ hercne nu þurh wulcne ræd' (l. 6452) (And then was the king dead – listen now through what counsel [how it happened]), he says of Constantine's death. 'Nu þu miht iheren⁄ of þan kinge Vortimere. / hu he spac wið Seint Germain' (ll. 7398–99a) (Now you may hear of the king Vortimer, how he spoke with St Germain); here he writes as if we are about to witness physically such a meeting. Less than forty lines later, he changes scene and brings us with him: 'Vo we ʒet a Uortigerne⁄ alre kinge si he ærmest. / he louede Rouwen⁄ of þan hæðenne cunne' (ll. 7431–2) (Let us turn again to Vortigern – may he be the most wretched of all kings: he loved Rouwenne of the heathen race). The transition from holy king who speaks with saints to wretched king who loves a heathen should not go unremarked as further evidence of Laʒamon's real perception of extremes as religious, not cultural or national, as well as of an implied turning from one to the other.

Such transitions using 'we' become common in Laȝamon from this point on whenever an abrupt scene change occurs; he clearly has a sensitivity about not losing a reader or listener. In fact, several phrasings even suggest that we too are participating in his narrative shifts. 'Let we hit þus stonden/ ꝛ speken of þan kinge', he writes, as if we are in conversation: let us leave Aldulf holding Gloucester thus and talk about how Vortigern is taken and bound by Hengest (l. 7645). Later, he uses the same form: 'Lete we nu ane while/ þeos ferde bilæue. / and speke we of Arðure aðelest kinge' (ll. 12680–1) (Let us now for a short while leave this host and speak of Arthur noblest of kings). Again, the scene has been changed, from Munt Giu and the army of Roman allies to Arthur's camp. A similar transition occurs in the St Michael's Mount episode with the giant: 'Lete we nu þene eotend bi-lafuen/ and atlien to þan kinge' (l. 12974) (Let us now leave the giant and turn to the king). Instead of 'speaking' we now 'turn', what may seem a minor change or an overemphasis on the vocabulary used. But the Arthurian section is by far the fastest-moving section of the work, and the change from speech to movement echoes in later examples of transition. 'Lette we nu beon Cadwaðlan. and ga we to Edwine aȝan' (l. 15201) (We will let Cadwalan be now and go we to Edwin again), says Laȝamon, taking us away from good Cadwalan and his Irish shelter with King Gille Patric to turn to Edwin's pillaging. Even at the very end of the history, once Cadwalader has gone to Rome and Merlin's prophecy is invoked, 'Ga we nu to Yuni a–ȝan/ ꝛ to Iuore his wedde-broþere' (l. 16079) (Go we now to Yuni again and to Ivor his blood brother). We turn from the future, and prophecy, and Rome (the link of all three will be increasingly important in this discussion), and return to Britain, and a set of circumstances not unfamiliar to Laȝamon himself: the endurance of Wales for the Welsh.

Laȝamon's use of the pronoun 'we' in historical narrative is not unprecedented, and in fact may indicate in part a debt to his Anglo-Saxon heritage, a debt invoked by scholars who discuss his archaisms. Cecily Clark has some interesting observations on changes in the narrative mode of the *Anglo-Saxon Chronicle* (ASC) that accord with aspects of Laȝamon's writing in his use of 'we', cause-and-effect and the ethical implications of historical events.[21] She found that objectivity, as we term it, begins to be discarded by the late ninth century (recall Gervase's indignation), paralleled by more complex syntax. Entries for the 890s use syntactical subordination to give insight into purpose and motivation. In addition, by 892, the chronicler begins to exist in the ASC itself, that is, he refers to himself as 'we', as if to identify with or speak for the whole people. As the tenth and eleventh centuries progress, Clark notes that diction becomes richer, with more emotive adjectives and adverbs, though these are still relatively scarce. By the mid-eleventh century, partisanship is expressed by an enhanced sense of causation: 'Events are not happening willynilly . . . but are determined by previous acts.'[22] While it is worth noting that one of the manuscripts of the Chronicle is the Worcester fragment, it is so called because it found its way there, not because it was written there, and we have no idea whether Laȝamon actually saw that manuscript himself. He seems, however, to have no problem injecting himself into his text or taking us with him, and neither conflicts with the validity of the text, perhaps because such interjections in historical contexts were centuries old by his time, or at least sanctioned by an older text. Thus, while romances might also have encouraged such language, it may well have an older and perhaps more native pedigree for Laȝamon.

As cited before, when writing about Arthur and his kingship, Laȝamon comments on the difference between oral and written accounts, and the problem of truth.

> Ne al soh ne al les/ þat leod-scopes singeð.
> ah þis is þat soððe/ bi Arðure þan kinge.
> nes næuer ar swulc king/ swa duhti þurh all þing.
> for þat soðe stod a þan writen/ hu hit is iwurðen.
> ord from þan ænden/ of Ar[ð]ure þan kinge.
> no mare no lasse/ buten alse his laȝen weoren.
> Ah Bruttes hine luueden swiðe/ ⁊ ofte him on liȝeð.
> and suggeð feole þinges/ bi Arðure þan kinge.
> þat næuere nes i-wurðen/ a þissere weorlde-richen.
> inoh he mai suggen/ þe soð wule uremmen.
> seolcuðe þinges/ bi Arðure kinge. (ll. 11465–75)

(Neither all truth nor all lies do the people's poets sing,
but this is true about Arthur the king.
There was never before such a king, so doughty through all things,
for that truth stood in the writings, how it happened,

from beginning to end about Arthur the king,
neither more nor less but just as his customs were.
But the British loved him so much, and often lie about him,
and say many things about Arthur the king
that never happened in this worldly kingdom.
He might say enough who will tell the truth
of the remarkable things about King Arthur.)

Leod-scopes (poets of history?) tell neither all the truth nor all lies, but written texts can be relied on; this same idea occurs in Wace, which many scholars have noted as evidence of his superior ability (over Laʒamon's) to distinguish historical truth from myth.[23] What makes oral narratives less reliable? In Laʒamon's opinion, the Britons love Arthur too much, and so increase his reputation in accordance with that love. He adds the tempering remark that telling the truth is marvellous enough, perhaps with the implication that he is describing himself here. He does *not* tell us how to arrive at truth, but implies that written sources preserve truth in a set form, whereas oral sources can be influenced by opinion, perhaps even changing opinion. These views support Stock's summary of how oral-aural culture verifies or checks anything:

> [M]en communicate not only by what they say but by how they behave ... The meaning of words is not generalized into a series of standard definitions which can then act as points of reference ... in oral tradition, one cannot check what is recalled against a presumably 'correct' version of events. Hence, the constitution of the social group, together with its 'folk-memory,' determines the relationship of the new elements to the old. The past, whether conceived abstractly or concretely, can be present, if relevant to ongoing cultural needs. Oral culture is therefore conservative, if only in the literal sense of the term.[24]

Why then would Laʒamon refer back and forth between oral and written forms? Perhaps the answer may lie partly in what Morse characterizes as a spectrum of choices:

> 'History' was the central secular category of long verisimilar narrative. Though it appeared to be obvious what 'history' meant, the breadth and variety of narratives, in verse and in prose, that described themselves (or were described by readers) as histories suggests that complex processes were at work and that playing within the definitions of history occupied

many writers. Calling a text 'historical' might have a legitimating function. It might defend the embroidering of a narrative based on another narrative . . . 'Historical', though, might be thought of as an exemplary narrative based upon events which had occurred at some point in the past, told in order to move and persuade its audience to imitate the good and eschew the evil, a 'true tale about the past' which included a vast range of what modern readers would regard as invented material and inappropriate, if implicit, moralizing . . . In the different conceptual space of the Middle Ages, 'true' might mean 'in the main' or 'for the most part' true, or even, 'it could have happened like this'. The problems of factuality were not resolved by medieval writers, even late-medieval legal writers, and the constant elaboration towards fiction created tensions between some recognizable, even extractable, central claims and narrative methods of conveying the author's sense of how the past was to be interpreted. In this sense history was a broad church, teaching by precept and example.[25]

Here, the range of what we might see as genres or disciplines becomes augmented by the issue of truth or accuracy; Morse's suggestive analogy of history to a church reinforces what Laʒamon himself saw as the source of ethical and moral judgements, but also a site that used both oral and written forms to extend its teachings. Another answer to the invocation of both forms for Laʒamon in particular may lie in his physical location in Britain itself and in the turbulent history and dramatic changes between Wales and England during the later twelfth century.

The Welsh Connection

In 1171–2, Henry II of England concluded an accord with the Welsh princes that stabilized relations for decades: no English king invaded Wales again for forty years. In addition, besides respect for Wales itself and severe punishment of English lords who invaded Wales, the period after the accord defined what became known as the March of Wales. R. R. Davies describes the March as created by warfare, but owing its development over the next century to three major factors: (1) the resurgence of native Welsh power; (2) the attitude of the English Crown, and its power to back up the accord; (3) the enterprise of individual barons in the March area.[26] Laʒamon lived close enough to the March to experience and know of successful multicultural or hybrid structures in which the English and the Welsh coexisted (though not without conflict), during a period in which Welsh culture, rather than being trampled, thrived.

Françoise Le Saux tackles the problematic question of Laȝamon's sources, but she pays particular attention to the possibility of Welsh sources. Because the Welsh remained primarily an oral culture quite late due to the conservative bardic traditions (our manuscripts of the *Mabinogi* and its accompanying tales, for instance, date primarily from the twelfth century or later[27]), the question of Welsh sources and Laȝamon's access to them fits into our discussion of his attitudes towards oral and written sources. (In fact, since such a small minority could read, it is fair to say that all European cultures of the time were still primarily oral, but some, including the Welsh, continued to keep their celebration of history as central to that oral tradition.) Le Saux summarizes the long contest between those who find Welsh influence and those who reject it, arguing that opinions have been influenced by prevalent attitudes towards Celts and especially Welsh minority culture. For example, she cites Imelmann's view that the Welsh did not mix enough to have an impact on the poet, Wyld's emphasis on the 'Englishness' of Laȝamon in order to avoid the accusation that the poet slavishly transliterates Wace, and Gillespy's choice to stress Laȝamon's German inheritance.[28] Pilch, however, 'enthusiastically advocates the case in favour of [Welsh sources]',[29] as indeed does Le Saux, bringing her experience of an MA dissertation written for the University of Wales Swansea, on Welsh sources.[30] (A recent reviewer of her book has again questioned whether Welsh sources could possibly be important; the critical tug-of-war continues.[31]) The usual reasons given for considering Welsh sources are summarized by Le Saux: (1) Laȝamon often gives better forms (that is, more accurate) of Celtic names than Wace does; (2) he has Welsh episodes and names not found in Geoffrey or Wace; and (3) he changes the story in favour of the Britons, not the Saxons, at times.[32] As Le Saux notes, we unfortunately have no way of knowing what manuscript of Wace Laȝamon used, and so have no information on its notations. While Le Saux accepts that Laȝamon knew no Welsh, she does not bar the use of Welsh sources. I accept Le Saux's position; given Laȝamon's location and the historical conditions, how he could *avoid* Welsh tradition needs proof, not the opposite view.

In any case, there is some evidence recoverable for Celtic influence, with the closest surviving sources existing in Wales. Le Saux argues for a higher than expected correspondence between Laȝamon and the

Armes Prydain, a Welsh poem traditionally associated with Taliesin and dated to after 900: 'The accumulation of correspondences between *Armes* and lines 10398 sqq. of the *Brut* [involving an elaborate metaphor about a fox] makes the probability of Laʒamon having used the Welsh poem high enough for the connection to be taken seriously.'[33] Because she rules out any first-hand knowledge of Welsh, Le Saux notes that Pilch confirmed that many of the Welsh names

> must have been transcribed from an oral source. This would suggest a limited amount of familiarity with Welsh (especially Welsh Arthurian) tradition, but no intimate knowledge of it. Laʒamon obviously had sufficient contact with his Welsh neighbours to be able to transcribe the most famous Welsh names correctly, and had access to specific information: but in an incomplete form. In other words, he knew Welsh people, who were prepared to provide him with whatever information he required, within certain limits.[34]

So far, Le Saux's evidence is not overwhelmingly compelling, especially in the much abbreviated form here. But several other features make a much stronger case for her view. Laʒamon stresses the character of Merlin more than do his sources, and he includes two new scenes: that of Merlin's trance, something reminiscent of descriptions of Celtic poets at work, and Uther's search for Merlin which finds him with a hermit. An ancient poet Myrddin was honoured in Wales along with the likes of Aneirin and Taliesin, and indeed the poet's reputation merges with the growing reputation of the Arthurian character later.[35] (The reasons for emphasizing Merlin will be taken up in the next chapter under prophecy.) Le Saux also cites Bullock-Davies's work on multilingual translators in the eleventh and twelfth centuries, called *latimers*.[36] Every court and baronial household needed one for conducting business in a multilingual area (like the March), but by travelling and knowing several areas and tongues, such people would not only be useful for business transactions, but for what they heard along the way, including tales.

In fact, Laʒamon's *Ernleʒe* (now usually referred to as Areley Kings) was on a major commercial route between London and Wales,[37] being on the Severn, the valley of which was 'the cardinal route into Wales' for reaching the central borderland.[38] Tatlock noted ferries in the seventeenth century at Redstone, Laʒamon's

Radestone, likely to be an ancient crossing, whereas two other ferries are documented by the early fourteenth century at Upper Areley (six miles north) and at Bewdley (three miles north).[39] Elizabeth Salter notes too:

> Areley-Kings was part of the manor of Martley, and in the diocese of Worcester. Martley seems to have been a royal manor in its earliest days: a fishery at 'Ernel', or Areley, with lands attached to it, was granted by the Empress Maud to the Cistercian Abbey of Bordesley on its foundation in 1136 . . . The manor of Martley remained in the king's hands until 1196.[40]

She adds:

> the ford over the Severn at Redstone was at one time the chief road across the river and, as the fourteenth-century *Gough Map* indicates, Areley-Kings must have been on the main road and water routes from Worcester to Bridgnorth.[41]

Such direct links between Worcestershire and Wales possibly a mere three miles from Laȝamon's church make it unlikely that he had no exposure to the Welsh. Davies notes that Welsh was also spoken in lowland Shropshire and Herefordshire, and that Archbishop Baldwin of Canterbury needed interpreters on his tour of the country in 1188 at Usk and at Radnor (Gerald of Wales confirms this fact).[42] He adds that storytellers and poets moved freely around Wales, 'both in imagination and in person', citing a tradition of the imaginary tour of Wales called *cylch Cymru*. But the twelfth-century process of carving Wales into dioceses and parishes provides even more ways that Laȝamon could have had access to information. Davies notes that not a single surviving parish church in all of Wales predates the mid-eleventh century, and connects this to the reorganization of the Welsh church and its increasing links to Rome. Wales was brought under the metropolitan control of Canterbury, but pressed for metropolitan status for St David's (which, interestingly, Laȝamon refers to by its Welsh name, Deuwi, l. 2413 *inter alia*). As Davies puts it:

> In the eleventh century, Rome was no more than a distant shrine, a pilgrimage centre . . . [I]t was the first half of the twelfth century which witnessed the transformation. Formal and regular links with Rome now became the norm: letters were exchanged; cardinals were lobbied; papal

sanction became recognized as the most secure insurance for all ecclesiastical title . . . papal legates were dispatched on visits to Welsh sees, the first recorded example being . . . in 1125; Welsh bishops, or at least those of the two southern sees [those closest to Laȝamon], became regular visitors to the papal court.[43]

Stronger circumstantial evidence concerns Laȝamon's apparent use and knowledge of triads, a mnemonic device common to oral Celtic literatures but collected and recorded in written form in Wales before they were lost elsewhere.[44] They also survive in isolated occurrences, much as in Laȝamon, in various stories converted to written form, as in the *Mabinogion* (the Four Branches of the *Mabinogi* and accompanying tales). Interestingly, Laȝamon seems to use the form, but his details do not match the triads we have in written form, something perhaps predictable if in fact he got his information from an oral source. For example, he comments that Malgus was the fairest man 'wið-uten Adam ⁊ Absolon. / swa alse þe boc us suggeð҄ þa æuere iboren weore' (ll. 14380b–1) (that ever was born, except for Adam and Absalom, just as the books tell us). While the mention of a book suggests a written source (not in Welsh but Welsh-influenced?), the form of a triad suggests Wales. In fact, a close triad exists (TYP #48), naming three men who had Adam's beauty: Absalom, Jason and Paris. As Le Saux notes, the *Brut* version shows a biblical bias, dropping Jason and Paris, perhaps something expected given previous points on Christian perspectives in Laȝamon. It may in turn reflect the bias of his source, either a Latin Welsh text or a fellow churchman from Wales. She also notes Laȝamon's stress on Arthur as a survivor with only two others (a triad), 'Þa nas þer namare҄ i þan fehte to laue҄ / of two hundred þusend monnen. þa þer leien to-hauwen҄ / buten Arþur þe king ane҄ ⁊ of his cnihtes tweien' (ll. 14263–5) (There were no more alive in that fight, of two hundred thousand men who there lay hacked to pieces, except Arthur the king alone and two of his knights) and the description of the battle of the Sosie valley as the third greatest fight known: 'Swa al swa suggeð writen҄ þæ witeȝen idihten. / þat wes þat þridde mæste uiht҄ þe auere wes here idiht' (l. 13716–17) (Just as is said in the writings the wise have compiled, that was the third greatest fight that ever was fought here). While she cites Indo-European fascination with threes (somewhat weakly),[45] no particular Anglo-Saxon or Middle English fascination with this number aside from the Trinity and related numerological virtues exists in the sources. By Occam's razor, Welsh influence in the form of triads seems the simplest explanation, and Christianity's use of the Trinity would only strengthen Laȝamon's predisposition to the use of threes.

In fact, despite the rareness of explicit Christian sentiment expressed in his own voice, Laȝamon does include a short passage on the Trinity. He inserts it to describe how Christ was born in Kinbelin's reign. As Le Saux notes, in Wace the information is bare (Christ came from heaven, he is God but became man for us, and he suffered for our redemption). Laȝamon expands it by evoking all three persons of the Trinity:

> He is ihaten Iesu Crist/ þurh þene Halie Gost,
> alre worulde wunne/ walden englenne.
> Fæder he is on heuenen/ froure moncunnes.
> Sune he is on eorðan/ of sele þon mæidene.
> ⁊ þene Halie Gost/ haldeð mid him-seoluen/
> þene gast he wel daleð. to þan þe him beoð leoue. (ll. 4524–9)

> (He is called Jesus Christ through the Holy Ghost,
> all the world's joy, ruler of angels.
> Father he is in heaven, solace of mankind,
> Son he is on earth of the best of maidens,
> and holds the Holy Ghost with himself.
> He gives the spirit generously to those who are beloved of him.)

Le Saux notes that Tatlock heard an echo of Sabellianism, but she herself notes that the 'distinction between the persons of the Trinity according to their "locus" reminds one somewhat of Origen's hierarchy within the Trinity according to their function'.[46] In neither case does she accept the attribution, concluding that 'Laȝamon was no theologian, for all that he was a priest, and . . . he was somewhat lacking in perception regarding the finer points of doctrine'. What she glosses over is that Laȝamon's version makes the Trinity much more immediate and significant: heaven and earth are linked through persons of the Trinity, and by sending out the Spirit, Christ can hold those who love him as closely as he holds the Spirit by which he moves such followers. The next scene in both Wace and Laȝamon has Teilesin (Taliesin), a prophet, interpreting the birth for Kinbelin, '⁊ heo hit ilæfdon/ þat Teilesin heom seide' (l. 4537) (and they believed it, what Teilesin told them); the connection for Laȝamon between Spirit and prophecy is thus much clearer, and notably linked to a name he would know well from Wales. Why these links are important will emerge better in a fuller discussion later. Here it is worth noting that a medieval commonplace also links the Trinity and literacy, in the three fingers a monk used to hold his pen while copying sacred texts.

Texts, Community and Prophecy

Returning to orality and literacy, however, we can see how triads, the Trinity and the link of Christianity and books bring us full circle back to Laȝamon's own concern with oral and written sources. Having mentioned evidence for an oral element, I can now turn to his references to what seem to be written texts, keeping in mind what Stock said about treating some information as if it were a text when it is not. Laȝamon does not limit texts to manuscript form, though most of his references seem to be to books. He nevertheless mentions written letters and messages quite often, and also includes a few references to what might be viewed as perceptible magic properties associated with writing. With one possible exception, however, the use of writing and texts is confined to the highest classes.

In the Leir episode, after Leir angrily disowns his daughter Cordoille, the king of France, Aganippes, sends a messenger to request her in marriage. Leir responds in writing. '[H]e letten writen a writ/ wel hit lette dihten' (l. 1573) could mean that he himself, illiterate, had a letter written in a manner in keeping with his status. Laȝamon comments, 'Þus *spec* þes kinges *writ*' (l. 1575) (Thus spoke the king's writ), an interesting mix of vocabulary in our current discussion. Upon receiving the message that he may marry Cordoille, though with no more than the clothes she wears, Aganippes 'hit lette raden/ leof him weren þa runen' (l. 1596) (had the letter read; dear to him were the runes/letters). Again the implication is that he cannot, or does not in these circumstances, read; the writing itself communicates status between the kings, as does having someone else compose, or write, or read. (Bzdyl takes the meaning further in his translation, with Leir having 'ordered a letter to be written handsomely' and Aganippus 'pleased at its handsome lettering'.[47]) Other occasions for writing signal the importance of the event for Laȝamon as well. Belin and Brennes send a messenger carrying 'writ-runan' to Rome (l. 2868) just before their famous victory. Later, in parallel scenes, Arthur and Luces exchange written messages, interestingly supplemented with oral statements, as in 'mid write ⁊ mid worde' (l. 12479), and the delivery of Arthur's letter after a lengthy statement by Luces's returning twelve messengers, 'her we habbeoð an honden⁄ writen þat he sende' (l. 12638) (we have here in hand the writing that he sends).

One of two other references to writing not in books concerns the previously mentioned West-mering stone. Maurius has 'þer-on grauen. sælcuðe run-stauen' (l. 4967) (engraved thereon excellent rune-staves) which tell how he slew Rodric and overcame the Picts. Crocia (Crocea) Mors, the sword which kills anyone whose blood it draws, is the second example of engraving or perhaps of runes as we know them. Laʒamon introduces it in a way now familiar when he wishes to include his audience: 'Nu þu miht iheren sulke[ð] word' (l. 3803) (Now you may hear excellent words). The sword is the emperor's weapon, but has unusual power:

> for nas næuere þe ilke bern. þe auere i-boren weoren⁄
> þat of þen ilke sweorde. enne swipe hefde⁄
> þat he of his likame. lette ænne drope blod⁄
> þat he nes sone dæd. neore he noht swa dohti. (ll. 3812–15)

(for there was not ever any warrior who ever was born
who, if he had one swipe from this same sword,
if he from his body lost a single drop of blood,
was not shortly dead, no matter how valorous he might be.)

A further detail mentioned just before this, however, seems the cause of such extraordinary deadliness: 'Wæs þe stelene brond⁄ swiðe brad ⁊ swiðe long. / þer-on weoren igrauen⁄ feole cunne *boc-stauen*' (ll. 3806–7) (The steel blade was very broad and quite long. Thereon were engraved many kinds of book-staves). This may be a small clue to the survival of Germanic or Anglo-Saxon attitudes towards runes, such as is evidenced in *Beowulf* with Grendel's mother and the sword in her lair. Similar attitudes towards magic (not always an evil activity in the Middle Ages[48]) appear in the context of books mentioning 'Karliun bi Uske': 'Summe bokes suggeð to iwisse⁄ þat þa burh wes biwucched. / and þæt is wel isene⁄ soð þat hit sunde' (ll. 12114–15) (Some books say truly that the burg was bewitched, and that is easily seen that it seems true). Books and truth are proven linked, which provides additional authority for Laʒamon's unspecific references.

When Leir dies, his daughter buries him in Janus' temple in *Leirchestre*, 'al swa þe b[o]c tellet' (l. 1860) (as the book tells). Discussing Galli as a British place name to mark the place of Gallus' death, Laʒamon comments that 'a þere Ænglisce boc/ he is ihaten Wale-broc' (l. 5407) (in the English book it is called Walbrook); the English name is not referenced in Bede, the named English source of the prologue, so he may be referring generally to something he had run across in his reading, or instead merely making a comment about what the English would call it in their books if they instead of the British referred to it. (Notice that books and English are linked, while the British are not so connected.) Elsewhere, twice he refers to the Sibyl's book of prophecies. 'Sibeli hit sæide/ hire quides weoren soðe. / and sette hit on bocke/ uolke to bisne' (ll. 12547–8) (Sibyl said it, her pronouncements were true, and she set it in a book to warn the people); here Laʒamon confirms that what was oral has been proven true because it was written down and so could be verified. He refers to the Sibyl again at the very end of his work, linking her written, Roman prophecies with Merlin's oral, Welsh ones: 'Merlin þe wise/ hit seide mid worde' (Merlin the wise said it in words) and 'Sibillie þa wise/ a bocken hit isette' (Sybil the wise set it in books) (ll. 16064, 16066). Again the contrast of oral and written occurs as part of the evocation of fulfilled and promised history. Laʒamon also occasionally simply refers to books as general sources, as when he comments that 'Nis hit a nare boc idiht' (l. 10313) (it is not written in any book), or 'seoððen hit seið in þere tale' (l. 11422) (then it says in the tale), or perhaps as when he speaks of the Sosie valley as the third greatest battle 'Swa al swa suggeð writen/ þæ witeʒen idihten' (l. 13716) (just as it says in the writings the wise have compiled). He once even refers backwards in his own work, 'al swa þes boc her telleð bi-uore/ a þissen spelle' (l. 3531) (just as this book tells here before in this story); his previous reference (to Lud building Lundenne) occurs in lines 1023–9.

As with the references to Merlin and the Sibyl, however, he often combines references to the two types of sources. While the lack of knowledge of the twenty giants 'a leoda ne a spella' (l. 903) (among the people or in tales) has been mentioned already, Laʒamon refers to oral and written sources perhaps in the interest of completeness or simply as a variant on the inexpressibility motif. It may just as easily indicate the relative balance of both sources in his time and place. So he can write 'Nes hit nohwhar iseid⁄ no a bocken irad' (l. 14623) (it is nowhere said nor in any book read) that so fair a people perished as did Caric and his men. Later he writes virtually the same phrase to describe the arrival of Saxon hordes against Cadwalan at Hatfield: 'Næs he boren nauere⁄ in nauer nare burhȝe. / þe mihte in æi spelle⁄ þat oðer uolc telle. / nas hit nauere isæid⁄ no on bocken irad⁄ / þat æuer ær weore⁄ æi swa muchel ferde' (ll. 15574–7) (He was not ever born, not in any burg, who might in any tale tell of that other folk; it was not ever said nor ever in books read that ever before was such a mighty army). Again, he gives equal due to sources, especially if those oral sources are privileged by prophecy or the weight of common agreement among people. Such common agreement, what Stock referred to above as 'the constitution of the social group, together with its "folk-memory"', may explain partly why Laȝamon also includes proverbs or aphorisms.

Proverbs often occur in the context of communal councils, where advice is offered or common wisdom invoked. Thus Membricius, advising Brutus and his nobles, advises taking the wealth of natives and leaving the country because 'þe riche haueð muchel rum⁄ to ræsen biforen þan wrecchen' (l. 504) (the rich have plenty of room to get the better of the wretched), and he wishes to forestall any retribution against his own folk if they stay. Arthur too seems to invoke conventional wisdom after his first dream. He groans and cries to God, 'let þu mi sweuen⁄ to selþen iturnen' (May you allow my dream to turn to good). His man Angel (an apt name) asks him to tell it so that good may come of it, and Arthur responds, 'Bluðeliche . . . to blisse hit iwurðe' (ll. 12763, 12766) (gladly . . . may it turn to joy). In other instances, Laȝamon has characters comment in ways that suggest they are repeating well-known perceptions. When Childric has been driven to the wood of Calidon after an initial victory over Arthur he laments, 'of[t] hit ilimpeð a ueole cunne þeoden. / þer gode cnihte<s>⁄ cumeð to sturne fihte. / þat heo ærest biȝiteð⁄ after heo hit leoseð' (ll. 10364–6) (often it happens to many kinds of people where good knights come to fierce battle, that they first win a victory, and after, they lose it). Arthur speaks in a similar fashion when he hears that Frolle has accepted his challenge to single combat: 'for hit bicumeð kinge⁄ þat his word stonde' (l. 11841) (it becomes a king that his word should stand). Roland Barthes would see this use of common wisdom as an instance of popular proverbs which 'foresee more than they assert, [because] they remain the speech of a humanity which is making itself, not one which is',⁴⁹ an interesting comment in light of Bakhtin's ideas on novels and society, or even in relation to prophecy. Barthes is contrasting popular proverbs with 'second-order language which bears on objects already prepared', for example, a maxim, or what he refers to as bourgeois aphorisms: 'The foundation of the bourgeois statement of fact is *common sense*, that is, truth when it stops on the arbitrary order of [the speaker].'⁵⁰ Le Saux comments on proverbs in a way which seems more like Barthes's aphorisms, noting for example the correlation between Laȝamon's 'i-wurðe þet iwurðe/ i-wurðe Godes wille' and ll. 504–5 in the Middle English *Proverbs of Alfred*, 'wurþe þat i-wurþe / wurþe godes wille' (let it happen as it will happen, let it happen according to God's will). (The correlation was first noted by Skeat in 1907.) The *Proverbs* is a text arguably categorized as Barthes's truth presented arbitrarily by the writer. But Le Saux also notes that the *Proverbs* manuscript closest to what occurs in the *Brut* (Maidstone Museum A 13) is of a later textual tradition.⁵¹

In a few other locations, Laȝamon himself interjects a viewpoint in a way that seems to draw from common and perhaps oral opinion and wisdom and add Laȝamon's own expansion. Morpidus the king, hearing of a sea beast that has ravaged his people, goes off to fight it in a scene reminiscent of *Beowulf* in which his men wait in the city, and his spear and sword break in the neck of the beast which then slays both him and his horse. Laȝamon comments that the king was too keen (an echo of 'most eager for fame'), 'for þe mon is muchel sot/ þe nimeð to him-seoluen. / mare þonne he maȝen walden/ he sæl halden þe raðer. / for unræd is swiðe ræh' (ll. 3247–9a) (for that man is a great fool who takes on himself more than he can handle; he will instead fail sooner, for stupidity is very rash). In another comment on the wisdom of a ruler's move, Laȝamon grudgingly approves of Caesar's dispersal of treasure to buy the goodwill of the French: 'Whær is þe ilke mon/ þat me ne mæi mid mede ouer-gan. / þurh þa luue of þan feo/ feond-scipe aleggen. / makien feolle ifreond/ þæh heo weoren i-uæiede' (ll. 3845–7) (Where is there any man whom one may not overcome with bribes, through the love of riches allay animosity, to make many friends though they had been enemies?). Elsewhere, he comments on Caesar's accomplishments of calendar and law, and sighs, 'Wale þat eæuere ei sucche mon/ in-to [helle] sculde gan' (l. 3601) (Alas that ever such a man should have to go to hell); his opposition of heathens and Christians does not prevent him from admiring achievements for the good, yet he still applies the consequences of not believing to those he admires who are not Christian.⁵²

Laʒamon's last two authorial comments both deal with truth and come late in the text. The first has already been discussed, being the section where he comments on how the Britons love Arthur and so exaggerate tales of him. He adds his own comment to broaden the application:

> Swa deð auer-alc mon⹁ þe oðer luuien con.
> ʒif he is him to leof⹁ þenne wule he liʒen.
> and suggen on him wurð-scipe⹁ mare þenne he beon wurðe.
> ne beo he no swa luðer mon⹁ þat his freond him wel ne on.
> Æft ʒif on uolke feond-scipe arereð.
> an æuer-æi time⹁ bitweone twon monnen.
> me con bi þan læðe⹁ lasinge suggen.
> þeh he weore þe bezste mon⹁ þe æuere æt at borde.
> þe mon þe him weore lað⹁ him cuðe. last finden. (ll. 11456–64)

> (So does every man who loves another:
> if he is loved by him, then he will lie
> and tell of him more honour than he deserves.
> There is no man so wicked that his friend will not speak well of him.
> Afterwards if among the folk hostilities arise
> at any time between two men,
> one can tell lies about the hated one
> even though he were the best man who ever ate at table.
> The man who loathes him knows how to find fault.)

Subjectivity too often informs what is said about someone, and the exaggeration is in proportion to the excess of love or ill feeling. (Is this a further comment on the validity of oral forms which can be occasioned by personal feeling, as for instance a satire was for Irish poets?) Yet real devotion or loyalty can survive and even resolve such differences. When Penda sends a trusted man to beg mercy of Cadwalan, Laʒamon comments that he did as bid, 'for a is on treowe monnen⹁ treouðe ihalden' (l. 15496) (always in true men is honour/ truth found). He contradicts the earlier observation that all men can be bought, but such contradictions are bound to exist in a large body of folk wisdom with a view on everything or, as Barthes said, a humanity that is making itself, in process.

What is the point of delineating Laʒamon's clear perception and acknowledgement of orality and literacy, especially in the context of considering him as a writer? Again, Bakhtin's theories can illuminate something of what Laȝamon accomplished. In his essay 'Discourse in the novel', Bakhtin comments on an example of an illiterate peasant who

> nevertheless lived in several language systems: he prayed to God in one language (Church Slavonic), sang songs in another, spoke to his family in a third and, when he began to dictate petitions to the local authorities through a scribe, he tried speaking yet a fourth language . . . All these are *different languages,* even from the point of view of abstract socio-dialectological markers. But these languages were not dialogically coordinated in the linguistic consciousness of the peasant; he passed from one to the other without thinking, automatically: each was indisputably in its own place, and the place of each was indisputable. He was not yet able to regard one language (and the verbal world corresponding to it) through the eyes of another language.[53]

While Laȝamon grants orality its place, he has also apparently begun to integrate aspects of its tradition into his work. His language is self-referential, as when he repeats or echoes phrases, or constructs parallel scenes, or refers backwards to another place in his own book; but it also acknowledges differences in perception in oral tales (as when Britons speak of Arthur) while including oral forms as complementary to written ones (when something is neither said nor read). Instead of dismissing, attacking or ignoring orality, he struggles to evaluate it and include it, in effect allowing a dialogue between the two, where it does not compromise his higher concern with truth. That concern with truth should be seen as a highly personal concern (though one common to historians of his age), more so than has been allowed in the past, perhaps because Laȝamon was viewed as a translator or imitator and that was seen as less individualistic. The points above about his specific word choices involving wordplay, word creation, echoes and a dialogic relationship among sources as well as characters should be seen as evidence against neutralizing his personality in the work.

Laȝamon and Bakhtin: Back to the Future

Some of Bakhtin's comments help here. He rejects studying the word divorced from context or perception of its referential range: '*To study the word as such, ignoring the impulse that reaches out beyond it, is just as senseless as to study psychological experience outside the context of that real life toward which it was directed and by which it is determined.*'[54] He would see instead any literary effort as one of choice designed to communicate a narrowed view of reference in order to clarify intention:

> Every socially significant verbal performance has the ability . . . to infect with its own intention certain aspects of language that had been affected by its semantic nuances and specific axiological overtones; thus, it can create slogan-words, curse-words, praise-words and so forth.[55]

We can see here the same process as Laʒamon's creation of compound words in order to clarify an idea for which his vocabulary had no preformed choice. (The same might be said of Shakespeare's vocabulary enrichment.) In addition, while my isolated consideration of terms such as 'book' and *boc-spelle* may seem a case of 'ignoring the impulse that reaches out beyond [them]', as Bakhtin says in the initial quotation for this section, Laʒamon's own references using such terms occur precisely to open up his own text to encompass the authority of others.

As for Laʒamon as a person behind his work, Bakhtin would see his choice to translate, and so to choose and create within his language something from others, a prime example of dialogue in the textual sense:

> [T]here may be, between 'languages,' highly specific dialogic relations; no matter how these languages are conceived, they may all be taken as particular points of view on the world. However varied the social forces doing the work of stratification – a profession, a genre, a particular tendency, an individual personality – the work itself everywhere comes down to the (relatively) protracted and socially meaningful (collective) saturation of language with specific (and consequently limiting) intentions and accents . . . As a result of the work done by all these stratifying forces in language, there are no 'neutral' words and forms – words and forms that can belong to 'no one'; language has been completely taken over, shot through with intentions and accents. For any individual consciousness living in it, language is not an abstract system of normative forms but rather a concrete heteroglot conception of the world . . . Each word tastes of the context and contexts in which it has lived its socially charged life; all words and forms are populated by intentions. Contextual overtones (generic, tendentious, individualistic) are inevitable in the word.[56]

The apparent paradox of *limited* language being socially meaningful or collective brings to mind Stock's comments on how an oral culture preserves and alters its memory so as to determine the relationship of new elements to old. The constitution of the social group does the limiting/determining and the conserving; Laȝamon's audience, at least as he conceives it, is perceptible in his tailored version as much, or as little, as he is.[57]

For a parallel or analogy to oral and written in Laȝamon, Bakhtin comments on folkloric life ('a pre-class, agricultural stage': here we see Bakhtin's own limiting choices of reference) when discussing time and space in Rabelais (what Bakhtin terms his chronotope). He notes that such a stage is characterized by a feeling for time that had as its basis social everyday time, that is, the time of labour: holidays, the agricultural labour cycle, seasons, periods of the day, stages in the growth of plants and animals.

> This time is collective . . . differentiated and measured only by the events of *collective* life . . . This is the time of productive growth . . . Insofar as individuality is not isolated, such things as old age, decay and death can be nothing more than aspects subordinated to growth and increase . . . This is a time maximally tensed toward the future. It is a time when collective labour concerns itself for the future: men sow for the future, gather in the harvest for the future, mate and copulate for the sake of the future.[58]

Once societies form stratifications, 'individual life-sequences' emerge, and men lose their link to the life of nature: 'Food, drink, copulation and so forth lose . . . their link, their unity . . . they become a petty private matter; they seem to exhaust all their significance within the boundaries of individual life.'[59] To retain significance in a narrative, these private elements must become metaphorically enriched, symbolic in a larger context. For Bakhtin, 'their metaphorical enrichment is purchased at the expense of any dim traces of the past that might still remain . . . the *interior aspect* of life must be downplayed.' The collectivity of folkloric and oral culture is confined to the past: the individual life survives there, but its reference is different. To be meaningful, a larger context must be constructed in which individual lives are significant because of deeper, broader meaning. Rather than any one person emerging as a sufficient paradigm, the pattern created by individuals *in society* becomes important: the individual life in service to the society or community (from petty and private to metaphorically enriched) gives meaning. The significance is social.

Using the same ideas in terms of oral and written, the oral collectivity gives way to the individual reader; but that reader becomes important then as part of a textual community, for example, through the semantic range of words as understood and created by an audience. Laȝamon constructs such a community in a historical text where the land's history is one of cyclical warfare, in which individuals matter less than patterns – until the individual's calling is recognized: each man bears a responsibility to truth. Laȝamon fulfils his own by his true book (or is the Caligula manuscript prologue accurate in saying his *truer* word?), and by recording the promise of the future in an emphasis on prophecy. Divine justice will govern all. The last line of his work speaks of all proceeding according to God's will, 'i-wurðe þet iwurðeⁱ i-wurðe Godes wille'. Many have seen this phrase as evidence of a pervasive fatalism in Laȝamon or, at best, resignation or ambivalence.[60] For Laȝamon, however, it links word and Word, book and Book, and rather than an abrogation of responsibility, it is a call to listen, to read and to believe. The action of belief will fulfil prophecy and unite text, reader and God. Stock comments about the twelfth century:

> Alienation once again became a topic of discussion. Man, so to speak, not only anguished over a new separation from the paradise of familial relations in Eden, which were oral, intimate, and free from interpretive superstructures. Texts, as Hugh of St. Victor suggested, or rather, reading, study, and meditation based upon them, offered him a technical instrument for helping to restore the lost spiritual unity with God.[61]

Bakhtin's pre-class agricultural time of folklore unites here with the past of Eden; the alienation from community Bakhtin sees is a problem Laȝamon too faces, and tries to solve in his history. The *Brut* participates in the attempt to restore lost spiritual unity by uniting the oral activity of prophecy with the developing textual authority of the book. While this may seem somewhat ludicrous to a modern reader, regaining a more perfect communication with God was an active spiritual concern of this time. Laȝamon's past, more than being merely nostalgic or the voice of a culture now lost, becomes a measure of the future in his text. Bakhtin comments on the process by terming it 'historical inversion':

> [M]ythological and artistic thinking locates such categories as purpose, ideal, justice, perfection, the harmonious condition of man and society

and the like in the *past* . . . To put it in somewhat simplified terms, we might say that a thing that could and in fact must only be realized exclusively in the *future* is here portrayed as something out of the past, a thing that is in no sense part of the past's reality, but a thing that is in its essence a purpose, an obligation.[62]

Time collapses, as it will in infinity and the eternal, and the interpenetration of past and present, as in his book and through his acts as writer, foretells allegorically what must occur. Laȝamon, it should be noted, does *not* place 'what must only be realized exclusively in the *future*' in the past. He creates a communal goal beyond the end of his text's extent, akin to the open-ended or contemporary novel discussed earlier.

Bakhtin goes on to say that the future in myth is therefore robbed since everything worthwhile has been shifted to the past. Roland Barthes has similar reservations when discussing myths. For him, the mythical signification is 'never arbitrary; it is always in part motivated, and unavoidably contains some analogy.'[63] He goes on to add that myth is an inflexion (much as Bakhtin says it involves individualistic limitation of meaning), but that the function of myth is not to deny:

> its function is to talk about [things]; simply, it purifies them, it makes them innocent, it gives them a natural and eternal justification, it gives them a clarity which is not that of an explanation but that of a statement of fact.[64]

Elsewhere, he adds that 'myth has the task of giving an historical intention a natural justification, and making contingency appear eternal. Now this process is exactly that of bourgeois ideology.'[65] If Laȝamon had in fact been creating a past in order to justify a present, as in valorizing the Saxons and their violence, or even the Normans, Barthes's comments would raise serious questions about his propaganda and his 'purity'. For Laȝamon, however, the past of warfare and contention and error is only redeemed, or made metaphorically transcendent, if the future gives it significance. The catalyst for redemption is supernatural, beyond man's control but accessible to him. While this transcendence can appear as an abrogation of power or responsibility, in Laȝamon, the way to transcendence is active, the power literally immaterial, being faith.

He finds transcendence in his religion: it is a basic tenet of Christianity that, without the Fall, God would not have become man, fulfilling an earlier redemptive prophecy. Laȝamon is not exonerated of 'motivation' in his use of myth, in Barthes's phrase, nor of attempting to purify its material by saying its brutality is a measure of alienation from God. But he is not justifying the status quo or creating an ideology to justify a political present. Instead, Christianity does not sanction the past and its errors or betrayals; it offers a way of reading them that illuminates the future. Just as in oral culture, the social group decides how old and new relate, so Christianity can for Laȝamon draw on both oral and written authority and be verified, through prophecy and its promise of fulfilment, and through individual choice related to a community's welfare.

3
History, Prophecy and Possibility

No doubt the world is entirely an imaginary world, but it is only once removed from the true world.

(Isaac Bashevis Singer, 'Gimpel the Fool')

This chapter attempts to show how the disparate elements presented earlier link up and form a consistent reading of Laȝamon's text, though not by the book's own evidence anything like 'the' reading of it, using approaches that at least initially imitate contemporary ones for Laȝamon and the medieval readers after him.[1] To examine history and prophecy, I return to the temporal and finite to look at what Laȝamon stresses in history, and then expand to the transcendent context for finite occurrences. Here, recall his focus on the opposition of Christians and heathens, the concept of truth as paramount and the emphasis of betrayal versus keeping faith as the dominant repetitions in the work. But to create the links of finite and infinite, or natural and supernatural, it is more useful to begin with magic.

Magic and Divination: The Supernatural and Natural

Supernatural events and powers occur regularly in the *Brut*, from small details such as giants and monsters, probably as marvels of the past, to eagles, dreams and magic linked to prophecy. So Ruhhudibras the king, who built Winchester, Canterbury and Shaftesbury, dies after a great eagle spoke at the castle where he was: '[A]n muchel ærn specẻ a þon castle þer he set. / þet Ruhhudibras þe kingẻ him-seolf hit iherde. / ꝉ alle his cnihtesẻ þe mide him weoren. / Þes fuȝel tecnedeẻ faie-sið þes kinges' (ll. 1412–15) (A great eagle spoke from the castle where he sat, so that Ruhhudibras the king himself heard it, and all his knights who were with him. The bird prophesied the death of the king). The eagle was often connected with pagan prophecy or divination, and an echo of its flight is probably intended when Bladud, the king's successor, 'cuðe þene vuele craft/ þat he wið þene Wurse spæc' (l. 1421) (knew skills of evil so that he spoke with the Worse/Devil), and dies trying to fly after 'He ʒealp þat he wolde fleon/ on fuʒeles læche' (l. 1434) (he boasted that he would fly in the form of a bird). Eagles reappear at the Scottish loch when Arthur goes there; the details have been remarked as reminiscent of Anglo-Saxon sources, notably the mere where Beowulf finds Grendel's mother. Even some of the vocabulary echoes: 'Þat water is unimete/ brade nikeres þer ba[ð]ieð inne. / þer is æluene ploʒe/ in atteliche pole' (ll. 10851–2) (that water is immeasurably broad, water monsters swim therein; there is elven play in the terrible pool). On the sixty islands in the loch nest eagles and other great birds, 'arnes/ ⁊ oðere græte uoʒeles', which again are a prophetic sign:

> Þe ærnes habbeoð ane laʒe/ bi æuer-ælches kinges dahʒen.
> whænne-swa æi ferde/ fundeð to þan ærde.
> þeonne fleoð þa fuʒeles/ feor i þan lufte.
> moni hundred þusen/ ⁊ muchel feoht makið.
> Þenne is þat folc buten wene/ þat reouðe heom is to cumene.
> of summes cunnes leoden/ þe þat lond wulleð i-sechen.
> Tweien dæʒes oðer þreo/ þus scal þis taken beo.
> ær unkuþe men/ to þan lond liðen. (ll. 10856–63)

> (The eagles have a custom in each and every king's reign.
> Whenever any army comes upon that region,
> then the birds fly far into the air,
> many hundred thousands of them, and engage in a great battle.
> Then that folk knows without doubt that disaster is to come to them
> from some race of people who wish to seek that land.
> Two days or three, thus this sign will be
> before foreign men march into the land.)

Such 'tokens' have an ancient heritage, 'divinatory observation of the flight and cries of birds' having been described by Isidore of Seville in his *Etymologies* and drawn from classical writers such as Varro.[2] Anglo-Saxon texts also featured eagles and other prophetic birds, such as those which carry holy men in *Andreas* or, in *The Life of St Gregory* (ch. 16), the raven which Paulinus has shot after it sang as if proclaiming an omen.³

Dreams too link present and future with truth; oneiromancy, the interpretation of dreams, was popular throughout the Middle Ages.⁴ When Arthur has his first dream in which a dragon conquers a bear, it follows directly after Laȝamon's foreshadowing of Modred's and Wenhauer's treachery, still at best just begun, for Arthur has only just set sail for the Continent. None of his men dare put an evil reading on the dream, because they are afraid of the consequences and that such a reading will come true, as discussed above; everyone agrees that telling the dream aloud may turn it to good: 'Ne durste þer na cniht/ to ufele ræcchen na wiht. / leoste he sculden leosen/ his leomen þat weoren him deore' (ll. 12792–3) (Not a single knight there dared to interpret evilly in any way, lest he should lose his limbs that were dear to him). But a second dream, more detailed and chilling, confirms for Arthur that something has happened. As discussed earlier, Arthur's insistence on the horror of his dream finally causes the messenger to admit the truth. The details of the dream allow us to see how clearly and well Laȝamon uses symbolism and dreams to reflect the power of prophecy. Sitting atop his hall with Walwain before him, Arthur watches Modred and Wenhauer hew down the posts that hold up the roof. When the roof collapses, Arthur breaks his right arm in the fall and Walwain breaks both. To smite Modred, Arthur must use his left hand; he then hacks the queen into pieces which he throws into 'ane swarte putte' (l. 14001) (a dark pit). Then a golden lion, 'deoren swiðe hende. þa ure Drihten make[de]' (l. 14008) (a quite noble beast that our Lord made), grabs him by his middle and takes him into the sea with it, until the waves carry him to a fish which carries him to land. All wet, he begins to quiver, and that merges with his waking reaction. Clearly, the two traitors destroy the house and hall (in multiple senses) that Arthur creates. They incapacitate his champion and force Arthur to fight disabled. Injured, he still conquers them, and God's most beautiful creature takes him into the water. As a lion is often linked to Christ in bestiaries, and water to baptism, we can read a type of salvation here; but it is also true that the story will in fact be that Arthur crosses the water to Avalon, and then will return, just as the fish (again, Christlike, or perhaps like Jonah's whale) saves him. The dream will be confirmed, and Arthur himself does so: when Walwain and Angel and others die, he says, 'Ich wuste bi mine sweuene⸳ whæt sorȝen me weoren ȝeueðe' (l. 14145) (I knew from my dream what sorrows would befall me).

Bakhtin writes of dreams and visions as 'subjective playing with time', where '[t]ime begins to be influenced by dreams'. He also discusses how 'this violation of elementary temporal relationships and perspectives' creates a 'miraculous world' where space too distorts, 'an emotional, subjective distortion of space which is in part symbolic'.[5] (Bakhtin's example is the Montsalvat episode in *Parzival*.) No one could read the accounts of Arthur's dreams and doubt Laȝamon's understanding of the symbolic. In his work, however, Laȝamon keeps spatial distortion, and so perhaps subjective distortion, to a minimum. He carefully documents locations through place names and follows the campaigns of his rulers through the real world. His only concession to symbolic, subjective or emotional spatial distortion is Avalon. That exception proves crucial, for it conquers death. Like Dante, Laȝamon draws the world of dreams and visions into the temporal world in order to link eternity with his own present, using a Celtic and Christian space: Avalon. Why accept the link of Celtic and Christian in Avalon, and in connection with Arthur? Davies notes that the same period that saw the existence of great secular heroes like Arthur and other Welsh rulers had a parallel religious mythology that emerged in the eleventh and twelfth centuries along with Arthurian material. The fifth and sixth centuries, 'the age of saints', 'acquired in ecclesiastical mythology much of the status and mystique that the era of "the men of the North" (W. *gwŷr y Gogledd*) occupied in secular mythology'. Many were anxious to defend the reputation of the native Church in the face of Norman assault, and great Welsh lives of saints such as David and Cadog were written.[6]

In fact, Arthur is directly linked to Welsh saints by no fewer than seven Latin Lives written principally in Wales and western England. These works, discussed by Jeff Rider, 'form the most extensive body of surviving Arthurian texts written before, or at about the same time as, Geoffrey of Monmouth's *Historia Regum Britanniae* (c. 1136–38)'.[7] He cites a 'notable expansion of historiographical activity in the Anglo-Norman realm between 1090 and 1130', often as part of the need to defend charters and the reputation of saints against Norman scepticism and encroachment. He divides six of the Lives into two Welsh groups, a Llancarfan group (a Life of Cadog by Lifris, Lives of Cadog and Gildas by Caradoc, and a Life of Illtud by

Caradoc or a disciple) and a Cardigan group (Lives of Padarn and Carannog). A seventh, perhaps later, is the Breton *Vita Euflami* (Efflam). Rider comments that Geoffrey was undoubtedly influenced by these Welsh Lives in his concept of Arthur,[8] but that no fixed tradition of Arthur emerges from the material:

> It has often been written that Arthur plays the stock hagiographical role . . . but this is not strictly true. In only two of the ten episodes in which he appears in these Lives does Arthur play the role of the humbled royal antagonist who grants land or prerogatives to the saint . . . In other episodes he plays a role more heroic than royal, grants nothing, acts in concert with the saint, or is simply thrown in for 'historical' relief. The figure of Arthur in these Lives is, in fact, more remarkable for its diversity than for its unanimity.[9]

Such diversity and heroic status, nevertheless linked to saints, could indicate why he was so useful for Laȝamon's purposes. Arthur may be secular, but he is the greatest Christian Celtic king; even more, Christianity itself promises that death shall have no dominion. Arthur's 'magic' can be miracle too, the perfect Christian king betrayed but triumphant and ultimately resurrected. It is not too much to argue that Arthur provides Laȝamon the priest with a perfect secular and Christian hero whose attributes do not go unrecognized, and Merlin gives him a prophet's voice to record.

Both Arthur's and Merlin's connections with Christianity emerge clearly in the *Brut*, most likely due to Welsh influence on their depiction. Listen, for example, to the Christlike overtones in Merlin's prophecy of Arthur's fame, echoed but expanded from Geoffrey:

> of him scullen gleomen/ godliche singen.
> of his breosten scullen æten/ aþele scopes.
> scullen of his blode/ beornes beon drunke.
> of his eȝene scullen fleoni/ furene gleden.
> ælc finger an his hond/ scarp stelene brond.
> scullen stan walles/ biuoren him to-fallen.
> beornes scullen rusien/ reosen heore mærken.
> Þus he scal wel longe/ liðen ȝeond londen.
> leoden biwinnen/ 7 his laȝen sette/
> Þis beoð þa <ta>cnen of þan sune. þe cumeð of
>   U[ðe]re Pendragune. (ll. 9410–19)

(Of him shall minstrels pleasingly sing,
from his breast shall noble poets eat,
warriors will be drunk on his blood.
From his eyes shall fly fiery sparks,
each finger on his hand will be a sharp steel blade.
Stone walls will fall before him,
warriors shall shudder, their banners fall in battle.
Thus for a very long time he will go throughout the land,
conquering peoples and setting up his laws.
This is the sign of that son who is begotten of Uther Pendragon.)

It is also important that Merlin says this to his dear friend, 'leofe freond,' sent to find him, a holy hermit, before going to Uther's court. Again, this detail may be significant on several levels. Davies notes,

> Contemporaries indeed conceded that native Wales was not without its excellences in the practice of religion. Most notable were its hermits, living either individually . . . or in communities . . . Welsh law accorded a special status to such men (W. *diofrydogion*), not dissimilar to that of holy men and anchorites in other societies. Their word had an especial force in oath-taking and they frequently acted as mediators in local disputes . . . Even Gerald of Wales was forced to concede that 'nowhere will you find hermits and anchorites of greater spirituality than in Wales'.[10]

Given our previous discussion of oaths and betrayals, and the emerging argument that prophecy in Laȝamon is not merely political and secular, the role of the hermit gives Merlin's character some unexpected aspects.

But let us examine what Merlin can be in Laȝamon's text, and how his magic and prophecy link to the supernatural in Christianity, by looking first at other descriptions of prophecy and divination in the work. Only three references occur before the incident with Vortiger's walls that brings Merlin to court. Almost as soon as the history begins, Ascanius, son of Aeneas, sends for those 'þe cuþen dweomerlakes song' (l. 137) (those who know the sorcerous song) in order to know the future of an unborn child. His son Silvius fathered a child in secret, and Ascanius learns that the child will slay father and mother but will eventually gain honour. In fact, the mother dies in childbirth; the son Brutus mistakenly shoots his father while hunting, is banished, but eventually gains a reputation and returns. The language used is repeated later in the text: 'witen he wolde⁄ þurh þa wiðer-craftes' (l. 138) ([Ascanius] wished to know through evil powers) and 'Heo wrpen heore leoten/ þe Scucke wes bi-tweonen. / heo funde on þen crefte/ carefule leoðes' (ll. 140–1) (they cast their lots – the Devil was among them. They found by the arts songs full of pain). The dream motif also occurs early: Brutus comes upon Diana's temple during his travels. Diana is loved by the devil: 'Heo dude wnder craftes/ þe Scucke hire fulste' (l. 576) (She practised wondrous arts; the Devil aided her) and '[t]o hire weoren iwoned/ þa wnder-creftie men. / of þa [þ]ingen þa weren to kumen/ heo heom wolde cuðen. / mid tacnen ꝥ mid swefnen/ þonne heo weren on slæpe' (ll. 579–81) (with her were associated wondrously crafty men. Of the things that were to come she would inform them with signs and with dreams when they were asleep). Brutus himself shoots a white hind and wraps himself in its skin before her altar to take advantage of such prophetic dreams; she tells him of Albion and how he will make a new Troy: 'þet lond is swiþe wunsum/ wellen þer beoð feire. / wuniað in þon londe/ eotantes swiðe stronge. / Albion hatte þat lond/ ah leode <ne> beoð þar nane. / Þer-to þu scalt teman/ ꝥ ane neowe Troye þar makian' (ll. 622–5) (that land is so lovely: springs there are fair. Exceedingly strong giants live in the land. That land is called Albion, but there are no people there at all. There you shall breed and make there a new Troy). In both cases, though the prophecies be true, they are products of demonic aid. Laȝamon clearly mentions the Shuck, the Devil, as the real source of such power.

That connection soon changes. The only other mention of prophecy before Merlin concerns the birth of Christ. Just after the passage previously cited on the Trinity, when Kinbelin was king, a prophet named Teilesin came to court. Wace was the first to introduce him, anachronistically in terms of Welsh tradition, since he rightly belongs to the age of heroes some five centuries later than in Wace's text. Yet Welsh tradition also has Taliesin (Laȝamon's Teilesin) reincarnated periodically, and Foulon notes that 'the Welsh believed that Taliesin had passed through many incarnations, had borne a banner before Alexander the Great, and had been an instructor to Eli and Enoc'.[11] So such anachronism need not deny him his identification with the well-known prophet and poet of later times. In fact, two separate traditions exist, one historical, a poet who wrote for Urien Rheged, and a prophetic figure associated more with the Celtic Otherworld and magic, the bard of Elphin.[12] The two often end up combined. In Wace and Laȝamon, Taliesin is summoned to

Kinbelin's court by twelve wise men because of his powers of prophecy:

> feorliche þing fuleden him/ he wes ihaten Teilesin.
> heo heolten hine for witie. þurh his wit-fulne cræfte/
> 7 al heo hit ilæfdon. þat Teilesin heom seide/
> he seide heom selkuð i-noh/ 7 al heo hit funden soð
> he seide heom ælche ȝere. wæt heom to cumen weore. (ll. 4535–9)

> (Marvellous things attached to him; he was called Teilesin.
> They considered him a wise man because of his mental arts,
> and they believed everything that Teilesin told them.
> He told them a great many wonders and they found it all true.
> He told them every year what would happen to them.)

Kinbelin questions him on the 'seolcuðe leod-ronen' (l. 4549) 'wondrous rumours/accounts' about a child born in Bethlehem, because his people are very afraid. He has both heard and read of signs:

> Muchele is 7 stor þe eiȝe/ tacnen þer beoð on sterren.
> an monen 7 on seonnen/ eie is on mon-cunnen.
> Þis is widen icuð/ 7 þa writen me beoð to icume.
> 7 ic wolde iwiten æt þe/ þu ært mi wine deore.
> to whan þis tocne wule ten/ to wulche þinge temen. (ll. 4552–6)

> (Great and powerful is the terror – there are signs among the stars,
> in the moon and the sun. Awe fills mankind.
> This is widely known and the writing of it has come to me,
> and I wish to learn from you – you are my dear friend –
> what this sign will portend, what things it will breed.)

Taliesin chooses to emphasize the oral, normal enough in prophecy, by saying, 'Hit wes ȝare iqueðen/ þa quides beoð nu soðe' (l. 4559) (It was long ago prophesied; those prophecies are now come true); that such sayings (*quides*) are true should also echo with previous use of the term *quide* as a synonym for a will. This birth entails a bequeathal or inheritance that saves men from sin. Taliesin makes this salvation clear by conflating the birth with the harrowing of hell immediately after Christ's death: the child is born to be called 'Saviour' (*Hælend*) because he brings his friends out of hell (Taliesin names thirteen and adds that 'many thousand' more are saved, ll. 4560–9). Importantly, for the first time prophecy is linked not with demons but with Christianity; a Welsh poet and prophet becomes the link.

Merlin as Laʒamon's Prophet

Whether Laʒamon (or Wace) knew much of the traditions about Taliesin is problematic (see, for example, Bullock-Davies's work on *latimarii* and the exchange of stories at court), but the question has relevance for the dominant prophetic figure in Laʒamon's work, Merlin. Both Myrddin and Taliesin were considered Welsh poets as well as prophets, and appear together in a Welsh triad listing the Three Skilled Bards of Arthur's court: Myrddin son of Morfryn, Myrddin Emrys and Taliesin.[13] One text attributed to Myrddin himself goes by the name of *Ymddiddan Myrddin a Thaliesin* (The Dialogue of Myrddin and Taliesin). Jarman comments that it combines

> reflections by these two seers on two distinct events . . . an attack made, or believed to have been made, by Maelgwn Gwynedd on the kingdom of Dyfed in the first half of the sixth century . . . [and] a prophecy in general terms about the battle of Arfderydd . . . These references suggest that the author of the poem derived his material from the saga of Arfderydd rather than from the more particular legend of Myrddin.[14]

The two are companions in other tales, however, notably the *Vita Merlini* of Geoffrey of Monmouth. There, Thelgesinus/Taliesin joins Merlin in the woods late in life, to expound to Merlin upon 'the constitution of the universe, fishes, and islands. Both discuss the history and future of Britain.'[15] Merlin foretells the battle of Arthur and Modred, then is cured of his madness (and his prophetic powers) by a draught from a spring that miraculously appeared nearby. Thelgesinus discusses curative waters, 'which in his opinion evidence the dominion of God over nature', and Merlin, while purifying himself through fasting, 'holds forth upon the marvellous behaviour of birds'. Elsewhere he has spoken of how he knows the future, the past and various secrets of nature, including bird flight and star wanderings.[16] Clearly, Geoffrey went to some pains to distinguish between Christian and pagan ability: for Geoffrey, Merlin loses his prophetic powers when he becomes more like a saint. His prophecies, he implies, do not come from God.

Laȝamon too makes clear a distinction between the demonic and the divine. Occurrences of prophecy and omen before Merlin in Laȝamon were, as remarked, notably pagan except for the Taliesin episode. The occurrences of magic or divination *after* Merlin's appearance, excluding those of Merlin himself, are limited to a comment on astrologers at court, and the character of Pelluz. The astrologers at Arthur's court are carefully described as canons and clerics from the minster of St Aaron whose ability helps advise the king:

> Canunes þer weoren; þe cuð weoren widen.
> þer wes moni god clarc; þe wel cuðe a leore.
> muchel heo ferden mid þan crafte; to lokien in þan leofte.
> to lokien i þan steorren; nehȝe and feorren.
> þe craft is ihate; Astronomie.
> Wel ofte heo þan kinge; seide of feole þinge.
> heo cudden him on leoden; what him sculde ilimpen. (ll. 12121–7)

> (Canons there were who were widely known,
> many a good cleric was there who knew well his studies.
> Often they went with skill to look into the heavens,
> to look at the stars near and far.
> That art is called astronomy.
> Quite often they told the king of many things,
> they foretold to him in speech what would happen to him.)

In contrast, the only other stargazer is the evil Pelluz, 'an clarc þe com from Spaine' (l. 15218) (a clerk/cleric from Spain), who spies out every action of Cadwalan. Though described as 'clarc', Pelluz's Spanish background might raise doubts, given the mix of Muslim and Jewish cultures there in (for Laȝamon) a time of crusades. In addition, he serves Edwin, who took Brien's sister by force; Brien is Cadwalan's knight and the one who counselled Cadwalan to deny Edwin his crown. Pelluz uses his powers to see Cadwalan's every action and keep him from regaining the throne: '[F]eole craftes he cuðe; þa he isah in þan lufte. / on sterren and on sunne; and on þare sæ brade. / in-siht he cuðe; a winde and a mone. / of þan uisce þer he wlæt; and of wurmen þer heo crepe' (ll. 15220–3) (Many skills he knew when he looked in the heavens, on stars and on the sun, and on the broad sea. Insight he had into wind and moon, of the fish where it swam, of serpents where they creep). Only Brien's murder of Pelluz ends his magic, and not before an odd occurrence of unwitting cannibalism on Cadwalan's part due to Pelluz's forewarning to Edwin. Unable to come to Britain because of Pelluz, Cadwalan falls ill on an island near Yarmouth and craves animal flesh, 'deores flæsce'. As none exists on the island, Brien finally resolves to cut a piece of his own thigh. Cadwalan recovers unaware, though Brien pointedly comments when bringing the meat, 'ich habbe þe here i-broht/ breden alre deorest. / þat ich auere an æi borde/ beren bi-uoren kinge' (ll. 15268–9) (I have brought you here the dearest meat that I ever before have borne before a king at table). The pun of *deor* (animal) and *deorest* (dearest) is Laȝamon's own touch of irony, echoing Christian offerings of bread and 'flesh' (including an aural pun on the Middle English, where the words for bread and for meat, 'breden', l. 15268, here would sound alike).[17]

To return to the ways in which Merlin is different from Laȝamon's other figures connected with magic and divination: Jan Ziolkowski has written about Merlin in Geoffrey's *Vita* as a composite character with three aspects, namely

> one part a wild man engaged in shamanlike practices that were widespread in the pre-Christian era, one part a political prophet of a type still found in Wales when Geoffrey wrote, and one part a Christian prophet combining traits of Old Testament prophets and Christian saints.[18]

The shaman aspect involves astrology, trances, power from spirits and the ability to ride into the other world either with an animal companion or as an animal, frequently a bird. The political aspect in the *Vita* is couched in Galfredian metaphor, that is, using animals to represent notable figures. (We have seen that Laȝamon uses such images in the prophetic dreams of Arthur, and that his similes are one of his great ingenuities.) Thus Merlin will speak of a Cornish boar, meaning Arthur; Laȝamon also uses this particular example.

But Ziolkowski's final aspect, of a Christian saint and Old Testament prophet mixed, becomes the most intriguing for Laȝamon's depiction of Merlin's character. The question of whether Merlin was inspired by demons or by God was crucial. Ziolkowski notes that soon after the *Vita* came into circulation, medieval schoolmen examined the problems connected with the source of his prophetic powers in detail:

History, Prophecy and Possibility 111

By the end of the twelfth century they had already produced five systematic commentaries. Between 1174 and 1179 appeared the *Explanationes in prophetiam Merlini* (sometimes attributed to Alan of Lille) . . . The author of the treatise inclines to believe that Merlin was Christian and a bona fide prophet; but even if Merlin was not a Christian, the author points out that Job, the Sibyls, Balaam, Cassandra, and many others who were not Jewish were filled with the prophetic spirit by the Lord.[19]

Once again, Laȝamon participates in a contemporary issue and concern, and chooses a side. How he represents Merlin becomes crucial to understanding how he sees his history as functioning.

The initial setup of Merlin's appearance begins when Vortiger's walls at Mount Reir fall down each night. He sends

> æfter world-wise monne⸱ þa wisdom cuðen.
> ⁊ bad heom leoten weorpen⸱ ⁊ fondien leod-runen.
> fondien þat soðe⸱ mid heore siȝe-craften . . .
> Þas weorlde-wise men⸱ þer a twa wenden.
> summe heo wenden to þan wude⸱ summe to weien-læten.
> heo gunnen loten weorpen⸱ mid heore leod-runen.
> fulle þreo nihten⸱ heore craftes heo dihten.
> Ne mihten heo nauere finden⸱ þurh nauere nane þinge
> whær-on hit weore ilong⸱ þat þe wal þat wes swa strong.
> æuere-ælche nihte to-ras⸱ ⁊ þe king his swinc læs. (ll. 7733–5, 7738–44)

> (for the wordly-wise men who knew wise things,
> and bade them cast lots and attempt incantations
> to find the truth with their magical skills . . .
> These worldly-wise men went in two directions.
> Some went to the wood, some to crossroads.
> They began to work with their speech runes.
> A full three nights they prepared their arts.
> They could not ever find, not through a single thing,
> what was the reason that the wall that was so strong
> each and every night collapsed, and the king wasted his efforts.)

The 'worldly-wise' men break into two groups that use places associated with magic, woods and crossroads; they are unsuccessful. (Worth noting is the cross in the Caligula manuscript margin next to this section.) Next, Ioram comes and lies about knowing the cause. His advice to seek out a child with no father brings Merlin to court along with his mother.

Merlin's mother is now a nun, but she tells a tale about a golden knight who comes to her, she knows not from where, and by whom she conceives her son. Her heritage is royal, as she is Conan's daughter, and Vortiger treats her as if she were his kin, 'swulc heo his cun weore' (l. 7825). His curiosity about Merlin draws the story from her: at fifteen, she saw the fairest thing born: 'swulc hit weore a muchel cniht⁄ al of golde idiht. / Þis ich isæh on sweuene⁄ alche niht on slepe' (ll. 7840–1) (as if it were a great knight, made all of gold. This I saw in a dream each night while asleep). Vortiger sends for Magan the wise man:

> He wes a wis clærc⁄ ⁊ cuðe of feole cræften.
> he cuðe wel ræden⁄ he cuðe feor læden.
> he cuðe of þan crafte⁄ þe wuneð i þan lufte.
> he cuðe tellen⁄ of ælche leod-spelle. (ll. 7860–3)

> (He was a wise clerk and knew of many arts.
> He knew how to advise well, he knew how to see ahead,
> he knew about the arts that reside in the heavens,
> he knew how to tell about each people's history.)

Magan's designation as 'clærc' could imply Christianity, though not necessarily, given the use of the same term for Pelluz, and 'feor læden' implies seeing afar, prophecy or divination. Magan tells Vortiger about spirits that live between earth and heaven called *incubii demones*, implying that such a one fathered Merlin. He says, 'Ne doð heo noht muchel scaðe⁄ bute hokerieð þan folke' (l. 7877) (they do not do much harm, but they bother people). This is a particular group within a larger group of beings in the heavens, for earlier he says that they will all remain there until *Domes-dæi*, but that 'Summe heo beoð aðele⁄ ⁊ summe heo uuel wurcheð' (l. 7874) (they are some of them noble and some of them work evil).

Such questionable paternity makes Merlin the candidate Vortiger seeks. Merlin, however, scornfully challenges Ioram on his lies, asking for a contest in which each will give the cause of the nightly destruction, and the true seer will be known by the results. As mentioned in chapter 1, Merlin calls Ioram 'leod-swike', a traitor to his people, eventually proven by the discovery of the two dragons as Merlin foretold. Ioram and his seven followers are beheaded.

Vortiger presses Merlin for prophecy after Merlin tells the meaning of the white and red dragons. Merlin rebukes him as a fool for asking about the dragons, which refer to future kings: 'Ah ʒif þu weore swa wis mon⁊ ⁊ swa witter a þoncke / . . . ich þe wolde suggen⁊ of sorʒe þine' (ll. 8001, 8004) (But if you were such a wise man and so clever in thought . . . I would have told you of your sorrow). He reminds Vortiger of his betrayal of Constance and his bringing of the Saxons, then announces the arrival of Aurelius and Uther for vengeance. He foretells the deaths of Aurelius and Uther by poison, a pointed prophecy, given the earlier death by poison of Vortiger's son Vortimer at his wife's hands. He also prophesies that Uther's son, 'a wilde bar' (wild boar) from Cornwall (ll. 8031–2), will 'alle þa swiken⁊ swenien mid eiʒe' (l. 8034) (all the traitors destroy with terror).

His next appearance occurs at the request of Bishop Tremorien of Caerleon, who counsels Aurelius to send for him: 'We habbeoð ænne witeʒe⁊ Mærlins ihaten' (l. 8479) (We have a wise man called Merlin). Aurelius wishes to construct a memorial to those killed at Amesbury. He sends men to the four directions, but those who go to Wales, 'Wælsce londe', find Merlin near a well: 'Þe walle he lufode⁊ ⁊ ofte hine þer-inne. baðede' (l. 8498) (the well he loved and often bathed himself therein). The similarity to the miraculous spring of the *Vita* merges with the Celtic practice of well worship. The knights greet Merlin in the king's name and offer great rewards for his service, but Merlin rejects them, as Laʒamon has him reject all material reward. Merlin says he knew Aurelius and Uther 'beien⁊ ær heo iboren weoren. / þæh ich nauer nouþer⁊ mid eʒen ne iseʒe' (ll. 8520–1) (both before they were born, though I never saw either with eyes [in person]). He then bewails the fact that Aurelius will not live long, an incidental prophecy, and agrees to come to court. Laʒamon adds the comment, surely reflective of the problems discussed above regarding prophecy, 'Wale þat an worlde⁊ næs nan wite. / þat auere wuste here⁊ whes sune he weore. / buten Drihten ane⁊ þe wlæt al clane' (ll. 8539–41) (Alas that there was no wise man in the world who ever knew here whose son he was except the Lord alone who sees all). The reference to God's knowledge may be taken as an indication that Merlin is God's own mystery, not the Devil's. The tasks in which Merlin then becomes involved confirm that he does not operate under demonic inspiration. He immediately comments on his lack of materialism to Aurelius and links it to his powers; Aurelius asks him to tell of the world's course and the future.

> O Aurilie þe king⁊ þu fræinest me a sellic þing.
> loke þat þu na mare⁊ swulc þing ne iscire⁊

> For mi gæst is bæl iwis, þa a mire breoste is.
> and ȝef ich a-mong monnen, ȝelp wolde makien.
> mid glad-scipe mid gomene, mid god-fulle worden.
> mi gast hine iwarðeð, 7 wirð stille.
> 7 binimeð me min wit, 7 mine wise word for-dut.
> þenne weore ich dumbe, of æuer-ælche dome. (ll. 8548–55)

> (O Aurelius the king, you ask me an unusual thing.
> Look that you do not utter such a thing ever again,
> for my spirit within my breast is certainly distressed,
> and if I wished to make such a boast among men,
> with gladness and for entertainment with suitable words,
> my spirit would become angered and still,
> and take from me my wisdom and prevent my wise words.
> Then I would be dumb on each and every judgement.)

The company of men or peer pressure could cause a loss of calm that would steal his abilities: prophecy cannot be forced, or made to serve egotism or power. It is a gift. The source of that gift becomes somewhat clearer when Merlin builds Stonehenge. He tells how it stands in Ireland, and that when men are ill, they go to the stone: '7 heo wasceð þene stan, 7 þer-mide baðieð heore ban. / umbe lutle stu[n]de, heo wurðeð al isunde' (ll. 8578–9) (and they wash the stone and therewith bathe their bones; in a little while they become entirely healed). Such curative powers, reminiscent of those discussed by Taliesin in the *Vita*, also reflect common beliefs about relics and their virtues of healing in Christianity. Aurelius exclaims that the size of the stones and Merlin's claim that no man born could bring them from that place make the task impossible. Merlin replies, 'betere is liste, þene ufel strenðe' (l. 8590). *Ufel* can mean fierce as well as evil, and Merlin might be saying something akin to a variant on 'brains over brawn'; but, given the problematic question of his powers, he may well be asserting the intellect over (demonic) strength, with the intellect the spiritual aspect of man.

When Merlin fetches the 'Eotinde Ring', as Stonehenge is called, his men must first fight with King Gillomar's army. Gillomar swears 'a Seint Brændan, Ne scullen heo læden ænne stan' (l. 8642) (by Saint Brendan they shall not take away any stone). He goes on to make an exaggerated threat and boast, which Laȝamon concludes with 'Þus þe vnwise king, plaȝede mid worden. / ah al an oðer hit iwærð, oðer he iwende' (ll. 8652–3) (thus the unwise king played with words, but it happened completely otherwise than he thought). Apparently, Brendan is not sufficient to the task. Yet Merlin seems to call on supernatural power to move the stones, because he walks about the ring, three times within and without, muttering 'al-se he bede sunge' (l. 8702), as if singing prayers. As Laȝamon has elsewhere used different vocabulary to describe casting spells, he seems here to make the point that Merlin's power is not evil. He reinforces it once Stonehenge is re-erected at Amesbury. The ring is consecrated, and the ceremony takes place on a Christian feast, Whitsunday, and includes the creation of two bishops:

> Al þan Whitensunendæi⁄ þe king a þan uelde læi.
> hæt halȝien þe stude þe hæhte Stanhenge.
> Þreo dæies fulle⁄ wunede þe king stille.
> i þan þridde dæie⁄ heȝe wurðede his duȝeðe.
> he makede tweie biscopes⁄ wunder ane gode.
> Seint Dubriz;to Kaerliun⁄ to Eouuerwic. Seint Samson.
> beien heo iwurðen hali⁄ ꝥ mid Gode haȝe. (ll. 8731–7)

> (All of Whitsunday the king lay camped in the field,
> ordered hallowed the place that was called Stonehenge.
> Three full days the king remained still.
> On the third day he fully honoured his retainers.
> He made two bishops, wondrously good:
> St Dubriz for Caerleon, for York, St Samson.
> They were both holy and close to the high God.)

Brendan did not fail Gillomar; Merlin's side simply had divine blessing.

Merlin apparently stays at court, because later, when a comet appears with a dragon flashing rays of light at France and Ireland, Uther calls to him. He asks him to tell 'of þan tacne⁄ þe we i-sæȝen habbeoð' (l. 8932) (of the sign that we have seen). Then follows a passage on which many have commented as matching contemporary accounts of Welsh seers:

> Mærlin sæt him stille⁄ longe ane stunde.
> swulc he mid sweuene⁄ swunke ful swiðe.
> Heo seiden þe hit iseȝen⁄ mid heore aȝen æȝen.
> þat ofte he hine wende⁄ swulc hit a wurem weore.
> Late he gon awakien⁄ þa gon he to quakien. (ll. 8935–9)

(Merlin sat silent for a long while,
as if he suffered violently in a dream vision.
Those who saw it with their own eyes said
that often he himself moved as if a serpent.
Later he began to awake, then he began to shudder.)

He interprets the comet as representing Uther and his offspring, Arthur and his sister Æne, who marries Lot. He then 'gon to slume⁄ swulc he wolde slæpen' (l. 8979) (began to drowse as if he would sleep), presumably exhausted by his effort. The contemporary account of Gerald of Wales describes *awenyddion*,[20] though he classes them ambiguously, as possibly possessed by demons:

> When you consult them about some problem, they immediately go into a trance and lose control of their senses, as if they are possessed. They do not answer the question put to them in any logical way. Words stream from their mouths, incoherently and apparently meaningless and without any sense at all, but all the same well expressed: and if you listen carefully to what they say you will receive the solution to your problem . . . When they are going into a trance they invoke the true and living God, and the Holy Trinity, and they pray that they may not be prevented by their sins from revealing the truth.[21]

Once Aurelius dies, Uther succeeds and Merlin leaves court, though Uther would have had him stay. Uther has two dragon images made to remind him of Merlin's prophecy and also of the man himself, 'al for Mærlines l[u]ue⁄ swa swiðe he wilnede his cume' (l. 9086) (all for love of Merlin, so greatly did he desire his coming). One he used as a battle standard, the other he placed at the bishop's see in Winchester, along with his spear. (The latter sounds like a borrowing of the Carolingians' holy lance.) Once again, Laȝamon manages to link a sign of Merlin and his power both to the Church and to prophecy.

When Uther desires Ygærne, Ulfin counsels him to send for Merlin and win him with 'liste', the same word used by Merlin to describe power greater than strength. Because attempts to find Merlin failed earlier, Ulfin suggests sending a hermit who 'swor bi his chinne⁄ þat he wuste Merlin. / whar he ælche nihte⁄ resteð vnder lufte. / and ofte he him spæc wið⁄ ⁊ spelles him talde' (ll. 9364–6) (swore by his chin [his beard?] that he knew where Merlin rested each night under the skies, and often he spoke with him and told him tales). The sanctity of Welsh hermits, as well as their sanctity in romance, tells us once again that Merlin is in good company.[22] The hermit finds him in the woods and 'heo clupten heo custen، and cuðliche speken' (l. 9386) (they embraced, they kissed, and spoke as known friends). Merlin tells the hermit what his errand is before the hermit can, and includes a long prophecy of what Arthur will be like, including his never dying and his breast and blood as food for *scops* and warriors, adding, 'Þis beoð þa <ta>cnen of þan sune. þe cumeð of U[ðe]re Pendragune' (l. 9419) (these are the signs of the son who comes of Uther Pendragon). The repeated use of *tacnen*, signs, in Merlin's art confirms his prophetic powers. Merlin agrees to all because of his affection for the hermit ('and faren ich wulle for þire lufe', l. 9427a (and fare forth I will for love of you)), again linking him to Christian brotherhood, and he again refuses all reward. Instead, he tells Uther to reward Ulfin and the hermit, 'for ich am on rade. rihchest alre monnen. / ⁊ ȝif ich wilne æhte، þenne wursede ich on crafte' (ll. 9445–6) (for I am in counsel the richest of all men, and if I wanted wealth, then I would worsen in skill). Laȝamon may have felt such emphasis necessary, given that Merlin's next act is to shape-change not simply himself but Uther and Ulfin as well, and to deceive the wife of another. Merlin does not appear again in the text except as a source of prophecy; as a character, his last appearance occurs here. His words, however, are repeatedly revived, and Arthur becomes the fruit of his action. Neither his words nor Arthur are presented in a negative light.

At least ten more times, Merlin's prophecies are cited as fulfilled. After commenting on how the Britons exaggerate Arthur's reputation because of their love for him, the text adds (emphasis added):

> And swa hit wes iuuren iboded، ær he iboren weoren.
> *swa him sæide Merlin، þe witeȝe wes mære.*
> þat a king sculde cume، of Vðere Pendragune.
> þat gleomen sculden wurchen burd، of þas ki[n]ges breosten.
> and þer-to sitten، scopes swiðe sele.
> and eten heore wullen، ær heo þenne fusden.
> and winscenches ut teon، of þeos kinges tungen.
> and drinken ⁊ dreomen، daies ⁊ nihtes.
> þis gomen heom sculde i-lasten، to þere weorlde longe.
> *And ȝet him seide Marlin، mare þat wes to <co>mene.*
> þat al þat he lokede on، to foten him sculde buȝen.
> *Þa ȝet him sæide Mærlin، a sellic þe wes mare.*

> þat sculde beon unimete care، of þas kinges forð-fare.
> and of þas kinges ende، nulle hit na Brut ileue
> buten hit beon þe leste dæð، at þan muchele dome.
> þenne ure Drihte، demeð alle uolke. (ll. 11491–506)

> (And so it was revealed before he was born.
> *So Merlin himself*, who was a famous wise man, *said*
> that a king should come from Uther Pendragon,
> that minstrels would make a board from the king's breast
> and the most excellent poets would sit at it
> and eat as they wished before they went from there,
> and draw out wine draughts from the king's tongue,
> and drink and sing rejoicing by day and by night.
> This delight should last them to the end of the world.
> And *yet Merlin himself said* more that was to come,
> that all that he looked on should kneel at his feet.
> Then *again Merlin himself said* a wonder that was even greater,
> that there would be immeasurable sorrow from the king's departure,
> and no Briton will believe in the king's death
> unless it be the final death at the great Judgement
> when our Lord judges all folk.)

Arthur himself even seems prophetic as, just after this passage, he tells how he will go to Avalon to heal with Argante. Another cross occurs in the manuscript margin here; perhaps it indicates a link to Christianity through prophecy.

Merlin's next prophecy fulfilled occurs when Arthur fights and defeats the Romans:

> Þa wæs mid soðe ifunde، *þat Mærlin sæide whilen*.
> þat sculden for Ar[ð]ure، Rome ifullen afure.
> and þa wal of stanen، quakien and fallen.
> Þas ilke tacni[n]ge sculde beon، of Luces þan kæiseren.
> ꝛ of þan senature، þa mid him come of Rome،
> and of þan seoluen wisen، þæ þer gunnen resen.
> *þat Merlin i furn-daȝen seide*، al heo hit funden þere.
> swa heo duden ære. and seoððen wel iwhare،
> *ær Arður iboren weore. Merlin al hit bodede*. (ll. 13530–8)

> (Thus it was found to be true *what Merlin said once*,
> that because of Arthur Rome would go up in flames
> and the walls of stones would quake and fall.

> This same sign would be about Lucius the emperor
> and the senators who came with him from Rome,
> and the selfsame manner by which they began to collapse.
> *What Merlin in ancient times said*, they found it all there
> just as they did before and after on all occasions.
> *Before Arthur was born, Merlin revealed it all.*)

The same prophecy reoccurs less than 500 lines later, virtually verbatim: 'Þa wes hit itimed þereᴉ *þat Merlin saide while.* / þat Romwalles sculdenᴉ aʒein Ar[ð]ure to-uallen' (ll. 13964–5) (Then was it come to pass *what Merlin said once*, that Rome's walls should fall before Arthur).

A similar prophecy about the destruction of Winchester reiterates Arthur's battle prowess and Merlin's ability: 'Þa wes hit itimed þereᴉ *þat Merlin seide while.* / Ærm wurðest þu Winchæstreᴉ þæ eorðe þe scal forswalʒe. / *swa Merlin sæideᴉ* þe witeʒe wes mære' (ll. 14200–2) (Then was it come to pass *what Merlin said once*: 'Wretched you will become, Winchester; the earth shall swallow you up.' *So Merlin said, the truest prophet*). All three passages stress that Merlin made his prophecies sometime in the past, whereas the initial references merely comment that 'Merlin said it'. The repetition of *while* (once), *furndaʒen* (ancient times) and the phrase 'before Arthur was born' emphasizes the past. When Arthur goes forth to Avalon, however, the time frame shifts. While Geoffrey and Wace both use this extension into the future, Laʒamon develops it more fully and links it more closely to Merlin and prophecy in general.

Why argue that Laʒamon has deliberately stressed prophecy, as opposed to Wace's treatment of the same, with Wace arguably Laʒamon's most direct source? Because of the almost total absence of Merlin and his prophecies in the *Roman de Brut*. Jean Blacker-Knight comments that this omission is part of the depoliticization of the text (as compared to Geoffrey, Wace's source), illustrated by Wace's 'general reluctance to comment on the political ramifications of historical events' and his 'characterization and the exclusion of Merlin's prophecies'.[23] She states:

> Wace omits an extremely important section of Geoffrey's narrative, the *Prophetiae Merlini*, which comprises Book VII of that work; this omission, in fact, is the most dramatic example of Wace's draining of political import from the material associated with Arthur . . . Honesty and trepidation

notwithstanding, by stripping Merlin of his political predictions, Wace has removed a primary element in Geoffrey's characterization of the prophet-magician. Wace reports that Merlin was peerless as a diviner and engineer but affords only one glimpse of Merlin as a diviner – the scene where Merlin explains to Vortigern the significance of the two dragons . . . From this characterization, it was a short step to the portrayal of Merlin strictly as a magician – instead of as a sage – as seen soon after in such Old French prose romances as the thirteenth-century *Huth-Merlin*.[24]

Why not speak of Geoffrey's inclusion of prophecy, though more limited than what we find in Laʒamon, in the same way? Hanning argues, in *The Vision of History in Early Britain* (1966), that Geoffrey's view is fundamentally secular and political, not also concerned with Christian morality, say, as is Gildas:

> The secular interpretation of British history brought to birth by at least one of the authors of the *Historia Brittonum* can be said only to have reached a promising youth in that work. Its potential remained unrealized for over three hundred years, until Geoffrey of Monmouth's *Historia regum Britanniae*, appearing suddenly in twelfth-century England, offered to its first, amazed readers a comprehensive and spectacular vision of the British past largely free of Christian assumptions.[25]

His mention of the *Historia Brittonum* raises one of the points in his work where more recent scholarship must correct his argument. David Dumville, arguably the premier modern historian of early Britain and its chronicles, has worked for many years on a new critical edition of the *Historia Brittonum*,[26] commonly if inaccurately also referred to as Nennius' work. In the process of detailed re-evaluation of the manuscript traditions, Dumville uncovered evidence for what has come to be called the 'Sawley School'. Its relevance to the *Historia Brittonum*, importantly, links it with a Celtic and Welsh interest in historiography:

> I suggest that in the *Historia Brittonum*, we have an early example, perhaps the earliest, of a Welsh attempt at constructing a . . . synthetic history [similar to that of the Irish *Lebor Gabála Érenn*, its *Book of Conquests*]. It certainly does not represent the earliest work of harmonisation and synchronisation, for the secular men of learning, particularly concerned with genealogy, had already been at work, as Dr

Molly Miller has so ably shown us . . . I think that I have some evidence that, in twelfth-century Wales, a sort of super-*Historia Brittonum* was being written, again in Latin, of which we have some fragments preserved in a north English manuscript *ca* 1200.[27]

Dumville had written in 1977 about the Anglo-Norman Robert Banastre, who was driven from north Wales by Owain of Gwynedd in 1167, bringing his Welsh dependants to Lancashire with him. Evidence for Welsh personal names are common in Lancashire documents from the end of the twelfth century, showing how numerous the settlers were; they are even called 'Les Westroys' a century later in a petition of 1278. This community may help to explain the significant survival of Celtic-Latin texts in Sawley abbey, which Dumville postulates but also is careful not to push too far:

> A combination of a Cistercian appetite for history with a Welsh desire to preserve and mould living historical traditions could have been responsible for this substantial aspect of the remarkable activities of the Sawley school.
>
> I do not wish to pretend that Banastre's Welshmen (and the continuing cultural contacts with Wales in which their migration probably resulted) were responsible for all of the activity discussed above. Indeed, for the two or three texts procured before 1166, that is almost certainly out of the question; similarly, we cannot with any confidence attribute to this cause the availability at Sawley of Hiberno-Latin works. However, the background which this migration provides can hardly be ignored in seeking any solution to the problem of the sources and personnel of the Sawley school.[28]

Dumville's care in tracing and analysing manuscript evidence points out one of the difficulties in accepting Hanning's study as a whole: Hanning's view is overly homogenized, continuous and neat, with insufficient notice of the complicated textual traditions involved. While he clearly could not know in 1966 what Dumville uncovered later, he certainly knew, for example, of the difficulties in writing about Geoffrey's *Historia Regum Britanniae*. In 1951, a variant version was published (the standard version came to be called the 'Vulgate'), showing differences so significant that it was referred to as a separate recension.[29] This complicated manuscript tradition, along with an equally difficult textual tradition for the *Historia Brittonum* (a text Hanning several times cites as influencing Geoffrey in particular),³⁰ demonstrates the caution needed for linking a text like Geoffrey's to Laȝamon's work.

Le Saux is the one scholar who has recently tried to trace influences of Geoffrey on Laȝamon's text; her analysis is closely reasoned, example by example, for sixteen pages.³¹ I will highlight only her main conclusions as a result:

> Geoffrey of Monmouth's *Historia Regum Britanniae* was certainly one of the best-known works in Laȝamon's day; and, being the source of Wace's *Roman de Brut*, it is also ultimately the source of the English *Brut*. For Laȝamon not to have been aware of this would be somewhat astonishing – everything indicates that he was a man of considerable curiosity, even if certain critics have questioned the extent of his learning. One would therefore expect Laȝamon to have been personally familiar with the text of the *Historia*, which was widely read, and tremendously popular.³²

Citing the work of Wülcker (1876), Imelmann (1906) and Visser (1935), she discusses eleven cases of influence. She concludes after careful comparison that 'only six may be considered as potentially significant, and three are dubious . . . All the cases that plead strongly in favour of Laȝamon's indebtednesss to the *Historia* are related in one way or another to Merlin and his prophecies',³³ a conclusion of interest to our discussion here. In fact, she goes on to note that Caldwell's work, 'after a systematic comparison between Wace's text and that of the Variant *Historia*, was able to show that part at least of the *Roman de Brut* agrees consistently with the Variant Version'.³⁴ In further discussion of Wace's *Roman de Brut*, noting that we cannot determine the original version and that, as Tatlock noted, some passages in the *Brut* derive from the *Prophecies of Merlin* (the very section dropped by Wace, as shown earlier), Le Saux notes a possible compromise solution:

> [T]he prophecies were available not only as a separate book of the *Historia*, but were frequently added to Wace-manuscripts, as attested by Ivor Arnold . . . The copy of the *Roman de Brut* kept at Durham Cathedral, C IV 27.1, a thirteenth-century Anglo-Norman manuscript, includes an interpolation of 670 lines containing a French translation of the Prophecies of Merlin; MS Lincoln Cathedral no 104 (Anglo-Norman, C13) also adds some ten folios of prophecies (in French), at the Vortigern passage.³⁵

She ends her analysis by finding nearly insurmountable difficulties in determining specific instances of influence, but some evidence that influence exists:

> It is therefore reasonable to conclude that Laȝamon must have known at least the Vulgate *Historia*. The evidence does not suggest a systematic use of the work, though; there is no indication that Laȝamon bothered to check the *Roman* against the *Historia*. The sum of these different agreements does however indicate that the English poet had read the *Historia* at some time or another, and remembered enough of it to be able to 'complete' Wace in parts, as well as being more or less consciously influenced by it in his own, independent expansions ... It is therefore most probable that, even though Geoffrey of Monmouth is nowhere mentioned by name in the English *Brut*, the *Historia Regum Britanniae*, the 'best-seller' of the Middle Ages, should have been known by Laȝamon. The extreme closeness of Wace to his main source makes it difficult to detect specific areas of indebtedness to the *Historia*; but it may be considered as certain that Laȝamon knew the seventh book of Geoffrey's work, while incidental agreements between the English *Brut* and the rest of the *Historia* strongly suggest that his knowledge was not restricted to the *Prophetiae Merlini*.[36]

Given her finding that some of Laȝamon's material on Merlin came from Geoffrey, the major differences, as noted earlier, emerge. Geoffrey casts Merlin as demonically empowered or, in the *Vita*, saintlike only after the loss of his power. Yet Le Saux does find evidence that Laȝamon knew the *Vita Merlini*, 'and while the poem is clearly not a major source for the *Brut*, it is likely that it contributed to the portrayal of Merlin, and may have provided the starting-point for [some] scenes'.[37] Clearly, Laȝamon's *attitude* towards Merlin did not come from Geoffrey, regardless of incidental, borrowed detail, and this point demonstrates the major problem with identifying Geoffrey's aims in reporting any prophecies with those of Laȝamon in *his* use of prophecy.

It is true that Geoffrey has some concerns in common with Laȝamon. But Blacker-Knight comments that Geoffrey wrote 'with an eye to those in power, [and] operated within the tradition of Latin historiography, under the scrutiny of fellow historians'.[38] Hanning comments that Geoffrey had no moral dimension to his work, exalted the individual to make a clear separation of the individual from national history, and that Merlin, for Geoffrey, exemplifies human greatness creating history and its own destiny. Since, however, he has predicted Arthur's coming in his vatic seizure, he acts here too as an agent of inexorable history, bringing to fruition that which he knows must happen. It might be said that Merlin is Geoffrey's symbol for the artist-historian, whose insight into predetermined history gives him some control over the historical process. But he is also to be equated with the androgynous, passive-active form of history itself, and, as a crucial figure in a specific part of the *Historia*, with the British *regnum*, or with that part of its career which he oversees, viz., its rise to greatest eminence.[39]

Given these contentions, Geoffrey's aims and Laȝamon's are worlds apart. In fact, Laȝamon seems responsible for an innovative compromise: the integration of a Christian, moral perspective on history with a political and secular view parallel to Geoffrey's. The two men's politics, however, differed. Geoffrey (like Laȝamon) had appreciation, even if an overpossessive one, for the Britons, but it seems wrapped in egotism at best. He warns William of Malmesbury and Henry of Huntingdon against writing about British kings, since only he has the 'true' source of information. Blacker-Knight's note states,

> The Bern Manuscript – according to Griscom (33–34), one of the earliest and best of the *Historia* – contains an epilogue . . . 'Reges vero saxonum Willelmo Malmesberiensi et Henrico Huntendonensi quos de regibus Britonum tacere iubeo cum non habeant librum istum Britannici sermonis quem Gualterus Oxenefordensis archidiaconus ex Britannia advexit quem de historia eorum veraciter editum in honore predictorum principum hoc modo in Latinum sermonem transferre curavi' (XII, xx, 535–36). (The kings of the Saxons I leave to William of Malmesbury and Henry of Huntingdon. Concerning the kings of the Britons, I bid them to remain silent since they do not have that book which Walter, archdeacon of Oxford, brought with him from Brittany, the book containing the true story in the honor of the above-named princes, which I have taken care to translate into the Latin tongue.)[40]

(We should be careful in giving too much weight to this phrase attributed to Geoffrey, given earlier comments on Dumville's evaluation of Griscom and his colleagues' work. In particular, Dumville felt that Griscom and Faral generalized too freely from too limited a number of manuscripts.[41]) Blacker-Knight adds:

In essence, Geoffrey's purpose in writing his history of the rise and fall of British dominion in England was twofold: nationalistic and political (pragmatic). He aimed to show that, though the Britons once had legitimate claim to lordship over Britain through their Trojan ancestry, they lost control over the island because they continually fought among themselves . . . [P]resent and future kings were to learn from the example of the beleaguered Britons that the only way to secure and sustain peace was through united rule.[42]

Thus, she argues that Geoffrey is nationalistic, something I do not find in Laȝamon, and that his work presents a political message through analogy, much as Hanning argues and which we have seen is insufficient to encompass what Laȝamon does. The *currency* of Geoffrey's message may well be something Geoffrey had in common with Laȝamon, but his aims differed. For him, the true heirs of British power were those who lived in Brittany; he considered the Welsh too 'effete', in Gransden's term.[43]

Where do Laȝamon's recorded prophecies lead? Arthur is taken to Avalon, and 'Þa wes hit iwurðen⁄ þat Merlin seide whilen. / þat weore uni-mete care⁄ of Arðures forð-fare. / Bruttes ileueð ȝete⁄ þat he bon on liue' (ll. 14288–90) (Then it came to pass *what Merlin said once*, that there would be immeasurable sorrow at Arthur's going forth. Britons yet believe that he is alive). But after comments on how no man born of any woman could know more of the truth to say more of Arthur, Laȝamon adds, 'Bute while wes an witeȝe⁄ Mærlin ihate. / he bodede mid worde⁄ his quiðes weoren soðe. / þat an Arður *sculde ȝete⁄ cum* Anglen to fulste' (ll. 14295–7) (but once there was a prophet called Merlin; he foretold with words, his prophecies were true, that an Arthur *should yet come* to aid those in England/the English). Suddenly the emphasis shifts to the future and even the political; this same phrase which so confused Madden and others opens up the significance of Arthur, but more importantly, it extends the significance of prophecy past the time recorded in this book. It denies any closure to Laȝamon's history, and his acknowledgement of that fact receives support from his further references to Merlin and to the Sibyl. By contrast, Wace's text uses Arthur's departure to close off his story and significance:

> Maistre Wace, ki fist cest livre,
> Ne volt plus dire de sa fin

> Qu'en dist li prophetes Merlin;
> Merlin dist d'Arthur, si ot dreit,
> Que sa mort dutuse serreit.
> Li prophetes dist verité;
> Tut tens en ad l'um puis duté,
> E dutera, ço crei, tut dis,
> Se il est morz u il est vis.
> Porter se fist en Avalun,
> Pur veir, puis l'Incarnatiun
> Cinc cenz e quarante dous anz.
> Damage fud qu'il n'ot enfanz.
> Al fiz Cador, a Costentin,
> De Cornuaille, sun cusin,
> Livra sun regne si li dist
> Qu'il fust reis tant qu'il revenist. (ll. 13282–98)

(Master Wace, who made this book, will say no more of his end than the prophet Merlin did. Merlin said of Arthur, rightly, that his death would be doubtful. The prophet spoke truly: ever since, people have always doubted it and always will, I think, doubt whether he is dead or alive. It is true that he had himself borne away to Avalon, five hundred and forty-two years after the Incarnation. It was a great loss that he had no children. To Cador's son, Constantine of Cornwall, his cousin, he surrendered his kingdom, and told him to be king until he returned.)[44]

Wace's scepticism emerges here: not so much 'rightly', the prophet *may* tell the truth (*si ot dreit*), but much doubt over whether Arthur died or not remains. He cynically comments that it is unfortunate that Arthur had no children, but his kinsman Cador of Cornwall will reign until Arthur returns (*il fust reis tant qu'il revenist*). The entire sense of Arthur's passage and Merlin's role changes. In Laȝamon, Merlin promises a future Arthur to the English; in Wace, Arthur's dubious return makes such a future highly unlikely, and Merlin's prophecy (and prophetic character itself) is barely recorded, with marked doubt. The kingdom is handed over to a cousin, and even that is weakened by the sense that all is temporary, until Arthur returns.

Prophecy, Possibility and Preaching

The full context of Laȝamon's finale now needs examination to demonstrate the possibilities which prophecy and specific prophecies allow. Even several reigns later, when Arthur has been gone over a century, Laʒamon mentions Merlin three times, and the Sibyl once, in his last seventy-five lines. The first mention occurs in a suggestive context. Cadwalader, who will be the last British king, falls asleep on his knees in church, having gone there before attempting to gain back Britain. '[A] wunder ane fair mon' (l. 16007) (a wondrously fair man) appears to him in a vision or dream to inform him that he will never return. (The description, of an angel, reminds us of how Merlin's mother described her lover, ll. 7840–1.) Instead, the angel says he will go to Rome, be shriven of his sins, and die there to join God in heaven. 'Alemainisce men' (German men) will rule Britain, not the British, but then the angel finishes with the crucial addition:

> and næuermære Bruttisce men bruken hit ne moten.
> *ær cume þe time þe iqueðen wes while.*
> *þat Merlin þe witeʒe bodede mid worde.*
> Þenne sculle Bruttes sone buʒen to Rome
> and draʒen ut þine banes alle of þene marme-stane.
> and mid blissen heom uerien uorð mid heom-seoluen.
> in seoluere and in golde in-to Brutlonde.
> Þenne sculle Bruttes ana balde iwurðen.
> al þat heo bi-ginneð to done iwurðeð after heore wille. (ll. 16020–7)

(and nevermore might British men have benefit of it
before the time comes that was prophesied
that Merlin the wise one revealed in words.
Then shall Britons straightaway turn to Rome
and withdraw all your bones from the marble tomb,
and with joy convey them forth in silver and in gold
along with them into Britain.
Then shall Britons become exceedingly bold;
all that they begin to do will happen according to their will.)

Somehow, the coming of 'an Arthur' links with the reclaiming of Cadwalader's bones from Rome and the accomplishment of all the British determine for themselves. The source of this dream vision becomes clear very soon, for the king sends for wise men to interpret the dream and they 'radden him to taken on al swa Godd him hafde itakned to don' (l. 16040) (advised him to take on all that God had given him a sign to do). Merlin's prophecies are confirmed as divinely inspired, the *tacnen* as from God. Thus, when Cadwalader sends

Yuni and Iuor back to his land in Wales to live as brothers, he comments:

> Yuni hit wes itacned me/ alse ʒe scullen nu i-seo.
> for Merlin þe wise/ hit seide mid worde/
> al of mine for[ð]-fare/ ꝉ of mire unimete care.
> and Sibillie þa wise/ a bocken hit isette.
> þat ich scal iuullen/ mines Drihtes wille. (ll. 16063–7)

> (Yuni, it was a sign to me as you shall now see,
> for Merlin the wise said it in words;
> all about my departure and about my inordinate sorrow,
> and the wise Sibyl set it in books,
> that I should fulfil the will of my Lord.)

The curious aspect of this comment and connection to Merlin is that the phrase 'unimete care' (immeasurable sorrow) was used of Arthur's going (see, for example, l. 11503 as quoted), and the previous mention of the Sibyl concerned the three kings who would win Rome, Belin, Constantine and Arthur (ll. 12545–55). Laʒamon then continues with an account of how Cadwalader does indeed join Pope Sergius in Rome and die there, and adds the final reference to Merlin and the prophecy he promised or set fast with words:

> His ban [Cadwalader's] beoð iloken faste/ i guldene cheste.
> and þer heo scullen wunie/ þat þa daʒes beon icume<ne>.
> þa Merlin ine iuurn daʒen/ vastnede mid worden.
> Ga we nu to Yuni a–ʒan/ ꝉ to Iuore his wedde-broðere . . .
> Þæs Bruttes on ælc ende/ foren to Walisce londe. (ll. 16076–9, 16088)

> (His bones are locked fast in a golden chest
> and there they shall stay until that day is come
> that Merlin in ancient times promised with words.
> Turn we now to Yuni again and to Ivor his bound brother . . .
> The Britons from every corner went to the land of Wales.)

The Welsh remain in their land to this day, 'and ʒet wunie[ð] þære/ swa heo doð auere-mære' (l. 16090) (and still dwell there as they will do evermore), and the English rule the country. Laʒamon has linked God's will to Merlin's prophecy, and the future of the English (those who live in England) to some future Briton of Welsh tradition; the vision's statement (see p. 127) that the Britons will 'iwurðeð after heore wille' (l. 16027) links directly to the history's last phrase about God's will. The British lost the land and its rule, 'þat næuere seoððen mære׀ kinges neoren here' (l. 16093) (so that never more since were they kings here), yet the prophecy promises a future tied to the Welsh. Laȝamon adds, '*Þa ȝet ne com þæs ilke dæi׀ beo heonne-uorð alse hit mæi. / i-wurðe þet iwurðe׀ i-wurðe Godes wille. Amen*' (ll. 16093–5) (*Thus far that same day has not come; be it henceforth as it may*, it will happen as it happens: it will happen according to God's will. Amen). The pregnancy of this phrasing only becomes clear when Laȝamon's emphasis of prophecy is fully recognized and his aim clarified.

What does prophecy allow? The existence of a promise as well as faith, an interaction of choice on both sides, divine and human. Why would prophecy be so important to Laȝamon, and to our understanding of his history? In part, because it changes the form of his text to something open-ended and in part because it links up with his location near the March and with contemporary trends in Welsh and English history of the twelfth and thirteenth centuries. God becomes a partner with the British through prophecy linked to Rome and Christian supernatural power (relics). British will is fulfilled because it is identified with God's will in a new covenant that involves the future of the island: prophecy is the direct intervention of the eternal or timeless into time, and Merlin becomes not just a Welsh figure but a prophet as divinely inspired as any in Scripture. Cadwalader's vision links with Merlin's prophecy and Laȝamon's account; 'al þat [Bruttes] bi-ginneð to done׀ iwurðeð after heore wille' (l. 16027) (all that the British begin to do happens according to their will) because 'i-wurðe þet iwurðe׀ i-wurðe Godes wille' (l. 16095) (what happens happens, according to God's will). We can begin to understand why the omission of prophecy and Merlin's role as crucial keys, and their role for the Welsh especially, has caused us to miss the significance of a substantial emphasis Laȝamon intended. He is *not* abrogating power or responsibility and turning it all over to God as a man resigned to bad luck or nostalgic about the past. The intersection of the divine and the mortal occurs in a real world setting. It allows for historical change sanctioned, even promised, by a power outside history but accomplished by men.

Sheila Delany's comments on utopias offer a point for discussion here, though some would see her views on them as idiosyncratic. Typically, scholars have seen the Middle Ages as having no utopian visions, but Delany argues with this point and joins those who have been 'gleaning bits of utopian spirit – what Ernst Bloch calls "the hope principle"'.[45] She defines utopian thought as

> that which offers alternatives to the way we live now, whether these alternatives be collective or individual, mass or elite, political or psychological. Utopia offers other models, and it is infused with the conviction of genuine possibility. The lack of such historical present possibility has been my criterion for excluding from my discussion millennial and apocalyptic literature, fairytale and myth (including paradisal or golden-age myth), and the topos of the *locus amoenus*. These modes usually have other purposes than the utopian: they aim to account for the status quo, to reconcile us to it, to teach us about it or to transcend it: anything but to change it.[46]

She therefore discusses heresy and alchemy, but rejects such concepts as Cokaygne, which she terms a fantasy, and Joachism, since Joachim de Fiore, while foreseeing a historical change, envisions one where people will be resurrected persons with spiritual bodies and so 'will have no remaining human weaknesses, and therefore no need for social coercion. Since this vision is not imagined of real people in real time, it is not pertinent' to Delany's views of utopias.[47] At first glance, the Arthurian world seems a utopia, singularly devoid of betrayal until the very end, but it also seems to fit Delany's excluded topic of a golden-age myth, Bakhtin's valorized past. Prophecy, however, can change that, as Christianity provides continuity. Merlin's prophecies, divinely sanctioned, are real historical possibilities for Christians; as such, the prophecies deal with 'real people in real time', even if the time of fulfilment is unknown. If we object that Arthur and things Arthurian were essentially viewed as myth, we ignore the historical reality of Welsh belief in such a figure and the influence of that belief on Laʒamon. We also ignore the fact that Laʒamon's time *is* the future of the time about which he writes.

Davies, in his history of the Welsh from 1063 to 1415, comments that, given Welsh views of their failure to keep Britain and their resentment of the Saxons (*Saesson* being a specific term in Welsh, usually insulting, perhaps even the reason why Laʒamon can distinguish between heathen Saxons and the Angles), they 'could hardly have borne their sense of loss had it not been relieved by a prospect of deliverance'. The Welsh referred to themselves as Britons well into the twelfth century, and a united Britain was the focus of their hope; 'Thus, according to the native law-texts, the triumphant song which the chief court poet was required to intone as the royal warband returned from a plundering foray was 'The Sovereignty of Britain' (*Unbeniaeth Prydain*).'[48] Crucial to preserving this view were 'luxuriant elaborations of a corpus of prophecy'. Davies's comments are worth quoting in full here to stress their importance for reading Laʒamon:

> Such prophecies were certainly in circulation in Wales well before the advent of the Normans but they were augmented with the passage of each generation. They were associated in particular with the person of Myrddin or Merlin, a poet-prophet whose original connections seem to have been with the sagas of the Old North but whose career and exploits, like those of other North British heroes, were gradually relocated in legend in Wales. Hope was the great theme of the Merlinic prophecies – hope of delivery from, and extermination of, the Saxons and hope of the advent of a messianic deliverer who would once more restore the Britons to their rightful control of the Island of Britain . . . These Merlinic prophecies were the staple political ideology of medieval Welshmen. 'They boast,' commented Gerald of Wales, 'that in a short time their countrymen shall return to the island and, according to the prophecies of Merlin, the nation of foreigners as well as its name shall be exterminated, and the Britons shall exult again in their old name and privilege in the island.'[49]

As political ideology, Merlin's prophecies were utopian by Delany's definition because they were perceived as real and possible and of the immediate future. Laʒamon's text makes it clear that such prophecies are real; his innovation, probably due to his own heritage and to witnessing the cooperation of the March area, was to de-emphasize the extermination of the race of Saxons in favour of exterminating their paganism. He then recreates them in the term Angles, a race entirely Christian but representing those who live in England who will all benefit from an Arthur's coming. By conflating British hope with Christian prophecy, he makes political ideology co-operative and divinely sanctioned, and an Arthurian kingdom, where all (noble) men are brothers seated equally, feasible. We ignore the power of such views at the expense of Laʒamon's accomplishment; Davies comments that the 'importance of such prophecies, as indeed of Welsh historical mythology in general, should not be under-estimated in any analysis of contemporary political attitudes and behaviour'.⁵⁰ It is not irrelevant to understand their importance in an era of new relationships between England and Wales; Gerald of Wales was himself the grandchild of a mixed marriage, and Geoffrey of Monmouth was born in a border area but was frequently at the English court and in Oxford. Davies notes especially Geoffrey's fondness for Caerleon on Usk as 'a tribute to the captivating power of the Welsh frontierlands on the Norman imagination', and the compliment was returned through Welsh translations of his work.

What of the intersection of Laȝamon, poetic form and the prophetic material he uses? Because Wace's text also takes the form of poetry, we could easily dismiss Laȝamon's choice as imitative, but we do have examples of Anglo-Saxon poetry as history, such as the various castings of biblical history (Genesis, Judith, Exodus) and of saints (Elena, Andreas) and even of cult objects (*The Dream of the Rood*), all notably religious/Christian, or the shorter poetic forms or excerpts found in the *Anglo-Saxon Chronicle*. But, curiously, James Kugel asks in his introductory essay to a volume on *Poetry and Prophecy*, 'is there something in the form itself of the prophetic corpus in Hebrew which might encourage the identification of poetry and prophecy?' While admitting that such a question appears simple-minded, he notes that there is no prosodic structure in biblical poetry corresponding to 'those well-known structural elements of our own poetry, meter and rhyme', but that most songs, proverbs and sayings in the Bible are characterized by

> repeated use of a generally binary sentence in which part *A* is separated from part *B* by a slight (and usually syntactic) pause, and part *B* is separated from the next line by a fuller stop (the two pauses thus often corresponding to a comma and period in an English sentence).⁵¹

These alternating pauses and stops appear even in translation and are drawn this way in Kugel:

```
    A                         B
_____ / _____ //
```

The resemblance to the Old English line is clear, but perhaps more striking is its resemblance to Laȝamon's lines. Le Saux quotes Dennis Donahue's thesis (later a book) on *Thematic and Formulaic Composition in Lawman's Brut*:

Because of the structure of Lawman's lines, Lawman's ideas are generally not run on . . . Even when a thought continues for several lines each line is end-stopped. The continuity of thought is picked up and maintained in each succeeding line through the introduction of a new subject and/or verb or repetition of the old.[52]

While clearly we cannot claim that Old English and Laȝamon's verse take their form from biblical prophecy, the coincidence is worth noting in Laȝamon's case, given his emphasis, if only as a curious fact. (It is akin to many critics' comments on how he manages to *sound* like Old English poetry even when he clearly is not writing Old English.) Perhaps it is another indication of his keen ear and talent for innovative imitation.

In addition, the classification of poetry as ethics provides a link between Laȝamon's work and interest in prophecy, and his vocation as priest. The identifying factor for classifying poetry has to do with behaviour, and poetry such as Statius' *Thebaid* is classed as ethics even when we see it as narrative history. Allen comments:

[T]o define ethics in medieval terms is to define poetry, and to define poetry is to define ethics, because medieval ethics was so much under the influence of a literary paideia as to be enacted poetry, and poetry was so practically received as to be quite directly the extended examples for real behaviour.[53]

What has been called Laȝamon's moralizing is therefore entirely in keeping both with his role as commentator and with expectations of what ethics entails.

Le Saux has commented that 'if we had not been told in the Prologue that the poet was a priest, we could not have guessed it',[54] something she attributes to Laȝamon's minimal interest in theology. It is true that exegetes or patristic scholars will find little to entertain them; but she perhaps brings to priesthood a preconceived notion of what a priest would know. Laȝamon is far from the country priest others have made him, as previously noted, but he is clearly not part of the elite theological group developing in Paris's universities or in other areas of the twelfth-century 'renaissance'. His concerns seem especially geared to a non-clerical audience, as she herself notes elsewhere,[55] and such theological elaborations (some of which he drops from Wace's text) would not serve as well as clear indications on ethical behaviour, homilies even. Yet, to us, advocating Merlin's prophecy seems an uneasy, even risky, choice for him to make instead of theological explanations. Again, Minnis's work clarifies why it could have attracted Laȝamon as commentator.

Minnis records an anonymous commentator's view that biblical prophets

> aimed at improving the people through their preaching. In order to make their divine message accessible, they employed a 'mode of preaching' appropriate to the people's capacities. This *modus praedicandi* was 'vulgar' so that everyone could understand it, using only simple words, words which were familiar to ordinary people.[56]

Laȝamon would have been familiar with preaching as a means to communicate morality and ethical behaviour; his use of prophets and prophecy suggests that he may have recognized a common goal between what he did as a preacher and what prophecy involved, though he in no way sees himself as a prophet. The twelfth century saw the first works in the Middle Ages specifically written as manuals for preaching. Guibert de Nogent prefaced his early twelfth-century commentary on Genesis with a book on how to give a sermon, the *Liber quo ordine sermo fieri debeat*. The translator, Joseph M. Miller, comments,

> Admittedly, negative assertions are not easily proved; nevertheless a serious examination of J.-P. Migne's collections of medieval documents indicates that none of the writers from the period between the death of Augustine (430) and the First Crusade (1095) had attempted any organized manual for preachers; rather they had confined themselves to exhortations concerning the need for the preacher to live a virtuous life and to know the Bible.[57]

Several comments from Guibert's work show concerns Laȝamon may well have had. In writing of how the evangelists used Old Testament phrases to make hearers more attentive, Guibert comments that 'we [preachers] learn simple stories to please some, and we *bring into the sermon the histories of old* and we embellish our words like a painter using many different colors on the same canvas' (emphasis added).[58] Elsewhere he warns against using the allegorical method exclusively or to excess:

it seems to do little more than strengthen our faith . . . even if it is proper for us to teach prophecy, therefore, and to repeat it often to our hearers, it is no less fitting – indeed it is more so – for us to say those things which they can apply in their daily lives. We speak more easily and confidently about the nature of virtue than about the mysteries of faith . . . treatment of this type of subject matter will be absolutely clear to everyone, especially since each will retain within himself, as if written in a book, something which he has drawn from the tongue of the preacher to help in temptation.[59]

Without arguing that Laȝamon read Guibert, I would say Guibert's comments (and later, Alain de Lille's *Summa de arte praedicatoria*, though that is more of a text on rhetoric for specific situations) show a context turning to concerns of how to make men see a virtuous way in their own lives. Indeed, if the Prologue records anything of Laȝamon's own thoughts, we should recall the injunction there that we 'leornia þeos runan' (l. 31, Caligula A.ix only), that is, that we study and learn this counsel. Guibert specifically comments on using past history, favours moral tales over complex allegory and uses the striking idea that a good sermon (an oral text) will write itself on a listener – the listener will become a book – to drive home the lasting value of relevant and accessible sermons, raising again the fluidity of oral and written contexts. His comment on prophecy may seem to work against Laȝamon's emphasis and my own argument for it; but he is speaking of prophecy as too difficult and distant, and more specifically of *fulfilled* prophecy (Old Testament prophecies fulfilled by the New Testament – he says we now have the sacraments). To write of already fulfilled prophecy, and risk confusing an audience, is discouraged. Laȝamon, of course, writes of a *popular* (current) prophecy, one related to real-life expectations, and therefore not what Guibert discusses as something to avoid.

To return to roles, the prophet, such as Merlin, 'does not assert the revelation he has received as his own property but claims God as its *auctor* . . . the prophet fulfilled the roles of *scriptor* and *compilator* in relation to the *auctor* God.'[60] Laȝamon simply becomes the commentator on Merlin's divine message, writing a Welsh prophetic figure as an embellished Christian prophet. Perhaps this perception of roles, as commentator on a *compilator*, influenced how Laȝamon alters and presents Merlin in context. Robert of Basevorn, though writing after Laȝamon in his 1322 *Forma praedicandi*, comments that a preacher should not dwell too long on the same point nor should he repeat more often than is right. He should hastily progress from one thing to another as the matter allows. An exception may be made when – without deviating too far from the matter – he finds along the way a source of edification into which, as I might say, he turns his stream of language as into a neighbouring valley. When he has sufficiently filled the place of added instruction he turns back into the channel of the intended sermon.[61]

Arthur and Merlin provide just such an occasion of edification without deviating too far in the *Brut*, and they allow a useful emphasis of Laʒamon's concerns. Once again the oral and literary intersect. A closer pair of forms hardly exists than preaching and prophecy, which depend on exactly the balance of oral and written that Laʒamon acknowledges and incorporates into his history.

Returning to the figure of Merlin, and to the political ramifications of Welsh belief in a saviour ruler promised by Merlin, helps in considering why Laʒamon's *Brut* had less of an impact than we expect, given my argument. The political aspect may explain this apparent rejection in Laʒamon's time. The promise of a Welsh ruler who would expel the English king in favour of one of Wales's own clearly has political threat to it. For the Welsh, this was not a myth, but a practical belief, something that was to be fulfilled in history. Laʒamon identifies this potential with the figure of Merlin. Laʒamon too seems to accept that Merlin and God have produced prophecies to foretell a real future; though he creates a future where all who live on the island are 'English' and so the rightful subjects of 'an Arthur', his modifications are an aberration of what the Welsh themselves passionately believed and hoped for. Their extension of the March boundaries more than a century after the accord with Henry shows how practical their desire to regain Britain could be. Their necessary coexistence demonstrates how Laʒamon could envision a future that contained both, but the survival of the March was short-lived and his Christian optimism concerning integration misplaced:

> By the thirteenth century the distinctiveness of the March within the dominions of the king of England was becoming ever more apparent. It was of Wales and yet it was not part of native Wales (*pura Wallia*); its lords were subjects of the king of England and held their lordships of him (albeit by the loosest and most nominal of feudal ties), yet it was no part of the institutional and legal structure of the kingdom of England. It was a

land which lay between Wales and England, attached to each of them but separate from both. One of the badges of identity and individuality was its law, the law of the March (L. *lex Marchie*). The separate status of that law was announced for the first time in no less august a document than Magna Carta (1215).[62]

As previously noted, this same King John of Magna Carta fame was buried in this very area, at Worcester, close to the time in which the *Brut* was written.

Unhappily, difficulties between the Welsh and the English increased in the thirteenth century, and, within a century of the accord, the English had claimed large sections of the March as well as of Gwynedd. What had been extensive gains for the Welsh in property and power were now eroding, and the Welsh themselves were seen increasingly as a threat to be managed and quelled. Their dangerous belief in Merlin's prophecies became a real political threat of anarchy and rebellion in both the secular and the religious realms, for, if God sanctioned Welsh prophets and superiority, both Church and state would lose in England. Perhaps that fear explains both the potency of the belief and an order from Canterbury in the 1280s. Davies notes:

[t]he Welsh were sustained by it [their belief] in the last dark days of native independence, and one of the first acts of the archbishop of Canterbury after the conquest of 1282–3 was to order that the Welsh be weaned from their ancient prophecies.[63]

He adds that it probably did not work, given the force of the prophecies, but it may indeed have inhibited the copying of texts about Merlin especially, and about the fulfilment of his British prophecies in England in particular. While I would not argue that Laȝamon's text is censored or neglected entirely because of his love of Merlin, the order may explain in part why no widespread influence seems to survive. Laȝamon was not ambivalent: he was instead an innovative compromiser who saw real prophecy, the true hand of God, in Merlin and in British tradition, especially in its laudable and ancient Christianity. He comments on that prophecy in a way that creates a better political reality for all. Unfortunately, his close identification with Welsh heroes and subjects may have cost him his reputation as a historian, as not everyone could transcend the threat of his vision to see its accomplishment. It would take the total subjugation of Wales, notably accomplished by the suppression of the Welsh language, in the time of Henry VIII to make the prophecies both popular and acceptable as a political tool, this time in the hands of the English royalty.[64]

And yet perhaps we can hear an echo of what Laȝamon envisioned both in the *Alliterative Morte Arthur*'s allusion to a *Brut* ('as the Bruytte tellys', l. 4346) and even more, in the masterpiece of the Midlands, *Sir Gawain and the Green Knight*. Gawain too values his troth as his life; he epitomizes the perfect blend of secular and sacred knighthood as well as the ridiculousness of excess and the fallibility of men. Arthur and Merlin may here have been degraded past serious attention, but Gawain stands forth to disown even the smallest falsehood. When Bercilak confronts him, the language will sound familiar to Laȝamon's readers. Bercilak says:

> For þe forwarde þat we fest in þe fyrst nyȝt,
> And þou trystyly þe trawþe and trwly me haldez,
> Al þe gayne þow me gef, as god mon schulde.
> þat oþer munt for þe morne, mon, I þe profered,
> þou kyssedes my clere wyf – þe cossez me raȝtez.
> For boþe two here I þe bede bot two bare myntes
>   boute scaþe.
>   Trwe mon trwe restore,
>   Þenne þar mon dred no waþe.
>   At þe þrid þou fayled þere,
>   And þerfor þat tappe ta þe. (ll. 2348–57)

> (And fully and faithfully you followed accord:
> Gave over all your gains as a good man should.
> A second feint, sir, I assigned for the morning
> You kissed my comely wife – each kiss you restored.
> For both of these there behooved but two feigned blows
>   by right.
>   True men pay what they owe;
>   No danger then in sight.
>   You failed at the third throw,
>   So take my tap, sir knight.)[65]

Trawþe (trustworthiness) continues to matter, and *trwe* must return *trwe*. Gawain, overcome by his lack of faith, exclaims:

> Lo! þer þe falssyng, foule mot hit falle!
> For care of þy knokke cowardyse me taȝt

> To acorde me with couetyse, my kynde to forsake,
> þat is larges and lewté þat longez to kny3tez.
> Now am I fawty and falce, and ferde haf ben euer
> Of trecherye and vntrawþe: boþe bityde sor3e
>   and care. (ll. 2378–84)

(Behold there my falsehood, ill hap betide it!
Your cut taught me cowardice, care for my life,
And coveting came after, contrary both
To largesse and loyalty belonging to knights.
Now am I faulty and false, that fearful was ever
Of disloyalty and lies, bad luck to them both!
               and greed.)

Bercilak laughingly tells him he was overcome by the goddess Morgan, mistress of Merlin, and that no one can prevail against her. But the source of Gawain's aspirations emerges most clearly in the last lines:

> Þus in Arthurus day þis aunter bitidde,
> þe Brutus bokez þerof beres wyttenesse;
> Syþen Brutus, þe bolde burne, bo3ed hider fyrst,
> After þe segge and þe asaute watz sesed at Troye,
>   iwysse,
> Mony aunterez here-forne
> Haf fallen suche er þis.
> Now þat bere þe croun of þorne,
> He bryng vus to his blysse! AMEN. (ll. 2522–30)

(In the old days of Arthur this happening befell;
The books of Brutus' deeds bear witness thereto
Since Brutus, the bold knight, embarked for this land
After the siege ceased at Troy and the city fared
          amiss.
Many such, ere we were born,
Have befallen here, ere this.
May He that was crowned with thorn
Bring all men to His bliss! Amen.)[66]

Here Britain's heritage unites with Christianity in an echo of La3amon's vision of the future: suffering and betrayal will be vindicated, if 'þou trystely þe trawþe', or, as La3amon put it, 'for a is on treowe monnen׃ treouðe ihalden' (l. 15496).

Laȝamon and Bakhtin: Textual and Narrative Potential

We need finally to return to Bakhtin to give a sense of why Laȝamon's accomplishments have not been recognized, and to demonstrate what his narrative attempts. In a late essay called 'The problem of speech genres', Bakhtin comments that speech genres are 'the drive belts from the history of society to the history of language', because historical changes in language styles are linked to changes in speech genres.[67] A speech genre is a sphere in which the language used develops its own 'relatively stable types' of utterances, where utterances include both oral and written language. The choice of a particular speech genre is determined by the nature of the given sphere of communication, semantic/thematic considerations, the concrete situation of the communication, the personal composition of its participants and so on.[68]

He then goes on to identify something he considers a major flaw in linguistic study, the 'fictions' of listener and understander as passive partners of the speaker. For Bakhtin, this fiction stems from a basic misunderstanding of utterances themselves and the functions of language:

> it is still typical to underestimate, if not altogether ignore, the communicative function of language. Language is regarded from the speaker's standpoint as if there were only *one* speaker who does not have any *necessary* relation to *other* participants in speech communication. If the role of the other is taken into account at all, it is the role of a listener, who understands the speaker only passively.[69]

But, as Bakhtin notes, speakers generally do *not* expect passive understanding that merely duplicates the speaker's/writer's ideas. Even as the listener listens, that listener takes an active, responsive attitude towards what is communicated, whether acting upon the utterance (as in following a command), responding aloud or delaying reaction with silent reception or understanding. The last is probably most applicable to reader reception.

Because *our* reception of Laȝamon has been passive, in that we no longer believe in the same Christian view of salvation history or in the particular prophecy he emphasizes (that is, communication fails due to historical, social changes), we have undervalued or devalued Laȝamon's accomplishment. As Bakhtin puts it:

Any utterance . . . has, so to speak, an absolute beginning and an absolute end: its beginning is preceded by the utterances of others, and its end is followed by the responsive utterance of others (or, although it may be silent, others' active responsive understanding, or, finally, a responsive action based on this understanding). The speaker ends his utterance in order to relinquish the floor to the other or to make room for the other's active responsive understanding. The utterance is not a conventional unit, but a real unit, clearly delimited by the change of speaking subjects.[70]

We, perhaps unlike Laȝamon's medieval readers, have not 'taken the floor', nor did we know what to say. Bakhtin writes that the reader or listener uses utterances to sense what he calls the speaker's 'speech plan' or 'speech will' which determines the entire utterance, its length and boundaries:

> We imagine to ourselves what the speaker *wishes* to say. And we also use this speech plan, the speech will (as we understand it), to measure the finalization of the utterance. This plan determines both the choice of the subject itself . . . as well as its boundaries and its semantic exhaustiveness.[71]

By imposing our own perceptions, from a different historical and social perspective, we have missed the potential of Laȝamon's narrative.

Earlier on, Laȝamon's work was described as akin to a historical novel. This phrase is not meant as a facile or simplistic identification. The interaction of author, characters and reader discussed above characterizes the complex genre of the modern novel, a complexity reserved for the modern period in general and not granted to what we see as pseudo-history in the twelfth century. Yet that interaction, the communication which Bakhtin emphasizes as a primary function of language, opens the boundaries of a text like the *Brut* in the hands of a preacher. Instead of a slavish imitation or dead-end epic, the *Brut* emphasizes the individual and the active repercussions of personal honour and choice. Choice relates to an overarching historical or political continuum, but the end of the text remains essentially unfinished. As I have argued, Laȝamon's desired response, from a responding and understanding reader who perceived his moral direction, would be to look for the prophecy's completion as part of the text's boundaries and 'semantic exhaustiveness'. Such a completion is most certainly beyond the boundaries of the text, but accords with the intent of a sermon or homily; it intersects with historical and social reality and even demands ethical participation in that reality to bring about completion. The openness or incompleteness of the text cannot be finalized until the prophecy is fulfilled. This combination of narrative potential and moral, individual potential through prophecy and preaching seems to me to be Laȝamon's true accomplishment and vision as a writer. He goes beyond romances and saints' lives, which, while emphasizing a hero's life and perhaps indicating a moral direction, can at best only offer a model for imitation. Such imitation would also be finite, limited to the lifetime of the respondent as surely as the text is to the lifetime of the hero. The valorized past cannot transcend time in the way that a narrative concerned with unfulfilled prophecy and the response of the reader can. By ending so far in the past, Laȝamon emphasizes that we readers *are* the future of his history and his past, a view often cited as common among twelfth-century readers of Arthurian material especially. Our lives and choices link directly to the end of his work, revolutionizing the boundaries and breaking the limits of the historical text. We can write not only his past, but our future, returning to the Eden of which Stock wrote, where communication, Bakhtin's basic function of language, is perfected.[72] No one would claim Laȝamon's communication is perfect. However, his insights on narrative strategies to suggest such fulfilment, and the techniques he used to experiment with form, do qualify him as something of a prophet for future literary endeavour.

Epilogue

So . . . I speak to you as I might speak to all those who most possess my thoughts – to Shakespeare, to Thomas Browne, to John Donne, to John Keats – and find myself unpardonably lending you, *who are alive, my voice, as I habitually lend it to those dead men – Which is as much to say – here is an author of Monologues – trying clumsily to construct a Dialogue – and encroaching on both halves of it. Forgive me.*

Now if this were a true dialogue – but that *is entirely as you may wish it to be.*

A letter of Randolph Henry Ash, character and poet in the novel *Possession: A Romance*, by A. S. Byatt.[73]

Appendix:
Overview of Laȝamon's *Brut*

Because of the length of the text and the unfamiliarity of many of its sections, I borrow Bzdyl's eight section headings in his translation to provide a brief summary of Laȝamon's history of Britain from its settlement to the death of the last British/Celtic king, Cadwalader. Of necessity, not all characters or incidents appear here.

I. *The Founding and Growth of Britain* (ll. 36–2139). Beginning with the destruction of Troy, Laȝamon mentions Aeneas, Ascanius and Silvius, but focuses on Silvius' illegitimate son Brutus and the prophecy that makes him great and brings him to Britain. After various battles in Greece and the winning of his queen Ignoge, Brutus settles and is succeeded by his three sons. The section continues with many legendary figures and tales, such as Humber of the Huns, Locrin who betrays his wife with his lover Astrild who lives secretly in an earth house, Ebrauc (from whom York took its name), Bladud and his wings, and Leir (in this version, Cordoille lives to rule but after being captured by her nephews, commits suicide). We also see the fraternal rivalry of the brothers Fereus and Poreus, in which Fereus dies in battle and their mother Iudon murders and dismembers Poreus in revenge, and the reign of Donwal, who as high king unites the Britons after gathering an army unlike any seen since Brutus' days. When he dies after a forty-year reign, his sons Belin and Brennes succeed.

II. *The Power of Britain* (ll. 2140–3586). The brothers Belin and Brennes dominate this section as the finest warriors, rulers and conquerors of Rome before Arthur. Though initially the two compete for kingship, through their mother Tonwenn's memorable intercessions on the battlefield, the brothers reconcile and create a kingdom of Britain and the Continent. Their successors lose some of their gains, but include notable figures such as Guencelin and his queen Marcie (of Marcian/Mercian law), the attacks of the Duke of Moray, the separation and reconciliation of the brothers Argal and Elidur (a parallel to Belin and Brennes themselves), Lud and the naming of his city for him (Kaer Lud, London), and Cassibellaunus, brother to Lud, who gave over the kingdom to his nephews Androgeus and Tennancius when they came of age. Their enmity allowed the Roman invasion that forced Britain to pay tribute.

III. *The Romans in Britain* (ll. 3587–6304). The focus here is on Julius Caesar and how Britain lost its dominance through treachery and enmity. Cassibellaunus, Androgeus and Tennancius each reign and then lose, but after them, Kinbelin reigns, and Christ is born at this time. Kinbelin receives this news from the prophet Teilesin, and thus a link of Christianity and prophecy (not to mention Wales) is established. After Kinbelin, Wither reigns, and has many battles with Claudius' troops, until by treachery the Roman Hamun kills him. Arviragus succeeds and marries Claudius' daughter Genuis, and several relatively uneventful reigns ensue. Luces, however, becomes the first Christian king, and churches and bishops appear. Other notables in this section include Coel, his daughter Helena who would find the True Cross, Maximian (Diocletian's man responsible for martyring Alban, Julian and Aaron), and Conan, who wishes to marry Ursula and so is the reason she and her virgins suffer. (In this version, Ursula is raped by the leader Melga and then turned over to his men as a whore.) Melga and Wanis, both pagans, lay waste the country. Finally, after many civil wars and repeated petitions to the Romans to get them out of trouble with their own rulers, the Britons are told that Rome has abandoned its interests in the island: they must solve their own problems.

IV. *Vortiger and the Coming of the Saxons* (ll. 6305–8100). Archbishop Guencelin warns the people of the pagan threat, sails to Brittany for help, and returns with Constantine, Conan's son; his success as a king is undermined later by repeated treacheries aimed at his sons Constance, Aurelius Ambrosius and Uther once they succeed him. This section contains the examples of Hengest and Vortiger as traitors, the fateful marriage of pagan Rouwenne to Christian Vortiger, and the ensuing betrayals and destruction. Merlin also appears here, a truthsayer and prophet who unwillingly attends the court and has Christian aspects despite his link to magic. Bzdyl ends the section at Vortiger's death, burnt in his castle by Aurelius and Uther.

V. *British Triumphs* (ll. 8101–9891). Aurelius captures Hengest, and Octa and Ebissa falsely accept baptism in a treacherous plan that frees Hengest, though he is later executed. Merlin reappears to move Stonehenge from Ireland, Appas poisons Aurelius, and Uther succeeds as king after benefiting from Merlin's visions. Merlin leaves, and Octa and Ebissa renounce Christianity to take advantage of Aurelius' death, but Uther, with Gorlois's help, captures them. Meanwhile, Uther lusts for and gains Ygerne, Gorlois's wife, engendering Arthur; Octa and Ebissa escape but are finally killed, and their Saxon successor is Colgrim. Colgrim's spies manage to poison Uther.

VI. *Arthur: Building an Empire* (ll. 9892–12341). Clergy fetch Arthur from Brittany (he is fifteen); he returns and engages Colgrim's men. But Childric the Roman also invades Britain against Arthur, and Arthur must forge alliances and win battles in Britain, following Colgrim over the Avon to kill him and his brother Baldolf and then chasing Childric until his knight Cador kills the emperor. The section also includes an excursion to Scotland, where women and clergy beseech Arthur's mercy, and Arthur and his men encounter a magical lake. Having established order in the island, Arthur takes Wenhaver as his wife, and obliges the kings of Ireland, Scotland, Iceland, Orkney, Gotland and Winetland to accept him as their lord. His court is enriched by many cultures, but after a riot incited by envy, Arthur creates the Round Table to quell resentment. Laȝamon comments on the fame of Arthur with Britons, and then begins Arthur's conquests of France/Gaul, conquering Flanders and Boulogne first before his confrontation alone on an island with the king of Paris, Frolle. Arthur returns to Britain; a brief description of the greatness of Caerleon follows, and his coronation and the attendance of many peoples is described at length.

VII. *Arthur: Rome and Modred* (ll. 12342–14296). Emperor Luces demands that Arthur become his man and make amends for killing Frolle. (This scene becomes the opening of the later *Alliterative Morte Arthur*.) Invoking the heritage of Belin and Brennes, Arthur refuses, and this section is primarily concerned with Luces's invasion, Arthur's defence, Gawain's status as Arthur's right-hand man and the subsequent conquest by Arthur of the continent and Rome in accordance with Merlin's prophecies. The encounter with the St Michael's Mount giant occurs here too, but, more importantly, Arthur has prophetic dreams and discovers the treachery of his wife and his nephew Modred. Modred dies at Camelford on the River Tamar, and Arthur is taken away by the elf queen Argante after he confers the kingdom on Cador's son Constantine.

VIII. *The Saxon Conquest of Britain* (ll. 14297–16096). Constantine succeeds, but little is said of him or of his successors. More important is the pagan threat of Gurmond, a warrior who swears he will rule only countries he has conquered for himself. He gathers many pagan allies, including Isembred of France who renounces his Christianity, and he besieges the British Carric at Cirencester, overcoming him by lighting tinder-packed shells tied to sparrows which then return to nest in the city and cause it to burn. Carric escapes but never returns. Laȝamon tells how for 105 years no Christianity is known in Britain, and then proceeds to tell of Gregory's mission led by Augustine. Rivalries continue, however, between Britons and Saxons, and especially between Edwin and Cadwalan for the kingship. Edwin is helped by an evil sorcerer from Spain, Pelluz, but Pelluz eventually is killed by Brian, Cadwalan's man, and Cadwalan later kills Edwin. He allies with Penda against Oswald, and Penda kills Oswald (the saint) through treachery, later killing Oswy, Oswald's brother, too. Many of Cadwalan's men see Penda, despite the alliance, as an enemy, but when Cadwalan dies, they accept Cadwalader, his son and Penda's nephew, as king. Because of famine and depopulation, Cadwalader abandons his country, goes to Brittany and remains there for eleven years. When things in Britain improve, fifty thousand Saxons land and settle, choosing Athelstan as king of all England. Though Cadwalader plans to reclaim his throne, a vision warns him that Britons will not rule until the time Merlin had foretold comes, when they reclaim Cadwalader's bones from Rome. He divides Wales between his heirs; then he and his wife do penance in Rome and die there. The Britons embrace Welsh culture and wait: 'God's will be done.'

Notes

Introduction: Critical Views

1. C. S. Lewis, 'The genesis of a medieval book', in *Studies in Medieval and Renaissance Literature*, collected by Walter Hooper (Cambridge: Cambridge University Press, 1966), 18.
2. Gretchen Ackerman, 'Sir Frederic Madden and Arthurian scholarship', in *King Arthur through the Ages*, vol. 2, ed. Valerie M. Lagorio and Mildred Leake Day (New York: Garland Publishing, Inc., 1990), 33.
3. E. G. Stanley, 'The date of Laȝamon's "Brut"', *Notes and Queries* n.s. 15 (1968), 85–8.
4. Elizabeth J. Bryan, *Collaborative Meaning in Medieval Scribal Culture*, Editorial Theory and Literary Criticism (Ann Arbor: The University of Michigan Press, 1999), 183, 187.
5. Bryan, *Collaborative Meaning*, 48.
6. Laȝamon, *Laȝamon: Brut*, 2 vols., ed. G. L. Brook and R. F. Leslie, Early English Text Society, vols. 250 and 277 (Oxford: Oxford University Press, 1963 and 1978).
7. Laȝamon, *Laȝamon's Brut, or Chronicle of Britain: A Poetical Semi-Saxon Paraphrase of the Brut of Wace*, 3 vols., ed. and trans. Sir Frederic Madden (London: Society of Antiquaries, 1847).
8. Laȝamon, *Laȝamon's 'Brut': Selections*, ed. J. N. Hall (Oxford: Oxford University Press, 1924). Laȝamon, *Selections from Laȝamon's 'Brut'*, ed. G. L. Brook (Oxford: Oxford University Press, 1963; reprinted 1983, 2nd edition revised by J. Levitt).
9. Laȝamon, *Layamon's Brut: A History of the Britons*, trans. Donald G. Bzdyl, Medieval and Renaissance Texts and Studies 65 (Binghamton: Medieval and Renaissance Texts and Studies, 1989). This translation abbreviates some scenes and should not be considered a fully accurate version.
10. Laȝamon, *Laȝamon's Arthur: The Arthurian Section of Laȝamon's Brut (Lines 9229–14297)*, edition and translation with introduction, textual

notes and commentary by W. R. J. Barron and S. C. Weinberg (Harlow: Longman Group UK Ltd, 1989).
11   Laȝamon, *Laȝamon's Brut or Hystoria Brutonum*, ed. and trans. W. R. J. Barron and S. C. Weinberg (Harlow: Longman Group Ltd, 1995).
12   Lawman, *Brut*, trans. Rosamund Allen (London: J. M. Dent & Sons Ltd., 1992).
13   . Carolynn VanDyke Friedlander, 'The first English story of King Lear: Layamon's *Brut*, lines 1448–1887', *Allegorica* 3 (1978), 42.
14   Marie-Françoise Alamichel, 'Lawamon et Shakespeare: de Leir à Lear', *Études anglaises Grand-Bretagne – États-Unis* 45.2 (April–June 1992), 162–76.
15   As noted by his private secretary and later editor of unpublished pieces, Walter Hooper, in the introduction to *Studies in Medieval and Renaissance Literature* (see note 1), viii.
16   Françoise Le Saux, *Laȝamon's Brut: The Poem and its Sources*, Arthurian Studies 19 (Cambridge: D. S. Brewer, 1989).
17   Richard Wülcker, 'Über die Quellen Layamons', *Beiträge zur Geschichte des deutschen Sprache und Literatur* 3 (1876), 524–55.
18   Le Saux, *Laȝamon's Brut*, 185.
19   Mark Girouard, *The Return to Camelot: Chivalry and the English Gentleman* (New Haven: Yale University Press, 1981).
20   Henry Cecil Wyld, 'Laȝamon as an English poet', *Review of English Studies* 6 (1930), 2.
21   Daniel Donoghue, 'Laȝamon's ambivalence', *Speculum* 65 (1990), 537.
22   James Noble, 'Laȝamon's "ambivalence" reconsidered', in Françoise Le Saux (ed.), *The Text and Tradition of Layamon's Brut*, Arthurian Studies 33 (Cambridge: D. S. Brewer, 1994), 170–82.
23   Jorge Luis Borges, 'The innocence of Layamon', in *Other Inquisitions 1937–1952*, trans. Ruth L. C. Simms, Texas Pan-American Series (Austin: University of Texas Press, 1964), 161.
24   Kelley M. Wickham-Crowley, '"Going Native": anthropological Lawman', special issue: *Theoretical Approaches to Lawman's Brut*, *Arthuriana* 10.2 (Summer 2000), 5–26.
25   Borges, 'The innocence of Layamon', 162.
26   Daniel Donoghue, 'Laȝamon's ambivalence', 537 and 563.
27   Ibid., 543.
28   Ibid., 558.
29   Ibid., 562.
30   R. R. Davies comments that, despite the plurality of Wales and its internal strife, 'those who did not speak Welsh (W. *anghyfiaith*) were immediately designated as aliens (W. *estron*); so it was that the English came to be branded as a 'foreign alien-tongued people' (*estron genedl anghyfiaith*). Language was becoming one of the badges of national

identity.' R. R. Davies, *Conquest, Coexistence, and Change: Wales 1063–1415* (Cardiff/Oxford: University of Wales Press/Oxford University Press, 1987), 17. Perhaps better known than the Welsh terms, Old English *wealas*, for foreigners/alien-speakers (particularly British- or Celtic-speakers), is the source of the term Welsh; thus, language as a sign of difference and identity was certainly recognized by both peoples.

31 Daniel Donoghue, 'Laȝamon's ambivalence', 560.
32 Ibid., 557, n. 81.
33 Ibid., 558.
34 Ibid., 563.
35 If Donoghue had drawn on Wulfstan's *Sermo Lupi ad Anglos* more fully, he might have found a view similar to Laȝamon's fifty years before the Normans came. After mentioning Gildas and his rebuke of the sins of the British, Wulfstan says, 'And it is true what I say; we know of worse deeds among the English than we have anywhere heard of among the Britons' ('⁊ soþ is þæt ic secge, wyrsan dæda we witan mid Englum þonne we mid Bryttan ahwar gehyrdan'). While both groups practise evil, the British are better. From Wulfstan's sermon in *Anglo-Saxon Prose*, trans. Michael Swanton, Everyman series (Rutland, Vt.: Charles E. Tuttle, 1993; reprint, 1996), 184. Old English version: *The Homilies of Wulfstan*, ed. Dorothy Bethurum (Oxford: Clarendon Press, 1957), ll. 187–9, 274–5. It can also be found in Dorothy Whitelock's *Sermo Lupi ad Anglos*, 3rd edn rev. (London: Methuen & Co. Ltd, 1963), ll. 195–7, 66.
36 For those wishing a brief review of the material covered in the *Brut*, the appendix at the back of this book contains a short summary.

1 Language as Personal History

1 Bzdyl, *Layamon's Brut*, 29, n. 19.
2 Laȝamon, *Brut*, vol. I, ed. G. L. Brook and R. F. Leslie, Early English Text Society, vol. 250 (London: Oxford University Press for The Early English Text Society, 1963), 5.
3 In G. Hickes, *Antiquae Literaturae Septentrionalis Liber Alter* (Oxford, 1705).
4 The form is ambiguous in number in the two manuscripts, and several scholars have read the reference to 'a book' read by a priest as a reference to his Missal or even to the Bible. Rosamund Allen's note for this line covers the variety of interpretations. Because it is possible that the reference is not to a personal library, but to books borrowed from others at Redstone, Worcester or even the manor at Areley Kings, it need not relate to how many books the author owned.
5 John Morris (ed.), *Domesday Book* (Chichester: Phillimore, 1982), vol.

16: *Worcestershire*, ed. Frank and Caroline Thorn, 174d, 176b, 177b, entries 8, 13; 15, 7; 23, 8.

6   A. J. Minnis, *Medieval Theory of Authorship: Scholastic Literary Attitudes in the Later Middle Ages*, 2nd edn (Philadelphia: University of Pennsylvania Press, 1988), 4–6, 11.

7   Daniel Donoghue, 'Laȝamon's ambivalence', 562: 'Their hesitation in choosing sides is part of the ambivalence of being torn between changing political structures.' We should also note here, though, that Donoghue may originally have developed his idea from Hanning, who wrote in his *Vision of History in Early Britain*, 'The political world of the Anglo-Norman historians was therefore one of greater complexity than they could compress into one consistent historiographical vision or system. Although any age presents enormous complexities to its chroniclers, in this case the genuine uniqueness of the Norman experience and the divided interests of the Christian but antiquity-loving historians combined to render impossible a unified approach to the past. Nor was this ambivalence the result of conscious choice.' See Hanning, 129.

8   Maureen Quilligan, *The Language of Allegory: Defining the Genre* (Ithaca: Cornell University Press, 1979), 286–7. She is quoting from Hardison's *Christian Rite and Christian Drama in the Middle Ages: Essays in the Origin and Early History of Modern Drama* (Baltimore: Johns Hopkins University Press, 1965) 12, 46–7.

9   Minnis, *Medieval Theory*, 10.

10 Roland Blenner-Hassett, *A Study of the Place-Names in Lawman's Brut*, Stanford University Publications, University Series, Language and Literature, IX, no. 1 (Stanford: Stanford University Press, 1950).

11 See, for example, Laȝamon, *Laȝamon's Arthur*, ed. and trans. Barron and Weinberg, xii

> Whether the *Brut* was written ten years before the turn of the century or twenty years after will have made little difference to the cultural context at the level of English life familiar to a country priest. In his western backwater social circumstances changed slowly.

Note also that while we may now see his location as peripheral, in Laȝamon's time his area was a hotbed of political, religious and military activity. Indeed, King John, who had trouble with his nobles, signed Magna Carta and ruled 1199–1216, was buried in Worcester Cathedral – the same cathedral cited as a possible location for the library with some of Laȝamon's written sources. Rosamund Allen has in fact argued for 1216 as the date of Laȝamon's composition, in '*Eorles* and *beornes*: contextualizing Lawman's *Brut*', and connects Laȝamon closely with John's reign. See *Arthuriana* 8.3 (Fall 1998), 4–22, a special issue on Laȝamon edited by James Noble.

12 Elizabeth Salter, 'Culture and literature in earlier thirteenth-century English: national and international', in Derek Pearsall and Nicolette Zeeman (eds), *English and International: Studies in the Literature, Art and Patronage of Medieval England* (Cambridge: Cambridge University Press, 1988), 34–5.
13 Bzdyl notes this possibility, *Layamon's Brut*, 282, n. 18.
14 Brian Stock, *The Implications of Literacy: Written Language and Models of Interpretation in the Eleventh and Twelfth Centuries* (Princeton: Princeton University Press, 1983), 60.
15 Incidental occurrences of *swike* forms are too numerous to discuss individually. They will therefore be cited briefly as endnotes during the discussion of major concentrations of related terms. Here I will note that Humber of the Huns, who killed the good Albanac son of Brutus, laid the land waste and 'leodene *bi-swikene*' (l. 1075) (betrayed the people); Locrin, made to take back his wife and abandon his lover Æstrilde, decides to hide his mistress in an earth house, 'for *swiken* he þohte' (l. 1175) (for he thought to deceive).
16 In between this episode and the next, Stater and Rudauc with his slaughtering Welshmen invade Donwal's territory after they have sworn oaths '*swiken* þat heo nolden' (l. 2046) (that they would not betray). Hearing the news, Donwal says, 'Nu heo beð *for-sworne⁄* mid heore *swike-dome*. / Bi Appollines ære⁄ ne ileue ich hem neuere-mare' (ll. 2058–9) (Now they are forsworn with their treachery. By Apollo's mercy I will not believe them ever again). Their death is a direct result of their lies, and justification enough: 'to-ȝene þene swerd broþeren⁄ þe beiene beoh *for-sworene*' (l. 2068) (against these sworn brothers who both are forsworn).
17 Occurrences of *swike*. Cassibellaunus believes that Caesar will not leave, and so waits until morning to attack. When he finds him gone, along with his opportunity to destroy Rome's claim on Britain, he says of the opinions and rumour given him, 'Nu wes þis ilke iseid⁄ me to *bi-swiken*' (l. 4004). Androgeus writes to Caesar for help against Cassibellaunus and claims it by stressing Cassibellaunus' betrayal of his word and his own trustworthiness, guaranteed by his life:

to þe ich mæne mi sær⁄
Androgeus þin aȝene mon þis nis nan *swike-dom⁄*
for þat weord þat ich þe sende. bi mine liue ich hit halde⁄
⁊ þu hit nult ileuen⁄ beoten hit læssinge beo.
ich hit wulle trousien⁄ þurh minne tir-fulne godd.
þurh mine lauerd Appollin⁄ þe leof me is on heorte. (ll. 4143b–8)

> (To you I mean to speak of my wronging,
> Androgeus, your own man. This is not any betrayal,
> for that word that I send you I hold as my life,
> and should you not believe it except as a lie,
> I will guarantee the truth of it through my glorious god,
> through my lord Apollin who is dear to my heart.)

He reiterates it upon their meeting, that everything written was true ('al mid soðe worden, alse þis write þe telleð', l. 4229), and that he will reinforce the written word with spoken oath: 'Þas weord ich wulle þe treosien. þurh mine tirfulne god, / þat ich hit wulle soðien. ase ich hit bi write suggen' (ll. 4234–5).

18 R. R. Davies, *Conquest*, 78.
19 'We are told in both [Geoffrey] . . . and Wace (9703–7) that Arthur conquered Iceland, but there is no mention of the king of Iceland or his son. No historical source for the names Ælcus and Escol is known.' Later, Geoffrey, Wace and Laʒamon refer to Iceland's king as Maluasius, Malvaisus and Malverus respectively. Neither Gonwais nor Doldanim exists in historical records outside Laʒamon's sources. Barron and Weinberg, notes to pp. 103 and 105, 269–70, in their edition of the Arthurian section of the *Brut*.
20 Bzdyl, *Layamon's Brut*, 256.
21 Le Saux, *Laʒamon's Brut*, 166.
22 Ibid., 230.
23 Daniel Donoghue, 'Laʒamon's ambivalence', 562.
24 Ibid., 537–8.
25 Recall how, for example, he pairs Saul and Agag with the deliberation over Hengest's fate. Even his inclusion of saints and saints' lives, such as Ursele, Milburga or Oswald, allows for *imitatio Christi* to function as analogy or typology.
26 *Anglo-Saxon Prose*, trans. Swanton, 178–9, 180, 181. In Old English, Bethurum, *Homilies of Wulfstan*, ll. 11–13, 267; ll. 71–6, 270; ll. 95–8, 271.
27 *Anglo-Saxon Prose*, 183, 184. In Old English, Bethurum, *Homilies of Wulfstan*, ll. 176, 184–89, pp. 274–5; ll. 195–7, 275.
28 Gervase of Canterbury, 'Prologus in Cronicam Gervasii', in *The Historical Works of Gervase of Canterbury*, vol. I: *The Chronicle of the Reigns of Stephen, Henry II., and Richard I., by Gervase, the Monk of Canterbury*, ed. William Stubbs (London: Longman & Co., 1879), 87–8. Translation is from *The Anglo-Saxon Chronicle*, trans. G. N. Garmonsway (London: Everyman's University Library, 1972; reprint, London: J. M. Dent & Sons Ltd, 1978), xviii.
29 See discussion in the following chapter, and Cecily Clark, 'The narrative mode of *The Anglo-Saxon Chronicle* before the Conquest', in Peter Clemoes and Kathleen Hughes (eds), *England Before the Conquest:*

Studies in Primary Sources Presented to Dorothy Whitelock (Cambridge: Cambridge University Press, 1971), 215–35.
30 M. M. Bakhtin, *The Dialogic Imagination: Four Essays*, ed. Michael Holquist, trans. Caryl Emerson and Michael Holquist (Austin: University of Texas Press, 1990), xxix–xxx.
31 Denis Donoghue, *Ferocious Alphabets* (New York: Columbia University Press, 1984), 30.
32 Bakhtin, *Dialogic Imagination*, 13.
33 Ibid., 11.
34 Ibid.
35 Ibid., 12.
36 Ibid., 15.
37 Ibid., xxvii–xxviii.
38 Ibid., xxviii.
39 Denis Donoghue, *Ferocious Alphabets*, 85–6.
40 Holquist, in Bakhtin, *Dialogic Imagination*, xxxi.
41 Salter, 'Culture and literature', 62.
42 Laȝamon, *Laȝamon's Brut, or Chronicle of Britain: A Poetical Semi-Saxon Paraphrase of the Brut of Wace*, ed. and trans. Sir Frederic Madden (London: Society of Antiquaries, 1847), vol. 3, 510, note for line 28651: 'Evidently an error for *Brutten*.'
43 Bakhtin, *Dialogic Imagination*, 17.
44 Ibid., 27–8.

2 The Potential of Writing and Community

1 Peter L. Allen, 'A frame for the text? History, literary theory, subjectivity, and the study of medieval literature', *Exemplaria* 3.1 (Spring 1991), 8.
2 Ibid., 7.
3 Ruth Morse, *Truth and Convention in the Middle Ages: Rhetoric, Representation, and Reality* (Cambridge: Cambridge University Press, 1991), 86–7.
4 Le Saux, *Laȝamon's Brut*, 189–92.
5 J. P. Oakden, *Alliterative Poetry*, 2 vols. (Manchester: Manchester University Press, 1930).
6 A. C. Gibbs, 'The literary relationships of Laȝamon's *Brut*' (Ph.D. thesis, Cambridge University, 1962).
7 Le Saux, *Laȝamon's Brut*, 191–2.
8 Ibid., 27.
9 Ibid., 31.
10 Ibid., 32.
11 Salter, 'Culture and literature', 48.
12 Morse, *Truth and Convention*, 48.
13 Ibid., 50, 51.

14 Such inexpressibility is also, however, found in Anglo-Saxon texts such as Wulfstan's *Sermo Lupi*, suggestively close to a list like those just discussed. Wulfstan comments that many are hurt by sin:

> Here are slayers of men and slayers of kinsmen and killers of priests and enemies of the monasteries; and here are perjurers and murderers; and here are whores and those who kill children and many foul fornicating adulterers; and here are wizards and witches; and here are plunderers and robbers and those who despoil, and, to be brief, countless numbers of all crimes and misdeeds . . . Alas, many might easily recall much more in addition, which one man could not outline in a hurry, to indicate how wretchedly it has gone. (Translation from Swanton, *Anglo-Saxon Prose*, 121.)

15 Stock, *Implications of Literacy*, 3–4.
16 Morse, *Truth and Convention*, 91, 92, 93.
17 Stock, *Implications of Literacy*, 73.
18 Salter, 'Culture and literature', 60.
19 Morse, *Truth and Convention*, 36, 38.
20 Bakhtin, *Dialogic Imagination*, 27–8.
21 Clark, 'The narrative mode', 215–35.
22 Ibid., 232.
23 See, for example, Charles Foulon, 'Wace', in Roger Sherman Loomis (ed.), *Arthurian Literature in the Middle Ages: A Collaborative History* (Oxford: Oxford University Press, 1959), 98:

> A precursor of the modern historian, Wace applied critical standards. 'The tales of Arthur are not all lies nor all true. So much have the story-tellers (*cunteür*) told and so much have the makers of fables (*fableür*) fabled to embellish their stories that they have made everything seem a fable.' This desire for accuracy, this scepticism, this common sense have been recognized by nearly all scholars. Even Tatlock applied to Wace the adjectives 'enquiring, critical, honest'.

24 Stock, *Implications of Literacy*, 15–16.
25 Morse, *Truth and Convention*, 6.
26 R. R. Davies, *Conquest*, 274–6, and Part III: 'The Age of Consolidation, 1172–1277', 213–330.
27 The earliest tale is *Kulhwch ac Olwen*, final redaction *c.* 1050–1100, with the four branches of the *Mabinogi* itself from twelfth-century manuscripts and fragments. The other material grouped with the four branches has manuscripts dated as follows: *Kyfranc Llud a Llevelys*, *c.* 1200–50; *Breudwyt Maxen Wledic, c.* 1150–1200; *Breudwyt Ronabwy*,

c. 1220–5; the three Arthurian romances of *Gereint vab Erbin, Iarlles y Ffynnawn* and *Peredur vab Evrawc* are dated to c. 1200. Summary of dates taken from D. Simon Evans, *A Grammar of Middle Welsh* (Dublin: The Dublin Institute for Advanced Studies, 1976), xxx.

28 Le Saux, *Laʒamon's Brut*, 121–4, *passim*. The entirety of chapter 6, 'The Welsh Sources', provides her views here, 118–54.

29 Ibid., 132. See Herbert Pilch, 'Layamon und die kymrische Literatur: Eine Erwiderung an W. Schirmer', *Zeitschrift für celtische Philologie* 29 (1962), 193–7, and his longer study, much relied on for its authority, *Layamon's 'Brut'. Eine literarische Studie* (Heidelberg: Carl Winter, 1960). In the article above, he is responding to a review of his book by W. F. Schirmer in *Anglia* 79 (1961), 76–81.

30 Françoise Le Saux, 'Laʒamon's Welsh sources: a critical review of Herbert Pilch's thesis' (MA diss., University of Wales, Swansea, 1984). Her views are also published in an article: 'Laʒamon's Welsh Sources', *English Studies* 67 (1986), 385–93.

31 'I suspect few will accept her ingenious postulation of a Welsh informant'; he prefers that 'Le Saux's argument . . . both appealing and persuasive, . . . be qualified by Daniel Donoghue's recent examination'. Donald L. Hoffman, *Quondam et Futurus: A Journal of Arthurian Interpretations* 1 (1990), 91–4.

32 Le Saux, *Laʒamon's Brut*, 125.

33 Ibid., 137.

34 Ibid., 134.

35 See Evans, *A Grammar of Middle Welsh*, xxiii, for a convenient summary of poems linked to a Myrddin. A fuller treatment of the poet is found in A. O. H. Jarman's inaugural lecture, *The Legend of Merlin* (Cardiff: University of Wales Press, 1960) and in his article 'The Welsh Myrddin poems', in R. S. Loomis (ed.), *Arthurian Literature in the Middle Ages* (London: Oxford University Press, 1959), 20–30.

36 Le Saux, *Laʒamon's Brut*, 143; the work commented on is Constance Bullock-Davies, *Professional Interpreters and The Matter of Britain* (Cardiff: University of Wales Press, 1966).

37 Ibid., 121.

38 R. R. Davies, *Conquest*, 29–30.

39 J. S. P. Tatlock, *The Legendary History of Britain* (Berkeley: University of California Press, 1950), 510. Chapter 23 is devoted to Lawman, 483–531.

40 Salter, 'Culture and literature', 67.

41 Ibid., 70.

42 R. R. Davies, *Conquest*, 17.

43 Ibid., 191–2.

44 *Trioedd Ynys Prydein*, ed. and trans. Rachel Bromwich (Cardiff: University of Wales Press, 1978); usually abbreviated as TYP.

45 Le Saux, *Laȝamon's Brut*, 149.
46 Ibid., 176–7.
47 Bzdyl, *Layamon's Brut*, 59.
48 See, for example, the comments issued by the University of Paris in 1398, summarized in Jeffrey Burton Russell, *Witchcraft in the Middle Ages* (Ithaca: Cornell University Press, 1972), 202: 'On September 19, 1398, the University of Paris affirmed that magic was efficacious and expressed its alarm that ancient errors were regaining their sway over the minds of men. It announced that there was a distinction between natural magic and magic going beyond natural means.' Nature, as God's creation, could not in itself make magic evil; only a pact with God's enemies could do so. See also Valerie Flint, *The Rise of Magic in Early Medieval Europe* (Princeton: Princeton University Press, 1991).
49 Roland Barthes, *Mythologies*, selected and trans. Annette Lavers (New York: Hill and Wang, 1972), 154.
50 Ibid., 154–5.
51 Le Saux, *Laȝamon's Brut*, 219–20.
52 He is echoing similar praise in Wace, but its point in Wace, according to Jean Blacker-Knight, is to make Caesar 'more a participant in a courtly system of values with greater relevance to the poet's own age than to the British history he is recounting. Thus Caesar is rendered noteworthy . . . because . . . [he] was worthy of being labeled "li vaillanz, li forz, li pruz, li conqueranz [valiant, strong, honorable, conquering]".' Jean Blacker-Knight, 'Transformations of a theme: the depoliticization of the Arthurian world in the *Roman de Brut*', in Mary Flowers Braswell and John Bugge (eds), *The Arthurian Tradition: Essays in Convergence* (Tuscaloosa: The University of Alabama Press, 1988), 67. The lines cited from Wace are ll. 3833–4.
53 Bakhtin, *Dialogic Imagination*, 295–6.
54 Ibid., 292. Italics are Bakhtin's.
55 Ibid.
56 Ibid., 293.
57 See also Rosamund Allen, 'The implied audience of Laȝamon's *Brut*', in Françoise Le Saux (ed.), *The Text and Tradition of Layamon's Brut*, Arthurian Studies 33 (Rochester: D. S. Brewer, 1994): 121–39.
58 Bakhtin, *Dialogic Imagination*, 206–7.
59 Ibid., 215.
60 For example, Daniel Donoghue, Le Saux and Martin Schichtman, who writes of Gawain as 'a man who recognizes his insignificance' and the 'sense of inevitability' that 'dominates' Laȝamon's work. Martin B. Schichtman, 'Gawain in Wace and Laȝamon: a case of metahistorical evolution', in Laurie A. Finke and Martin B. Shichtman (eds), *Medieval Texts and Contemporary Readers* (Ithaca: Cornell University Press, 1987), 116–17.

61 Stock, *Implications of Literacy*, 87. Schichtman, to his credit, unwittingly agrees, though he overstresses the Normans: 'For Laȝamon, living in Norman-occupied Britain, history was a means of showing his audience the way to God', 'Gawain', 119.
62 Bakhtin, *Dialogic Imagination*, 147.
63 Barthes, *Mythologies*, 126.
64 Ibid., 143.
65 Ibid., 142.

3 History, Prophecy and Possibility

1 We know he *was* read and examined soon after his writing, not simply because his work survives in two manuscripts, but because of the format of those manuscripts. In the twelfth century, changes in the layout of texts occurred because of increased interest in the study of texts. Stock notes such aids to study as running headlines, chapter titles and other rubrics, cross-references and author citations (p. 63). The Caligula manuscript contains marginal notations on major names of people and things (such as Belin or Crocea Mors) as well as crosses in the margins and extended Latin notes on historical background to events, such as Diocletian's persecutions when Laȝamon mentions a saint like Alban. Such evidence indicates a readiness to consult the text, not simply read it, and the Latin notes resemble those a student or commentator might add. Even the prologue may be an indication of studying the text, given that it fulfils expectations created by textual study among scholastics and that details such as changing sources to make all of them religious indicate a certain bias. Of course, he was also read much later as well, as Elizabeth Bryan's book and current research make clear.
2 Richard Kieckhefer, *Magic in the Middle Ages* (New York: Cambridge University Press, 1990), 11 and *passim*. See also Isidore of Seville, *Etymologies*, ed. Peter K. Marshall et al. (Paris: Les Belles Lettres, 1986).
3 For further discussion of what such birds could signify, see Sue Eastman Sheldon and Loren C. MacKinney, 'The eagle: bird of magic and medicine in a Middle English translation of the *Kyranides*', *Tulane Studies in English* 22 (1977), 1–20, and my article on 'The birds on the Sutton Hoo instrument', in Robert T. Farrell and Carol Neuman de Vegvar (eds), *Sutton Hoo: Fifty Years After*, American Early Medieval Studies 2 (Oxford, OH: American Early Medieval Studies, 1992).
4 Kieckhefer, *Magic*, 85–6:

> Popular oneiromancy might involve simple equation of dream content with future events: dreams about water, for example, might signal death by

drowning. On a more sophisticated level, the 'dream books' of writers such as Hans Lobenzweig (mid-fifteenth century) made careful allowance for the social status and physical condition of the dreamer, and contained complex rules for interpreting dreams.

Dante's references in his *Comedy* to dreams before waking always coming true is a reflection of pervasive belief.

5   Bakhtin, *Dialogic Imagination*, 154–5.
6   R. R. Davies, *Conquest*, 172–3.
7   Jeff Rider, 'Arthur and the saints', in Valerie M. Lagorio and Mildred Leake Day (eds), *King Arthur through the Ages*, vol. 1 (New York: Garland Publishing, Inc., 1990), 3.
8   Ibid., 8.
9   Ibid., 13.
10 R. R. Davies, *Conquest*, 178–9; the passage from Gerald is from his *Description of Wales*, published in vol. 6 of his *Opera*, ed. J. S. Brewer, J. F. Dimock and G. F. Warner, Rolls Series (1861–91), 204. Davies cites it as *DK*, I, xviii.
11 Foulon, *Wace*, 98.
12 Taliesin, *The Poems of Taliesin*, ed. and annotated by Sir Ifor Williams, English version by J. E. Caerwyn Williams, Mediaeval and Modern Welsh Series, vol. III (Dublin: The Dublin Institute for Advanced Studies, 1975), xv–xix.
13 The triad is translated in chapter 2 (p. 54) of *The Romance of Merlin: An Anthology*, ed. Peter Goodrich. The chapter, by John K. Bollard, contains a variety of translated texts and is entitled 'Myrddin in early Welsh tradition' (New York: Garland Publishing, Inc., 1990), 13–54.
14 Jarman, 'The Welsh Myrddin Poems', 25.
15 Jan Ziolkowski, 'The nature of prophecy in Geoffrey of Monmouth's *Vita Merlini*', in James L. Kugel (ed.), *Poetry and Prophecy: The Beginnings of a Literary Tradition*, Myth and Poetics Series (Ithaca: Cornell University Press, 1990), 153.
16 Ibid., 154, 156.
17 For more extensive discussion of this passage, see my forthcoming article, 'Cannibal cultures and the body of text in Laȝamon's *Brut*', in Rosamund Allen, Lucy Perry and Jane Roberts (eds), *Laȝamon: Contexts, Language and Interpretation*, King's College London Medieval Studies 19 (London: King's College London Centre for Late Antique and Medieval Studies, 2002), 351–69. A second article in the volume, by Lucy Perry, discusses the sexual aspects of the passage as well.
18 Ziolkowski, 'The nature of prophecy', 154.
19 Ibid., 159.
20 Ibid., 242, n. 17: 'The word *awenyddion* is the plural of *awenydd*, a word

that means poet-prophet and that derives from *awen* ("in-spiration") "oracular frenzy".'

21 Gerald of Wales, *The Journey through Wales and The Description of Wales*, trans. Lewis Thorpe (Harmondsworth: Penguin Books, 1978), 246–7; quoted in Ziolkowski, 'The nature of prophecy', 155.

22 It is perhaps not irrelevant that Laȝamon himself may have lived near and associated with a community of hermits, possibly one with a library. Salter writes (assuming Laȝamon's authorship of the prologue),

> Laȝamon's insistence that he lived 'near to Redstone', and, indeed, the ambiguity of the punctuation at that point in both manuscripts, so that it is impossible to know whether he 'read books' at Areley-Kings or at Redstone, raises a little speculation as to the exact significance of the references. Earlier historians were led to conclude that he had some close connection with the remarkable series of cliff-dwellings at Redstone, which housed a number of hermits as early as the twelfth and thirteenth centuries. Some recognised community must have dwelt there in Laȝamon's time; in 1182, Simon, clerk of 'Reddestan', is mentioned, and in 1260, protection was granted for 'the brethren of the House of Radestone'. The 'House of Radestone' never apparently developed into any more formal institution . . . we may wonder whether [Laȝamon] had any useful contact with the 'clerk' and the 'brethren' of a literary sort. (Salter, 'Culture and literature', 69–70)

23 Blacker-Knight, 'Transformations', 65.
24 Ibid., 70, 71, 72.
25 Hanning, *The Vision*, 121.
26 *The Historia Brittonum*, 10 vols., ed. D. N. Dumville (Cambridge: 1985–).
27 David N. Dumville, 'The historical value of the *Historia Brittonum*', in *Histories and Pseudo-histories of the Insular Middle Ages* (Aldershot: Variorum, 1990), 6–7. This book is a collection of offprints, in which each article is numbered by Roman numerals but retains its pagination from the original publication in which it appeared. All subsequent references here will be to the article number and page in this volume, followed by the original date of publication. For example, this citation would appear as VII, 6–7, 1986.
28 Dumville, XI, 48, 1977. See note 27 for an explanation of the citation form.
29 *The Historia Regum Britanniae: A Variant Version*, ed. Jacob Hammer (Cambridge, MA: Medieval Academy of America, 1951). This edition has been criticized as departing 'repeatedly from sound editorial principles' by Dumville, though he also notes in fairness that Hammer died long before he could do justice to the large numbers of manuscripts omitted by previous editions completed by Faral and Griscom. Recent

work has begun to deal more soundly with textual variants. See *The Historia Regum Britannie II: First Variant Version*, ed. Neil Wright (Cambridge: Brewer, 1987) and *The Historia Regum Britannie III: A Summmary Catalogue of the Manuscripts*, ed. J. C. Crick (Cambridge, 1989). Dumville's thoughts appear in 'An early text of Geoffrey of Monmouth's *Historia Regum Britanniae* and the circulation of some Latin histories in twelfth-century Normandy', XIV, 1–2. There are some 217 manuscripts known of the *Historia*.

30 See, for example, Hanning's comments that 'Geoffrey plainly demonstrates the separation of individual and nation, in a manner suggested by the secular account of Vortigern's death in *Historia Brittonum*', *Vision of History*, 151, and his contention that one source of Geoffrey's denigrating response to classical Rome's achievement is 'chapters 19–31 of *Historia Brittonum*', 163.

31 Le Saux, *Laȝamon's Brut*, 94–110.
32 Ibid., 94.
33 Ibid., 97.
34 Ibid., 101. She is reviewing Robert A. Caldwell, 'Wace's *Roman de Brut* and the *Variant Version* of Geoffrey of Monmouth's *Historia Regum Britanniae*', *Speculum* 31 (1956), 675–82.
35 Le Saux, *Laȝamon's Brut*, 99.
36 Ibid., 109–10.
37 Ibid., 116. Le Saux states that scenes like the poisoning of Vortimer and the hermit's finding of Merlin in the forest may have come from Geoffrey's *Vita*.
38 Blacker-Knight, 'Transformations', 56.
39 Hanning, *The Vision*, 171, 151; the quotation is on 154.
40 Blacker-Knight, 'Transformations', 205–6, n. 8.
41 Dumville, *Histories*, XIV, especially 22, but see entire section on the Bern version, 18–29.
42 Blacker-Knight, 'Transformations', 59–60.
43 Antonia Gransden, *Historical Writing in England c. 550 to c. 1307* (Ithaca: Cornell University Press, 1974), 205. 'Geoffrey emphasized that the present-day Welsh did not inherit the tradition of the ancient Britons. They were effete: it was the Bretons who were the heirs of British heroism.' She cites, in her note 181, Geoffrey's *Historia*, xii.19. Incidentally, she omits Laȝamon entirely from her study.
44 Wace, *Wace's Roman de Brut: A History of the British*, text and trans. Judith Weiss, Exeter Medieval English Texts and Studies (Exeter: University of Exeter Press, 1999), 332–5.
45 Sheila Delany, 'Run silent, run deep: heresy and alchemy as medieval versions of utopia', in *Medieval Literary Politics: Shapes of Ideology* (New York: Manchester University Press, 1990), 4.
46 Ibid.

47 Ibid., 5–6.
48 R. R. Davies, *Conquest*, 79.
49 Ibid.
50 Ibid., 80.
51 James L. Kugel, 'Poets and prophets: an overview', in James L. Kugel (ed.), *Poetry and Prophecy: The Beginnings of a Literary Tradition*, Myth and Poetics Series (Ithaca: Cornell University Press, 1990), 3.
52 Dennis P. Donahue, 'Thematic and formulaic composition in Lawman's Brut' (Ph.D. thesis, New York, 1976), quoted in Le Saux, *Laȝamon's Brut*, 29–30. The omission of university is hers.
53 Judson Boyce Allen, *The Ethical Poetic of the Later Middle Ages: A Decorum of Convenient Distinction* (Buffalo: University of Toronto Press, 1982), 12.
54 Le Saux, *Laȝamon's Brut*, 218.
55 Ibid., 164.
56 Minnis, *Medieval Theory*, 136.
57 Joseph M. Miller, Michael H. Prosser and Thomas W. Benson (eds), *Readings in Medieval Rhetoric* (Bloomington: Indiana University Press, 1973), 162.
58 Guibert de Nogent, 'A book about the way a sermon ought to be given', trans. Joseph M. Miller, in Miller, Prosser and Benson (eds), *Readings in Medieval Rhetoric*, 170.
59 Ibid., 171–2.
60 Minnis, *Medieval Theory*, 101.
61 Quoted in Minnis, *Medieval Theory*, 137; cited in n. 78, p. 253, as MS Bodley 738, fol. 76^v.
62 R. R. Davies, *Conquest*, 284–5.
63 Ibid., 80.
64 For a fuller discussion, see Caroline Eckhardt, 'Prophecy and nostalgia: Arthurian symbolism at the close of the English Middle Ages', in Mary Flowers Braswell and John Bugge (eds), *The Arthurian Tradition: Essays in Convergence* (Tuscaloosa: University of Alabama Press, 1988), 109–26.
65 All Middle English quotations from *Sir Gawain and the Green Knight*, ed. J. R. R. Tolkien and E. V. Gordon; 2nd edn, ed. Norman Davis (Oxford: Oxford University Press, 1967). *Sir Gawain and the Green Knight: A New Verse Translation*, trans. Marie Borroff (New York: W. W. Norton & Company, 1967).
66 While 'þe Brutus bokez' are clearly not Laȝamon's work alone, his work along with Wace's is the earliest and should be considered to be included in, and perhaps seminal to, the tradition.
67 M. M. Bakhtin, 'The problem of speech genres', in *Speech Genres and Other Late Essays*, trans. Vern W. McGee, ed. Caryl Emerson and Michael Holquist (Austin: University of Texas Press, 1986), 60, 78.

68 Ibid., 65.
69 Ibid., 67.
70 Ibid., 71–2.
71 Ibid., 77.
72 See above, p. 97: 'Man . . . anguished over a new separation from the paradise of familial relations in Eden, which were oral.' 'Texts . . . offered . . . to restore the lost spiritual unity with God.'
72 A. S. Byatt, *Possession: A Romance* (New York: Random House, 1990), 195.

Bibliography

Ackerman, Gretchen P., 'Sir Frederic Madden and Arthurian scholarship', in Valerie M. Lagorio and Mildred Leake Day (eds), *King Arthur through the Ages*, vol. 2 (New York: Garland Publishing, Inc., 1990), 27–38.
Ackerman, R. W., 'Sir Frederic Madden and medieval scholarship', *Neuphilologische Mitteilungen* 73 (1972), 1–15.
Alamichel, Marie-Françoise, 'The function and activities of women in Laȝamon's *Brut*', in Juliette Dor (ed.), *A Wyf Ther Was: Essays in Honour of Paule Mertens-Fonck* (Liège: Liège Language and Literature, Département d'anglais, 1992), 11–22.
——, 'King Arthur's dual personality in Layamon's *Brut*', *Neophilologus* 77, 2 (April 1993), 303–19.
——, 'Lawamon et Shakespeare: De Leir à Lear', *Études anglaises Grand-Bretagne – États-Unis* 45, 2 (April–June 1992), 162–76.
Allen, Judson Boyce, *The Ethical Poetic of the Later Middle Ages: A Decorum of Convenient Distinction* (Buffalo: University of Toronto Press, 1982).
Allen, Peter L., 'A frame for the text? History, literary theory, subjectivity, and the study of medieval literature', *Exemplaria* 3, 1 (Spring 1991), 1–25.
Allen, Rosamund, 'The implied audience of Laȝamon's *Brut*', in Françoise Le Saux (ed.), *The Text and Tradition of Layamon's Brut*, Arthurian Studies 33 (Rochester: D. S. Brewer, 1994), 121–39.
——, 'Counting time and time for recounting: narrative sections in Laȝamon's *Brut*', in Herbert Pilch (ed.), *Orality and Literacy in Early Middle English*, ScriptOralia 83 (Tübingen: Gunter Narr Verlag, 1996), 71–91.
——, '*Eorles* and *Beornes*: contextualizing Lawman's *Brut*', *Arthuriana* 8, 3 (Fall 1998), 4–22.
The Anglo-Saxon Chronicle, trans. G. N. Garmonsway (London: Everyman's University Library, 1972; reprint, London: J. M. Dent & Sons Ltd, 1978).

Bakhtin, M. M., *The Dialogic Imagination: Four Essays*, ed. Michael Holquist, trans. Caryl Emerson and Michael Holquist (Austin: University of Texas Press, 1990).
——, *Speech Genres and Other Late Essays*, trans. Vern W. McGee, ed. Caryl Emerson and Michael Holquist (Austin: University of Texas Press, 1986).
Barron, W. R. J., 'Arthurian romance: traces of an English tradition', *English Studies* 61 (February 1980), 2–23.
Barthes, Roland, *Mythologies*, selected and trans. by Annette Lavers (New York: Hill and Wang, 1972).
Bethurum, Dorothy, *The Homilies of Wulfstan* (Oxford: Clarendon Press, 1957).
Blacker-Knight, Jean, 'Transformations of a theme: the depoliticization of the Arthurian world in the *Roman de Brut*', in Mary Flowers Braswell and John Bugge (eds), *The Arthurian Tradition: Essays in Convergence* (Tuscaloosa: University of Alabama Press, 1988), 54–74.
Blake, N. F., 'Rhythmical alliteration', *Modern Philology* 67 (1969), 118–24.
Blanchet, Marie-Claude, 'L'Argante de Layamon', in *Mélanges de langue et de littérature du Moyen Age et de la Renaissance offerts á Jean Frappier*, vol. 1 (Geneva: Librairie Droz, 1970), 133–44.
Blenner-Hassett, Roland, *A Study of the Place-Names in Lawman's Brut*, Stanford University Publications, Language and Literature 9, no. 1 (Stanford: Stanford University Publications, 1950).
——, 'The English river-names in Lawman's *Brut*', *Modern Language Notes* 55 (1940), 373–8.
——, 'Gernemuðe: a place-name in Lawman's *Brut*', *Modern Language Notes* 57 (1942), 179–81.
—— and F. P. Magoun, 'The Italian campaign of Belin and Brenne in the Bruts of Wace and Lawman', *Philological Quarterly* XXI (1942), 385–90.
Bøgholm, N., *The Layamon Texts: A Linguistical Investigation*, Travaux du Cercle Linguistique de Copenhague III (Copenhagen: Einar Munksgaard, 1944).
Bollard, John K., 'Myrddin in early Welsh tradition', in Peter Goodrich (ed.), *The Romance of Merlin: An Anthology* (New York: Garland Publishing, Inc., 1990), 13–54.
Borges, Jorge Luis, 'The innocence of Layamon', in *Other Inquisitions, 1937–1952*, trans. Ruth L. C. Simms, Texas Pan-American Series (Austin: University of Texas Press, 1964), 158–62.
Bowen, E. W., 'Open and close "e" in Layamon', *Anglia* 16 (1894), 380–5.
Brandstädter, Walter Kurt, *Stabreim und Endreim in Layamons Brut* (Inaugural-Dissertation Albertus-Universität zu Königsberg i. Pr. Kirchhain N.-L.: Max Schmersow, 1912).
Brewer, Derek, 'The paradox of the archaic and the modern in Laȝamon's *Brut*', in Malcolm Godden, Douglas Gray and Terry Hoad (eds), *From*

Anglo-Saxon to Early Middle English: Studies Presented to E. G. Stanley (Oxford: Clarendon Press, 1994), 188–205.

Brown, A. C. L., 'Welsh traditions in Layamon's Brut', *Modern Philology* 1 (1903–4), 95–103.

Bruce, J. D., 'Some proper names in Layamon's *Brut* not represented in Wace's *Roman de Brut*', *Modern Language Notes* 26 (1911), 65–9.

Bryan, Elizabeth J., *Collaborative Meaning in Medieval Scribal Culture: The Otho Laȝamon*, Editorial Theory and Literary Criticism (Ann Arbor: University of Michigan Press, 1999).

——, 'Sir Frederic Madden's annotations on Laȝamon's *Brut*', in Herbert Pilch (ed.), *Orality and Literacy in Early Middle English*, ScriptOralia 83 (Tübingen: Gunter Narr Verlag, 1996), 21–69.

——, 'Theoretical approaches to Lawman's *Brut*', special issue: *Theoretical Approaches to Lawman's Brut*, ed. Elizabeth J. Bryan, *Arthuriana* 10, 2 (Summer 2000), 3–4.

——, 'Truth and the Round Table in Lawman's *Brut*', *Quondam et Futurus* 2 (1992), 27–35.

Bullock-Davies, Constance, *Professional Interpreters and The Matter of Britain* (Cardiff: University of Wales Press, 1966).

Burrow, J. A., 'Laȝamon's *Brut* 10, 642: Wleoteð', *Notes and Queries* n.s. 27, no. 1 (February 1980), 2–3.

Byatt, A. S., *Possession: A Romance* (New York: Random House, 1990).

Caldwell, Robert A., 'Wace's *Roman de Brut* and the *Variant Version* of Geoffrey of Monmouth's *Historia Regum Britanniae*', *Speculum* 31 (1956), 675–82.

Cameron, Angus F., 'Middle English in Old English manuscripts', in Beryl Rowland (ed.), *Chaucer and Middle English Studies in Honour of Russell Hope Robbins* (London: George Allen and Unwin Ltd, 1974), 218–29.

Cannon, Christopher, 'The style and authorship of the Otho revision of Laȝamon's *Brut*', *Medium Ævum* 62, 2 (1993), 187–209.

Clark, Cecily, 'The narrative mode of *The Anglo-Saxon Chronicle* before the Conquest', in Peter Clemoes and Kathleen Hughes (eds), *England before the Conquest: Studies in Primary Sources Presented to Dorothy Whitelock* (Cambridge: Cambridge University Press, 1971), 215–35.

Crick, Julia C., *The Historia Regum Britannie III: A Summary Catalogue of the Manuscripts* (Cambridge: D. S. Brewer, 1989).

Davies, H. S., 'Laȝamon's similes', *Review of English Studies* 11 (1960), 129–42.

Davies, R. R., *Conquest, Coexistence and Change: Wales 1063–1415* (Cardiff/Oxford: University of Wales Press/Oxford University Press, 1987).

Delany, Sheila, 'Run silent, run deep: heresy and alchemy as medieval versions of utopia', in *Medieval Literary Politics: Shapes of Ideology* (New York: Manchester University Press, 1990), 1–18.

Deskis, Susan E. and Thomas D. Hill, 'The wolf doesn't care: the proverbial and traditional context of Laȝamon's *Brut* lines 10624–36', *Review of English Studies* n.s. 46, 181 (1995), 41–8.

Dobson, E. J., 'Two notes on early Middle English texts', *Notes and Queries* n.s. 21, 4 (April 1974), 124–6.

Domesday Book, series ed. John Morris. *Worcestershire*, vol. 16: *Liber de Wintonia* compiled by direction of King William I, Winchester 1086, ed. Frank and Caroline Thorn (Chichester: Phillimore & Co. Ltd, 1982).

Donahue, Dennis, 'The animals tethered to King Arthur's rise and fall: imagery and structure in Lawman's *Brut*', *Mid-Hudson Language Studies* 6 (1983), 19–27.

———, *Lawman's Brut, an Early Arthurian Poem: A Study of Middle English Formulaic Composition*, Studies in Mediaeval Literature 9 (Lewiston: Edwin Mellen Press, 1991).

———, 'Lawman's formulaic themes and the characterization of King Arthur in the *Brut*', in Herbert Pilch (ed.), *Orality and Literacy in Early Middle English*, ScriptOralia 83 (Tübingen: Gunter Narr Verlag, 1996), 93–112.

Donoghue, Daniel, 'Laȝamon's ambivalence', *Speculum* 65 (1990), 537–63.

Donoghue, Denis, *Ferocious Alphabets* (New York: Columbia University Press, 1984).

Dumville, David N., 'An early text of Geoffrey of Monmouth's *Historia Regum Britanniae* and the circulation of some Latin histories in twelfth-century Normandy', in *Histories and Pseudo-histories of the Insular Middle Ages*, XIV (Aldershot: Variorum, 1990), 1–36; originally published in *Arthurian Literature* 4 (1985), 1–36.

———, 'Celtic-Latin texts in northern England, *c.* 1150–*c.* 1250', in *Histories and Pseudo-histories of the Insular Middle Ages*, XI (Aldershot: Variorum, 1990), 19–49; originally published in *Celtica* 12 (1977), 19–49.

———, 'The historical value of the *Historia Brittonum*', in *Histories and Pseudo-histories of the Insular Middle Ages*, VII (Aldershot: Variorum, 1990), 1–26; originally published in *Arthurian Literature* 6 (1986), 1–26.

———, *Histories and Pseudo-histories of the Insular Middle Ages* (Aldershot: Variorum, 1990).

———, ' "Nennius" and the *Historia Brittonum*', in *Histories and Pseudo-histories of the Insular Middle Ages*, X (Aldershot: Variorum, 1990), 78–95; originally published in *Studia Celtica* 10/11 (1975–6), 78–95.

Eckhardt, Caroline, 'Prophecy and nostalgia: Arthurian symbolism at the close of the English Middle Ages', in Mary Flowers Braswell and John Bugge (eds), *The Arthurian Tradition: Essays in Convergence* (Tuscaloosa: University of Alabama Press, 1988), 109–26.

Evans, D. Simon, *A Grammar of Middle Welsh* (Dublin: Dublin Institute for Advanced Studies, 1976).

Everett, Dorothy, 'Layamon and the earliest Middle English verse', in

Patricia Kean (ed.), *Essays on Middle English Literature* (Oxford: Oxford University Press, 1955; reprint, Westport: Greenwood Press, 1978), 23–45.
Fletcher, Robert Huntington, *The Arthurian Material in the Chronicles, Especially those of Great Britain and France*, 2nd edn expanded by Roger Sherman Loomis, Burt Franklin Bibliography and Reference Works Series 88 (New York: Burt Franklin, 1966).
Flint, Valerie, *The Rise of Magic in Early Medieval Europe* (Princeton: Princeton University Press, 1991).
Foulon, Charles, 'Wace', in Roger Sherman Loomis (ed.), *Arthurian Literature in the Middle Ages: A Collaborative History* (Oxford: Oxford University Press, 1959).
Frankis, P. J., 'Laȝamon's English sources', in Mary Salu and Robert T. Farrell (eds), *J. R. R. Tolkien, Scholar and Storyteller* (Ithaca: Cornell University Press, 1979), 64–75.
Friedlander, Carolynn Van Dyke, 'Early Middle English accentual verse', *Modern Philology* 76 (February 1979), 219–30.
——, 'The first English story of King Lear: Layamon's *Brut*, lines 1448–1887', *Allegorica* 3 (Summer 1978), 42–76.
Fries, Maureen, 'Women, power, and (the undermining of) order in Lawman's *Brut*', *Arthuriana* 8, 3 (Fall 1998), 23–32.
Geoffrey of Monmouth, *Historia Regum Britanniae: A Variant Version Edited from Manuscripts*, ed. Jacob Hammer (Cambridge: Mediaeval Academy of America, 1951).
——, *The Historia Regum Britanniae of Geoffrey of Monmouth*, ed. Acton Griscom (London: Longmans & Green, 1929).
——, *The Historia Regum Britannie of Geoffrey of Monmouth, I Bern, Burgerbibliothek MS 568*, ed. Neil Wright (Cambridge: D. S. Brewer, 1985).
——, *The Historia Regum Britannie II: First Variant Version*, ed. Neil Wright (Cambridge: D. S. Brewer, 1987).
——, *The History of the Kings of Britain*, trans. Lewis Thorpe (Harmondsworth: Penguin Books, 1966).
Gerald of Wales, *The Journey Through Wales and the Description of Wales* trans. Lewis Thorpe (Harmondsworth: Penguin Books, 1978).
——, *Opera: Description of Wales*, eds. J. S. Brewer, J. F. Dimock and G. F. Warner, Rolls Series (1861–91).
Gervase of Canterbury, 'Prologus in Cronicam Gervasii', in *The Historical Works of Gervase of Canterbury*, vol. I: *The Chronicle of the Reigns of Stephen, Henry II, and Richard I, by Gervase, the Monk of Canterbury*, ed. William Stubbs (London: Longman & Co., 1879).
Gildas, *The Ruin of Britain and Other Works*, ed. and trans. Michael Winterbottom (London: Phillimore, 1978).
Girouard, Mark, *The Return to Camelot: Chivalry and the English Gentleman* (New Haven: Yale University Press, 1981).

Glowka, Arthur Wayne, 'Laȝamon's heathens and the medieval grapevine', in Herbert Pilch (ed.), *Orality and Literacy in Early Middle English*, ScriptOralia 83 (Tübingen: Gunter Narr Verlag, 1996, 113–45).

——, 'Prosodic decorum in Layamon's *Brut*', *Poetica* (Tokyo) 18 (1984), 40–53.

Goodrich, Peter (ed.), *The Romance of Merlin: An Anthology* (New York: Garland Publishing, Inc., 1990).

Gransden, Antonia, *Historical Writing in England c. 550–c. 1307* (Ithaca: Cornell University Press, 1974).

Guibert de Nogent, 'A book about the way a sermon ought to be given', trans. Joseph M. Miller, in Joseph M. Miller, Michael H. Prosser and Thomas W. Benson (eds), *Readings in Medieval Rhetoric* (Bloomington: Indiana University Press, 1973), 162–81.

Hall, Joseph, *Selections from Early Middle English, 1130–1250*, 2 vols. (Oxford: Clarendon Press, 1920).

Hanning, Robert W., *The Vision of History in Early Britain: From Gildas to Geoffrey of Monmouth* (New York: Columbia University Press, 1966).

Harding, Carol E., *Merlin and Legendary Romance* (New York: Garland Publishing Inc., 1988).

Hilker, Wilfried, *Der Vers in Layamons 'Brut': Untersuchungen zu seiner Struktur und Herkunft*, Inaugural-Dissertation Westfälischen Wilhelms-Universität zu Münster (Westf.), 1965.

Hinckley, H. B., 'The date of Laȝamon's *Brut*', *Anglia* 56 (1932), 43–57.

The Historia Brittonum, 10 vols., ed. D. N. Dumville (Cambridge: Cambridge University Press, 1985–).

Hoffman, Donald L., Review of F. Le Saux's *Layamon's Brut: The Poem and its Sources*, in *Quondam et Futurus: A Journal of Arthurian Interpretations* 1 (1990), 91–4.

Hollister, C. Warren, 'Elite prosopography in Saxon and Norman England', *Medieval Prosopography* 2 (Autumn 1981), 11–20.

Holmes, Urban Tigner, Jr., 'Norman literature and Wace', in William Matthews (ed.), *Medieval Secular Literature: Four Essays*. Contributions of the UCLA Center for Medieval and Renaissance Studies I (Berkeley: University of California Press, 1965), 46–67.

Hulbert, James R., 'A hypothesis concerning the alliterative revival', *Modern Philology* 28 (1931), 405–22.

Isidore of Seville, *Etymologies*, ed. Peter K. Marshall *et al.* (Paris: Les Belles Lettres, 1986).

Jarman, A. O. H., *The Legend of Merlin* (Cardiff: University of Wales Press, 1960).

——, 'The Welsh Myrddin Poems', in Roger Sherman Loomis (ed.), *Arthurian Literature in the Middle Ages: A Collaborative History* (Oxford: Oxford University Press, 1959), 20–30.

Johnson, Lesley, 'Reading the past in Laȝamon's *Brut*', in Françoise Le Saux (ed.), *The Text and Tradition of Laȝamon's Brut*, Arthurian Studies 33 (Cambridge: D. S. Brewer, 1994), 141–60.

——, 'Tracking Laȝamon's *Brut*', *Leeds Studies in English* n.s. 22 (1991), 139–65.

Kalinke, Marianne E., 'Arthurian literature in Scandinavia', in Valerie M. Lagorio and Mildred Leake Day (eds), *King Arthur Through the Ages*, vol. I (New York: Garland Publishing, Inc., 1990), 127–51.

Keith, W. J., 'Laȝamon's *Brut*: the literary differences between the two texts', *Medium Ævum* 29 (1960), 161–72.

Kieckhefer, Richard, *Magic in the Middle Ages* (New York: Cambridge University Press, 1990).

Kirby, I. J., 'Angles and Saxons in Laȝamon's *Brut*', *Studia Neophilologica* 36 (1964), 51–62.

Kolbe, Max, *Schild, Helm und Panzer zur Zeit Laȝamons und ihre Schilderung in dessen Brut, verglichen mit der im Roman de Brut von Wace*, Inaugural-Dissertation, Universität Breslau (Trebnitz in Schles.: Maretzke & Märtin, 1891).

Kugel, James L. 'Poets and prophets: an overview', in James L. Kugel (ed.), *Poetry and Prophecy: The Beginnings of a Literary Tradition*, Myth and Poetics Series (Ithaca: Cornell University Press, 1990), 1–25.

Laȝamon, *Brut*, 2 vols., ed. G. L. Brook and R. F. Leslie, Early English Text Society, vols. 250 and 277 (New York: Oxford University Press, 1963 and 1978).

——, *Laȝamon's Arthur: The Arthurian Section of Laȝamon's Brut (Lines 9229–14297)*, ed. and trans. W. R. J. Barron and S. C. Weinberg (Harlow, Essex: Longman Group UK Ltd, 1989).

——, *Layamon's Brut: A History of the Britons*, trans. Donald G. Bzdyl, Medieval and Renaissance Texts and Studies 65 (Binghamton: Medieval and Renaissance Texts and Studies, 1989).

——, *Laȝamon's Brut, or Chronicle of Britain: A Poetical Semi-Saxon Paraphrase of the Brut of Wace*, 3 vols., ed. and trans. Sir Frederic Madden (London: Society of Antiquaries, 1847).

——, *Laȝamon's Brut or Hystoria Brutonum* (edition and translation), ed. W. R. J. Barron and S. C. Weinberg (Harlow: Longman Group Limited, 1995).

——, *Laȝamon's 'Brut': Selections*, ed. J. N. Hall (Oxford: Oxford University Press, 1924).

——, *Selęctions from Laȝamon's 'Brut'*, ed. G. L. Brook (Oxford: Oxford University Press, 1963; reprinted, 2nd edn revised by J. Levitt, 1983).

Lawman, *Brut*, trans. with an introduction by Rosamund Allen (London: J. M. Dent & Sons Ltd, 1992).

Lawton, David, *Middle English Alliterative Poetry and its Literary Background: Seven Essays* (Cambridge: D. S. Brewer, 1982).

Legge, Mary Dominica, *Anglo-Norman Literature and its Background*. (Oxford: Oxford University Press, 1963; repr. Westport, Conn.: Greenwood Press, 1978).
Le Saux, Françoise H. M., *Laȝamon's Brut: The Poem and its Sources*, Arthurian Studies XIX (Cambridge: D. S. Brewer, 1989).
——, 'Laȝamon's Welsh sources: a critical review of Herbert Pilch's thesis' (MA thesis, University of Wales, Swansea, 1984).
——, 'Laȝamon's Welsh sources', *English Studies* 67, 5 (October 1986), 385–93.
—— (ed.), *The Text and Tradition of Layamon's Brut*, Arthurian Studies 33 (Cambridge: D. S. Brewer, 1994), 170–82.
——, 'Listening to the manuscript: editing Laȝamon's *Brut*', in Herbert Pilch (ed.), *Orality and Literacy in Early Middle English*, ScriptOralia 83 (Tübingen: Gunter Narr Verlag, 1996), 11–20.
Lewis, C. S., 'The genesis of a medieval book', in *Studies in Medieval and Renaissance Literature*, collected by Walter Hooper (Cambridge: Cambridge University Press, 1966), 18–40.
Loomis, Roger Sherman (ed.), *Arthurian Literature in the Middle Ages: A Collaborative History* (Oxford: Oxford University Press, 1959).
——, 'Layamon's *Brut*', in R. S. Loomis (ed.), *Arthurian Literature in the Middle Ages* (Oxford: Oxford University Press, 1959), 104–11.
——, 'Notes on Laȝamon', *Review of English Studies* X (1934), 78–84.
Matheson, Lister M., 'King Arthur and the medieval English chronicles', in Valerie M. Lagorio and Mildred Leake Day (eds), *King Arthur Through the Ages*, vol. I (New York: Garland Publishing Inc., 1990), 248–73.
Maynadier, Gustavus Howard, *The Arthur of the English Poets* (New York: Octagon, 1907; repr. New York: Haskell House, 1966).
——, 'From Layamon to Malory', in *The Arthur of the English Poets* (New York: Haskell House, 1966), 197–217.
Millar, Robert McColl, 'Old English "þaet" and the demonstrative systems of Laȝamon's "Brut"', *Neuphilologische Mitteilungen* 95, 4 (1994), 415–32.
——, '"Reinterpretation" in the demonstrative systems of Laȝamon's "Brut"', *Neuphilologische Mitteilungen* 96, 2 (1995), 145–68.
Miller, Joseph M., Michael H. Prosser and Thomas W. Benson (eds), *Readings in Medieval Rhetoric* (Bloomington: Indiana University Press, 1973).
Minnis, A. J., *Medieval Theory of Authorship: Scholastic Literary Attitudes in the Later Middle Ages*, 2nd edn (Philadelphia: University of Pennsylvania Press, 1988).
Monroe, Benton Sullivan, 'French words in Laȝamon', *Modern Philology* 4 (1907), 559–67.
——, 'Studies in the phonology and vocabulary of Layamon's *Brut*', Ph.D. thesis, Cornell University, 1901.

Mooers, Stephanie, 'Networks of power in Anglo-Norman England', *Medieval Prosopography* 7 (Autumn 1986), 25–54.

Moorman, Charles, 'Literature of defeat and of conquest: the Arthurian revival of the twelfth century', in Valerie M. Lagorio and Mildred Leake Day (eds), *King Arthur through the Ages*, vol. I (New York: Garland Publishing Inc, 1990), 22–43.

Morse, Ruth, *Truth and Convention in the Middle Ages: Rhetoric, Representation, and Reality* (Cambridge: Cambridge University Press, 1991).

Mustanoja, Tauno F., 'Some reflections on Lawman's poetical syntax', in Michael Benskin and M. L. Samuels (eds), *So Meny People Longages and Tonges: Philological Essays in Scots and Mediaeval English Presented to Angus McIntosh* (Edinburgh: Middle English Dialect Project, 1981), 335–40.

Noble, James, 'Introduction', in special issue on Lawman's *Brut*, ed. James Noble, *Arthuriana* 8, 3 (Fall 1998), 1–3.

——, 'The larger rhetorical patterns in Laȝamon's *Brut*', *English Studies in Canada* 11, 3 (Sept. 1985), 263–72.

——, 'Variation in Laȝamon's *Brut*', *Neuphilologische Mitteilungen* 85, 1 (1984), 92–4.

Oakden, J. P., *Alliterative Poetry*, 2 vols. (Manchester: Manchester University Press, 1930).

Ogilvy, Jack D. A., *Books Known to the English, 597–1066*, Medieval Academy of America Publication 76 (Cambridge: Medieval Academy of America, 1967; revised and enlarged edition of *Books Known to Anglo-Latin Writers*, 1937).

Parry, Joseph D., 'Narrators, messengers, and Lawman's *Brut*', *Arthuriana* 8, 3 (Fall 1998), 46–61.

Perry, Lucy, 'Origins and originality: reading Lawman's *Brut* and the rejection of British Library MS Cotton Otho C.xiii', *Arthuriana* 10, 2 (Summer 2000), 66–84.

Pilch, Herbert, *Layamons 'Brut': Eine Literarische Studie*, Anglistische Forschungen 91 (Heidelberg: C. Winter, Universitätsverlag, 1960).

——, 'Layamon und die kymrische Literatur: Eine Erwiderung an W. Schirmer', *Zeitschrift für Celtische Philologie* 29 (1962), 192–7.

—— (ed.), *Orality and Literacy in Early Modern English*, ScriptOralia 83 (Tübingen: Gunter Narr Verlag, 1996).

Quilligan, Maureen, *The Language of Allegory: Defining the Genre* (Ithaca: Cornell University Press, 1979).

Rider, Jeff, 'Arthur and the saints', in Valerie M. Lagorio and Mildred Leake Day (eds), *King Arthur through the Ages*, vol. I (New York: Garland Publishing Inc., 1990), 3–21.

——, 'The fictional margin: the Merlin of the *Brut*', *Modern Philology* 87, 1 (August 1989), 1–12.

Ringbom, Håkan, *Studies in the Narrative Technique of Beowulf and Lawman's Brut* (Åbo, Finland: Acta Academiae Aboensis Humaniora ser. A, 36, no. 2, 1968).

Russell, Jeffrey Burton, *Witchcraft in the Middle Ages* (Ithaca: Cornell University Press, 1972).

Salter, Elizabeth, 'Culture and literature in earlier thirteenth-century English: national and international', in Derek Pearsall and Nicolette Zeeman (eds), *English and International: Studies in the Literature, Art and Patronage of Medieval England* (Cambridge: Cambridge University Press, 1988), 29–74.

——, 'Cultural patterns in twelfth-century England: Norman and Angevin', in Derek Pearsall and Nicolette Zeeman (eds), *English and International: Studies in the Literature, Art and Patronage of Medieval England* (Cambridge: Cambridge University Press, 1988), 4–28.

Schichtman, Martin, 'Gawain in Wace and La3amon: a case of metahistorical evolution', in Laurie A. Finke and Martin B. Schichtman (eds), *Medieval Texts and Contemporary Readers* (Ithaca: Cornell University Press, 1987), 103–19.

Schirmer, Walter F., *Die frühen Darstellungen des Arthurstoffes*, Arbeitsgemeinschaft für Forschung des Landes Nordrhein-Westfalen, Gewisteswissenschaften 73 (Cologne and Opladen: Westdeutscher Verlag, 1957).

——, 'Layamon's *Brut*', *Bulletin of the Modern Humanities Research Association* 29 (1957), 15–27.

Serjeantson, Mary S., 'The dialects of the west Midlands in Middle English', *Review of English Studies* 3 (July 1927), 319–31, especially 320–1 for La3amon.

Shapiro, Fred R., 'First use of the term *Middle English*', *Notes and Queries* n.s. 30 (June 1983), 237–8.

Sheldon, Sue Eastman and Loren C. MacKinney, 'The eagle: bird of magic and medicine in a Middle English translation of the *Kyranides*', *Tulane Studies in English* 22 (1977), 1–20.

Sheppard, Alice, 'Of this is a king's body made: lordship and succession in Lawman's Arthur and Leir', *Arthuriana* 10, 2 (Summer 2000), 50–65.

Sir Gawain and the Green Knight, ed. J. R. R. Tolkien and E. V. Gordon; 2nd edn, ed. Norman Davis (Oxford: Oxford University Press, 1967).

——, trans. Marie Borroff (New York: W. W. Norton & Company, 1967).

Smith, Roland M., 'Lawman's Gernemuðe', *Modern Language Notes* 60 (1945), 41–2.

Standrop, Ewald, 'Der Rhythmus des Layamon-Verses', *Anglia* 79 (1961), 267–86.

Stanley, E. G., 'The date of Layamon's *Brut*', *Notes and Queries* n.s. 15 (March 1968), 85–8.

——, 'Layamon's antiquarian sentiments', *Medium Ævum* 38 (1969), 23–37.
Stock, Brian, *The Implications of Literacy: Written Language and Models of Interpretation in the Eleventh and Twelfth Centuries* (Princeton: Princeton University Press, 1983).
——, 'Literacy and society in the twelfth century', in Glyn S. Burgess and Robert A. Taylor (eds), *The Spirit of the Court: Selected Proceedings of the Fourth Congress of the International Courtly Literature Society (Toronto 1983)* (Cambridge: D. S. Brewer, 1985), 1–4.
Stratmann, F. H., 'Das paragogische N im Laȝamon', *Anglia* 3 (1880), 552–3.
Strohm, Paul, 'Middle English narrative genres', *Genre* 13 (Fall 1980), 379–88.
Swanton, Michael (ed. and trans.), *Anglo-Saxon Prose*, Rowman and Littlefield University Library (Totowa, NJ: Rowman and Littlefield, 1975).
Taliesin, *The Poems of Taliesin*, ed. and annotated by Sir Ifor Williams, English version by J. E. Caerwyn Williams, Medieval and Modern Welsh Series III (Dublin: Dublin Institute for Advanced Studies, 1975).
Tatlock, J. S. P., 'Epic formulas, especially in Laȝamon', *Publication of the Modern Language Association* 38 (1923), 494–529.
——, 'Greater Irish saints in Lawman and in England', *Modern Philology* 43 (1945), 72–6.
——, 'Laȝamon's poetic style and its relations', in *The J. M. Manly Anniversary Studies in Language and Literature* (Chicago: University of Chicago Press, 1923; repr. Freeport, New York: Books for Libraries Press Inc., 1968), 3–11.
——, *The Legendary History of Britain* (Berkeley: University of California Press, 1950; reprint, New York: Gordian Press, 1974).
——, 'Irish costume in Lawman', *Studies in Philology* XXVIII (1931), 587–93.
Tiller, Kenneth J., 'The truth "bi Arðure þan kinge": Arthur's role in shaping Lawman's vision of history', *Arthuriana* 10, 2 (Summer 2000), 27–49.
Trautmann, Moritz, 'Über den vers Laȝamons', *Anglia* 2 (1879), 153–73.
Trioedd Ynys Prydein, ed. and trans. Rachel Bromwich (Cardiff: University of Wales Press, 1978).
Wace, *La Partie Arthurienne du Roman de Brut*, ed. I. D. O. Arnold and M. M. Pelan, Bibliothèque Française et Romane, Série B: Textes et Documents I (Paris: Librairie C. Klincksieck, 1962).
——, *Wace's Roman de Brut: A History of the British*. Text and trans. Judith Weiss. Exeter Medieval English Texts and Studies (Exeter: University of Exeter Press, 1999).
Watson, Jonathan, 'Affective poetics and scribal reperformance in Lawman's *Brut*: a comparison of the Caligula and Otho versions', *Arthuriana* 8, 3 (Fall 1998), 62–75.

Weinberg, Carole, 'Þat kinewurðe bed [a bed fit for a king]: thematic wordplay in Lawman's *Brut*', *Arthuriana* 8, 3 (Fall 1998), 33–45.

Whitelock, Dorothy, *Sermo Lupi ad Anglos*, 3rd ed. rev. (London: Methuen & Co. Ltd, 1963).

Wickham-Crowley, Kelley M., 'The birds on the Sutton Hoo instrument', in Robert T. Farell and Carol Neuman de Vegvar (eds), *Sutton Hoo: Fifty Years After*, American Early Medieval Studies 2 (Oxford, Ohio: American Early Medieval Studies, 1992), 43–62.

——, 'Cannibal cultures and the body of text in Laȝamon's *Brut*', in Rosamund Allen, Lucy Perry and Jane Roberts (eds), *Laȝamon: Contexts, Language and Interpretation*, King's College London Medieval Studies 19 (London: King's College London Centre for Late Antique and Medieval Studies, 2002), 351–69.

——, '"Going native": anthropological Lawman', in special issue: *Theoretical Approaches to Lawman's Brut*, *Arthuriana* 10, 2 (Summer 2000), 5–26.

——, 'Laȝamon's narrative innovations and Bakhtin's theories', in Françoise Le Saux (ed.), *The Text and Tradition of Laȝamon's Brut*, Arthurian Studies 33 (Cambridge: D. S. Brewer, 1994), 207–25.

Wülcker, Richard, 'Über die Quellen Layamons', *Beiträge zur Geschichte des Deutschen Sprache und Literatur* 3 (1876), 524–55.

Wyld, Henry Cecil, 'Laȝamon as an English poet', *Review of English Studies* 6 (1930), 1–30.

Ziolkowski, Jan, 'The nature of prophecy in Geoffrey of Monmouth's *Vita Merlini*', in James L. Kugel (ed.), *Poetry and Prophecy: The Beginnings of a Literary Tradition*, Myth and Poetics Series (Ithaca: Cornell University Press, 1990), 151–76.

Index

Aaron, St 109, 144
Absalom 86
Adam 86
Ælcus of Iceland 47, 51, 66, 152 n.19
Ælfric, King 77
Æne, sister of Arthur 116
Aeneas 4, 68, 105, 143
Æscil of Denmark 47–8
Æstrilde 151 n.15
Africa 50
Agag the Amalekite 67, 152 n.25
Aganippes, king of France 88
Alan of Lille (Alain de Lille) 111, 135
Alban, St 34, 144, 157 n.1
Albanac (Albanactus) 68, 151 n.15
Albin, St 16, 18, 20
Albion 106
Aldadus, Bishop 45, 67, 76
Aldolf (Aldulf) 45, 67, 79
Alfred the Great 27
Allen, Judson Boyce 133
Allen, Peter 63–4
Allen, Rosamund 4–5, 149 n.4, 150 n.11
Alliterative Morte Arthur 138, 145
ambivalence 7–11, 12, 20–3, 28, 97, 137, 150 n.7
Ambrosius, *see* Aurelius Ambrosius
Amesbury (Amberes-buri, Ambresburie) 37, 45–6, 51, 74, 113, 115
Anacletus 37
ancestors 2, 24, 28, 30, 33, 34, 42, 51, 61
Ancrene Riwle 67
Andreas 102
Andreas, St 132
Androgeus 65, 144, 151 n.17
Aneirin 84
Angel 91, 102
Anglia 6
Anglo-Saxon Chronicle (ASC) 56, 79–80, 132

Anglo-Saxon, *see* Old English
Anglo-Saxons, the 6, 7, 8, 10, 18, 21, 24, 42–6, 50–3, 57, 89, 131; Anglo-Saxon heritage 9, 13, 79; Anglo-Saxon law 27; Anglo-Saxon literature, texts 60, 101, 154 n.14; *see also* children of Rhonwen, *sæx*, Old English, Wulfstan
Annales Cambriae 50
Apollo (Appollin) 39, 71, 151 n.16, 151–2 n.17
Appas 46, 47, 145
archaism 9, 10, 11, 14, 53, 57, 63, 69, 70, 79; *see also* valorized past
Areley Kings (Ernleie, Ernleʒe) 15, 16, 18, 84, 85, 149 n.4, 159 n.22
Arfderydd, battle of 108
Argal 144
Argante 118, 146
Aristotle 19
Armes Prydain 84
Arnold, Ivor 122
Arthur 3, 5, 12, 14, 17, 27, 28, 29, 30, 31–2, 33, 34, 36, 37, 38, 40, 42, 47–9, 51, 53, 57, 60, 65, 66, 68, 69, 71–2, 74, 76, 79, 80–1, 84, 86, 88–9, 91, 93, 94, 101, 102–3, 104–5, 108, 109, 110, 116, 117–19, 124, 125–6, 127, 128, 130, 131, 136, 138, 139, 142, 143, 145–6, 152 n.19, 154 n.23; his armour 31; *see also* prophecy
Arviragus 68, 144
Ascanius, son of Aeneas 68, 105–6, 143
Astrild 143
Athelbert, king of Kent 35
Athelstan, king of England 146
auctor, -es 19, 20, 22, 135
auctoritas 19, 22
Auden, W. H. 14, 56
Augustine, St 12, 134
Augustine (Austin), archbishop of

Index

Canterbury 16, 18, 20, 34–5, 36, 68, 146
Aurelius Ambrosius 42, 45, 46, 66–7, 68, 74, 76, 113–14, 116, 144, 145
Avalon 60, 102, 103, 118, 119, 125
Avon, river 145
awenydd, -ion 116, 158 n.20
Awkward Age, The 60

Bacon, Roger 26
Baldolf 145
Bakhtin, M. M. 1, 13, 53, 56–62, 64, 65, 78, 92, 94–6, 97–8, 103, 130, 140–2
Balaam 111
Baldwin, archbishop of Canterbury 85
Banastre, Robert 121
Bangor 34–5, 68
Barron, W. R. J. 4
Barthes, Roland 91–2, 93, 98, 99
Bede, St 15, 16, 18, 53, 75, 90
Beduer (Bedivere / Bedwyr) 48
Belin (Beline) 28, 29, 39–40, 47, 68, 69, 71, 78, 88, 128, 143–4, 145, 157 n.1
Bell (Hall) 17–18
Beof of Oxene-uord (Oxford) 30
Beowulf 101
Beowulf 89, 92
Bercilak 138, 139
Bern manuscript 124
Bernard of Chartres 75
betrayal / treachery 12, 21, 29, 30–1, 32, 33, 36–55, 99, 151–2 nn.15–17; of family 38, 39, 40, 49; forger as traitor 38; of lord (*lauerd-swike*) 37; of people (*leod-swike*) 37, 45, 112; in *Sermo Lupi ad Anglos* 54
Bewdley 85
Bible, the 132, 134, 135
Blacker-Knight, Jean 119–20, 123, 124–5, 156 n.52
Bladud 68, 101, 143
Blenner-Hassett, Roland 24, 71
Bloch, Ernst 130
Bloy, León 9
Bollard, John K. 158 n.13
Bordesley 85
Borges, Jorge Luis 8–9
Boulogne 145
Brendan, St 114, 115
Brennes 28, 29, 39–40, 47, 66, 68, 69, 78, 88, 143–4, 145
Bridgnorth 85
Brien (Brian) 109, 110, 146

Britain (Brutaine, Brutene) 1, 3, 4, 7, 21, 23, 24, 25, 29, 40, 41, 43, 52, 57, 66, 68, 79, 82, 108, 110, 120, 127, 130, 131, 139, 143, 144, 145, 146
British / Britons, the, *see* Welsh, the
Brittany 34, 124, 125, 144, 145, 146; Bretons 160 n.43
Brook, G. L. 4, 15
Brown, A. C. L. 50
Browne, Thomas 142
Brutus 4, 24, 25, 37, 68, 91, 105, 106, 139, 143, 151 n.15
Bryan, Elizabeth 4, 157 n.1
Bullock-Davies, Constance 84, 108
Byatt, A. S. 142
Bzdyl, Donald G. 4, 15, 50, 88, 143, 144

Cadog, St 103
Cador of Cornwall 33, 69–70, 126, 145
Cadwalader 4, 21, 63, 68, 79, 127–8, 129, 143, 146
Cadwal(l)an 32, 50–1, 68, 79, 91, 93, 109–10, 146
Caerleon on Usk (Caer Usk, Caer Leon, Kær Usch, Kair Lion, Kaerliun, Kairliun, Karliun bi Uske) 35, 70–1, 72, 77, 89, 115, 132, 145
Caesar, Julius 26, 29, 65, 66, 68, 69, 92, 144, 151 n.17, 156 n.52
Caldwell, Robert A. 122, 160 n.34
Calidon 91
Caligula, *see* Cotton Caligula A.ix
Camber 68
Camelford 146
cannibalism 110, 158 n.17
Canterbury 100; archdiocese of 85, 137
Caradoc 103, 104
Carannog, St 104
Cardigan group of sts' lives 104
Carric (Caric, Karic, Kinric) 49–50, 68, 91, 146
Cassandra 111
Cassibellaunus (Cassibellaune) 26, 65, 66, 68, 71, 144, 151 n.17
Cenan, son of Androgeus 65
Chambers, R. W. 11
Chaucer, Geoffrey 6
children of Rhonwen 42, *see* Anglo-Saxons, the
Childric, emperor of Germany 28, 31, 33, 76–7, 91, 145
Christianity 13, 17, 21–2, 31, 36, 42–4, 46, 76, 88, 99, 104–5, 108, 112, 114,

118, 130, 139; British Christianity
  34–5, 137; birth of Christ 106–8; *see
  also* Christians, hermits, pagans,
  preaching, prophecy, relics, saints,
  trance
Christians 12, 13, 22, 33–5, 46, 47, 77,
  86, 130–1; and heathens 12, 30, 33,
  42–3, 46, 47, 66, 76, 92; literacy and
  75–7, 88; views of 124, 140
Church, the 20, 44, 116, 137
Cirencester 50, 146
Clark, Cecily 79–80
Claudius, Emperor 28, 65, 144
Coel 68, 144
Cokaygne 130
Colgrim 29, 33, 46–7, 145
Compendium Studii Philosophiae 26
Conan, father of Constantine 112, 144
Conan, nephew of Constantine 49
Constance (Costanz), son of
  Constantine, Conan's son 40–1, 42,
  44, 46, 113, 144
Constantine, Emperor 29, 68, 76, 128
Constantine, son of Cador 49, 126,
  146
Constantine, son of Conan, father of
  Uther 37, 46, 78, 144
Cordoille 39, 68, 88, 90, 143
Coriolanus 5
Cornwall 113, 126; *see also* Cador
Cotton Caligula A.ix (Caligula) 3–4, 14,
  15–17, 18–19, 39, 97, 111, 135, 157 n.1
Cotton Otho C.xiii (Otho) 4, 14–15, 17,
  18–19, 20, 39, 67
Crocia (Crocea) Mors 89, 157 n.1
Cunedaigius 39

Dante 103, 158 n.4
Dartmouth (Derte-muðen) 31, 32
David, St 103
Davies, R. R. 41–2, 46, 82, 85–6, 103,
  105, 130–2, 137
'De Leir à Lear' 5
Delany, Sheila 129–30, 131
Devil / Scucke / Wurse 65, 101, 106
dialogic text / relations / imagination 1,
  13, 61, 65, 78, 94, 95
dialogue 3, 13, 59–60, 77–8, 95, 142;
  translation as 95
Diocletian 144, 157 n.1
Doldanim of Gutlonde 47, 152 n.19
Domesday Book 17–19
Donahue, Dennis 132

Donne, John 142
Donoghue, Daniel 7–13, 20, 26, 53, 149
  n.35, 150 n.7, 156 n.60
Donoghue, Denis 57, 59–60
Donwal / Dunwale 39, 68, 143, 151 n.16
Dream of the Rood, The 132
dreams / visions 36, 48, 100, 102–3, 106,
  110, 112, 115–16, 127, 129, 145, 146,
  157–8 n.4; Arthur's dreams 36, 48,
  102–3, 110; in Diana's temple 106;
  Bakhtin on 103
Droitwich 17
Dubriz, St, bishop of Caerleon 115
Dumville, David 120–1, 124, 159–60
  n.29
Durham 122
Dyfed 108

eagle 100–2
Ebissa 145
Ebrauc 38, 143
*Ecclesiastical History of the English
  People* 18
Edwin (Edwine) 50, 79, 109, 110, 146
Efflam, St 104
Eleanor (Ælienor) of Aquitaine 16, 18
Elena, St 132; *see also* Helena
Elidur 144
England (Engle-lond) 7, 9, 10, 15, 16,
  18, 20, 24, 27, 32, 34–5, 51, 82, 103,
  125, 131, 132, 136, 137, 146
epic 57–8, 59, 61, 73
Ernleie (Ernleȝe), *see* Areley Kings
Escol 152 n.19
Essex (Æst-sæx) 30
Etymologies 101
Exodus 132
Explanationes in prophetiam Merlini 111

Fereus (Ferreus) 68, 143
Ferocious Alphabets 57
Flanders 145
Foliot, Gilbert, bishop of London 26
Forma praedicandi 135–6
Foulon, Charles 106
France 39, 68, 69, 115, 145, 146
Friedlander, Carolynn 5
Frolle 38, 91, 145
future, the 21, 94, 96, 97, 99, 113,
  125–6, 128–30, 136, 139, 142

Gabius 70
Galbraith, V. H. 11

Index

Galfredian metaphor 110
Galli (Walbrook, Wale-broc) 71, 90
Gallus 90
Gawain (Walwain) 29, 36, 48, 69–70, 102, 138–9, 145, 156 n.60
Genesis 132, 134
Genuis, daughter of Claudius 144
Geoffrey of Monmouth 3, 20, 27, 51, 53, 57, 60, 69, 83, 103, 104, 108–9, 110, 119–20, 121–5, 132, 152 n.19, 160 nn.30, 37, 43
Geomagog 27
Gerald of Wales 85, 105, 116, 131, 132
Germain, St 44, 78
Germany (Alemaine) 22, 23, 24
Gervase of Canterbury 55–6, 57, 80
Gibbs, A. C. 67
Gildas 11, 12, 53, 54, 55, 103, 120, 149 n.35
Gille Callæt 41
Gille Patric, King 79
Gillomar, King 114–15
Girouard, Mark 6–7
Glamorgan (Glom-margan) 39, 71, 77
Gloucester 79
Goethe, J. W. 58
Gonwais of Orkney 47, 152 n.19
Gorlois 145
Gornoille 39
Gotland (Gutlonde) 47, 145
Gough Map 85
Gransden, Antonia 125, 160 n.43
Greece 143
Gregory I, Pope 35, 36, 146
Grendel's mother 89, 101
Griscom, Acton 124, 159 n.29
Grosseteste, Robert 26
Guencelin, Archbishop 144
Guencelin, King 144
Guendoleine 68
Guibert de Nogent 134–5
Gurguint 68
Gurmond (Gurmund) 24, 35, 50, 68, 146
Gwynedd 137

Hall, J. 4
Ham (Cham) 15, 16
Hammer, Jacob 159 n.29
Hamun (Hamund) 28, 65, 144
Hanning, Robert W. 120, 121, 123–4, 125, 150 n.7, 160 n.30
Hardison, O. B. 21–2
Hatfield, battle of 91

Heavenfield, battle of 51
Helena (Helene), mother of Constantine 29, 76, 144; *see also* Elena, St
Hemeri 39
Hengest (Hengist) 22, 30–1, 33, 37, 42, 44, 45, 46, 50, 51, 67, 76, 79, 144, 145, 152 n.25
Henry II, king of England 16, 18, 82, 136
Henry VIII, king of England 138
Henry of Huntingdon 124
Herefordshire 85
heritage 2, 6, 8, 9, 21, 22, 25–6, 28, 30, 34, 61, 64, 131, 139
hermits 105, 116, 117, 159 n.22, 160 n.37
Historia Brittonum 120–1, 121–2, 160 n.30
Historia Regum Britanniae / Britannie 3, 20, 103, 119, 120, 121–5, 159–60 n.29
historians 36, 54, 55–6, 57, 81–2, 120, 121–5, 134, 150 n.7
historical inversion 97–8
history 21, 59, 63, 64, 73, 78–82, 120–5, 132–6
Holquist, Michael 57, 59, 60
Horsa 42
Howel 28
Hugh of St Victor 97
Humber 143, 151 n.15
Huth Merlin 120

Iceland 48, 145, 152 n.19
Ignoge, wife of Brutus 143
Illtud, St 103–4
Imelmann, Rudolf 83, 122
Ioram 37, 111, 112
Ireland 28–9, 45, 50, 114, 115, 145
Isemberd (Isembred) 65, 146
Isidore of Seville 101
Iudon (Judon) 68, 143
Iuor (Ivor, Yvor) 51, 68, 79, 128

James, Henry 59, 60
Japhet (Iaphet) 15, 16
Jarman, A. O. H. 108, 155 n.35
Jason 86
Jeremiah 19
Joachim de Fiore 130
Joachism 130
Job 111
John, king of England 137, 150 n.11
John of Salisbury 75

Index   179

Judith 132
Julian 144

Kaer Lud, see London
Karliun, see Caerleon
Keats, John 142
Ker, Neil 4
Keredic 22–3
Kinbelin 68, 69, 87, 106, 107, 144
Kinric, see Carric
Kugel, James 132

Lancashire 121
landscape 7, 18, 24, 33, 34
Laȝamon: biography 15–20, 36; name 23, 48; as priest, preacher 2, 13, 15–18, 21, 34, 53, 74–5, 87, 104, 133
Laȝamon's Brut: The Poem and its Sources 6
law / *laȝen* 23
Le Saux, Françoise 6, 7, 42, 50, 51, 52, 53, 67, 68–9, 83–4, 86–7, 92, 122–3, 132–3, 156 n.60
Lebor Gabála Érenn 120
Leicester (Kaer Leir, Leirchestre) 24, 90
Leir (Lear, Lir, Llŷr), King 5, 38–9, 68, 88, 90, 143
Leofnoth (Leovenath, Leouenad) 15, 16, 17–18, 19
Leslie, R. F. 4, 15
Leucais 17, 19
Lewis, C. S. 1, 6
Liber quo ordine sermo fieri debeat 134
Life of St Gregory, The 102
Lifris 103
Lincoln 28, 29
Lincoln Cathedral MS no. 104 122
Llancarfan group of sts' lives 103–4
Locrin 68, 143, 151 n.15
London (Kaer Lud, Kærlud, Lundene, Lundenne, Lundin, Lundres, New Troy, Trinovant) 24–5, 43, 72, 74, 84, 90, 144
Lot 74, 116
Luces, Emperor 17, 29, 37, 88–9, 118–19, 145
Luces, King 17, 68, 144
Lud, King 24, 68, 90, 144
Luke, St 17

Mabinogi 83, 86, 154 n.27
Madden, Sir Frederick 3–4, 5, 6, 60, 125
Maelgod 65

Maelgwn Gwynedd 108
Magan the wise man 26, 112
magic 100–2, 104–6, 108–11, 115, 145, 156 n.48; astrology 26, 108, 109, 110, 112; crossroads 111
Magna Carta 137, 150 n.11
Malgus (Malgo) 68, 86
Malin 38
Malverus / Maluasius / Malvaisus 152 n.19
manuscripts of the *Brut* 1, 3, 14–19; *see also* Cotton Caligula A.ix, Cotton Otho C.xiii
Map, Walter 26
Marcel 29
Marciane (Mærcene, Mærcie, Marcie), Queen 27, 144
Margadud, king of south Wales 32–3, 51
Maurius (Marius) 68, 89
Martley 85
Mason, Eugene 4
Maud, Empress 85
Maximien (Maximian), Emperor 29, 68, 144
Melga of Scythia 66, 67, 144
Membricius 91
Membriz 38
Mercia 27, 144
Merlin (Myrddin) 2–3, 12, 26, 37, 41, 42, 45–6, 53, 60, 66, 79, 84, 90, 104–5, 106, 108–9, 110–20, 122–4, 125–6, 127–9, 130, 131, 135–6, 137, 138, 139, 144, 145, 146, 155 n.35, 160 n.37
Middle English Dictionary 4
Middlesex (Middel-sæx) 30
Migne, J.-P. 134
Milburga 52, 152 n.25
Miller, Joseph M. 134
Miller, Molly 120–1
Minnis, A. J. 19–20, 23, 134
modus praedicandi 134
Moray, duke of 144
Modred (Moddred) 36, 37, 48–9, 102, 108, 145–6
Morgan (Margan), s. of Maglanus 39, 68
Morgan (goddess) 139
Morpidus, King 92
Morse, Ruth 64, 69–70, 73–4, 75, 81–2
Mount Cloard 66
Mount Reir 37, 111
Munt Giu 79

Myrddin, Myrddin son of Morfryn, Myrddin Emrys, *see* Merlin
myth 81, 98, 99, 130, 131, 136

nationalism / national identity 1, 5, 6, 7, 9, 10, 11, 12, 13, 20, 21, 22, 45, 52, 57, 125, 131, 136, 137, 148–9 n.30
Nennius 120
New Troy / Trinovant, *see* London
New Variorum Lear 5
Noah (Noe) 15, 16
Noble, James 8, 150 n.11
Norman Conquest 8, 10, 11, 53, 57, 58
Normandy 20
Normans 8, 10, 11, 20, 24, 25, 52, 149 n.35, 150 n.7, 157 n.61; Anglo-Normans 9, 26, 64, 150 n.7
novel 58, 59, 60, 61, 141

Oakden, J. P. 67
Octa 33–4, 45, 76, 145
Octaves 68
Old English 10, 12, 26, 28, 44, 67, 132, 133, 149 n.30
On the Continuity of English Prose from Alfred to More and His School 11
oneiromancy 102, 157–8 n.4; *see also* dreams
oral culture 2, 30, 36, 38, 92, 96–7; community 96–7; merits of oral and written 77, 80–3, 88, 90–1, 97, 99, 136; sources 64, 73–5, 84; Welsh and 84, 86; *see also* preaching, prophecy, written culture / sources
Origen 87
Orkney 47, 145
Ormulum 9
Oswald, St 32, 51, 146, 152 n.25
Oswy 32, 33, 146
Othere (Oðere) 65
Otho, *see* Cotton Otho C.xiii
Owain of Gwynedd 121
Oxford (Oxene-uord) 30, 132

Padarn, St 104
pagans 12, 30, 31–4, 42–7, 50, 66, 75, 78, 92, 131, 144, 146; see *also* Christians
Paris 133, 145; University of 156 n.48
Paris, prince of Troy 86
Parzival 103
Passent 46
Paul, St 19
Paulinus 102

Pearsall, Derek 69
Pelluz 109–10, 112, 146
Penda 32, 33, 50–1, 93, 146
Perrett, Wilfred 5
Perry, Lucy 158 n.17
Petreius 30
Pilch, Herbert 83, 84, 155 n.29
Piram, Archbishop 76
place names 2, 24–6, 28, 30–1, 39, 57, 58, 70–1, 103
Poetry and Prophecy 132
poison 22, 46–7, 49, 51, 76, 113, 145, 160 n.37
Poreus (Porreus) 68, 143
Possession: A Romance 142
preaching 54, 74, 75, 134, 135, 136, 141–2; manuals 134–6
'Problem of speech genres, The' 140
prologue 2, 14–21, 56, 73, 77, 159 n.22
prophecy: as narrative strategy 1, 53, 60–1, 91, 97, 104–20, 123–6, 131–6, 140–2; Christian prophecy 22, 36, 51, 99, 104–20, 128, 130–1, 135–7; Merlin's prophecy 79, 90, 104–20, 123–6, 134, 135–7; Taliesin's prophecy 87–8, 105–9; Welsh prophecy 12–13, 51, 87–8, 104–20, 129; *see also* dreams, eagle, Merlin, preaching, Sibyl(s), signs
Prophetiae Merlini 119, 122, 123
Prosenna 70
proverbs 3, 7, 52, 60, 91, 92; Barthes on 91–2
Proverbs of Alfred (Maidstone Museum A 13) 92
puns 2, 5, 23, 28, 30, 45, 48, 50, 58, 64–7, 110

Quencelin 29
Quilligan, Maureen 22

Rabelais, François 96
race 8, 10, 11, 12, 13, 52
Radnor 85
Redstone (Radestone, Radistone) 15, 16, 18, 84–5, 149 n.4, 159 n.22
Regau 39
relics 114, 116, 129, 132
responsibility 36, 54, 97
Return to Camelot, The: Chivalry and the English Gentleman 7
Rider, Jeff 103–4
Rival 68

Robert of Basevorn 135–6
Rockmoor 17
Rodric 89
Roman de Brut 68, 119–20, 122–3; see also Wace
Rome 28, 29, 40, 51, 78, 79, 85–6, 88, 119, 120, 127, 128, 129, 143, 144, 145, 146
Rouwenne (Rhonwen, Rouuenne) 22–3, 27–8, 42–5, 46, 76, 78, 144
Rudauc 151 n.16
Ruhhudibras, King 100–1
Rumareth 36

sæx 30, 45
St David's (Deuwi) 85
St Michael's Mount, giant of 48, 79, 145
saints 103–4, 110; Welsh saints 103–4; see also hermits
Salter, Elizabeth 10, 26, 60, 69, 74–5, 85, 159 n.22
Samson, St, bishop of York 115
Samuel 67
Saul, king of Jerusalem 67, 152 n.25
Sawley School 120, 121
Saxony ((Sex-londe) 32, 33, 35
Schichtman, Martin B. 156 n.60, 157 n. 61
Schiller, Friedrich 58
Scotland 101, 145
Seguine, Duke 66
Sergius, Pope 128
Sermo Lupi ad Anglos 54, 149 n.35, 154 n.14
Severn (Seuarne), river 3, 15, 16, 18, 21, 84, 85
Shaftesbury 101
Shakespeare, William 95, 142
Shem (Sem) 15, 16
Shropshire 85
Sibyl(s), the 12, 90, 111, 125, 127, 128
signs / *tacnen* 101, 115, 117, 127
Silvius, son of Ascanius 105, 143
Singer, Isaac Bashevis 100
Sir Gawain and the Green Knight 3, 138–9
Sosie valley 86, 90
Spain 109, 146
Speculum 8
speech genres 140
speech plan / will 141
Stanley, E. G. 4, 69

Stater 68, 151 n.16
Statius, P. Papinius 133
Stock, Brian 38, 73, 74, 81, 88, 91, 96, 97
Stonehenge (Eotinde Ring) 45, 74, 114–15, 145
Summa de arte praedictoria 135

Taliesin (Teilesin, Thelgesinus) 84, 87–8, 106–8, 109, 114, 144
Tamar, river 146
Tatlock, J. S. P. 84–5, 87, 122, 154 n.23
Teinewic 33
Tennancius (Tenauntius) 68, 144
Thebaid 133
Thematic and Formulaic Composition in Lawman's Brut 132–3
Tonuenne (Tonwenn), Queen 40, 143
trance, of seer 115–16, 124, 158 n.20; see also *awenydd, -ion*
treachery, see betrayal
Tremorien, bishop of Caerleon 113
Troy 24, 106, 139
truth 2, 26, 27, 77, 80–2, 93, 97, 138–9, 152 n.17; *treoðe / treouðe / trowþe* 12, 21, 47–8, 50–1, 93; *soð(e), seoð* 36, 39, 152 n.17; *soðfeste* 16, 19, 27, 56
Truth and Convention in the Middle Ages 69
typology 11, 53, 152 n.25

Ulfin 116, 117
Unbeniaeth Prydain (Sovereignty of Britain) 131
Upper Areley 85
Urien Rheged 106
Ursula, St 5, 144, 152 n.25
Usk 85
Uther Pendragon 31, 33–4, 37, 42, 46–7, 51, 66, 68, 74, 76, 84, 104, 105, 113, 115–16, 117, 144, 145
Utopia 129–31

valorized / epic past 53, 59, 61, 130, 142
Varro, M. Terentius 101
Verulam 34, 74
Vespasian 66
Vision of History in Early Britain, The 120
Visser, Gerard Johannes 50, 122
Vita Euflami 104
Vita Merlini 108, 110–11, 113, 114, 123, 160 n.37

Vortiger (Vortigern, Gwrtheyrn, Uortigerne) 22–3, 26, 30, 37, 40–3, 44–5, 46, 51, 66, 68, 76, 78, 105, 111, 112–13, 120, 122, 144, 160 n.30
Vortimer 27–8, 30, 42, 43–5, 46, 51, 68, 76, 78–9, 113, 160 n.37

Wace, (?) Robert 3, 4, 9, 14, 16, 18, 20, 51, 57, 60, 67, 68, 69–70, 81, 83, 87, 106–7, 108, 119, 120, 122–3, 125–6, 132, 133, 153 n.19, 154 n.23, 156 n.52, 161 n.66
Walbrook (Wale-broc), *see* Galli
Wales 2, 3, 20, 21, 32, 39, 46, 50, 51, 60, 79, 82, 84, 85–6, 103, 113, 121, 128, 131, 136, 137–8, 144, 146; March of 3, 13, 82–3, 84, 129, 131, 132, 136–7
Walter, archdeacon of Oxford 124
Wanis 144
'we', use of 78–80
wealas 149 n.30
Weinberg, S. C. 4
wells, worship of 113
Welsh, the / Britons 3, 7, 8, 11, 13, 21, 24, 41–2, 46, 52, 65, 79, 121, 127–30, 136, 148–9 n.30, 160 n.43; links to Rome 85–6; *see also* Arthur, Merlin, prophecy, Taliesin, Welsh sources
Welsh sources 83–8, 103, 120–1, 131; oral 84, 85
Wenhauer (Wenhaver) 36, 37, 48–9, 102, 145–6

Wessex (West-sæx) 30
West-mering stone 77, 89
Westroys, les 121
William of Malmesbury 124
Winchester 49, 101, 116, 119
Winetland (Winet-londe) 36, 145
Wither (Wiðer), King 28, 65, 68, 144
Worcester 10, 14, 85, 137, 149 n.4; cathedral 150 n.11; county 17, 85; diocese 85
Worcester fragment 80
Worcester 'Tremulous Hand' glossator 10
written culture / sources 2, 38, 49–50, 64, 73, 74, 75, 77, 80–2, 83, 86, 88–91, 94, 96, 97, 99
Wülcker, Richard 6, 122
Wulfstan 11, 12, 54, 74, 76, 149 n.35, 154 n.14
Wyld, Henry Cecil 7, 83

Yarmouth 110
Ygærne (Ygerne) 116, 117, 145
Ymddiddan Myrddin a Thaliesin 108
York (Eouuerwic) 115, 143
Yuni 51, 68, 79, 128

Ziolkowski, Jan 110–11